Genius After Psychoanalysis

PSYCHOANALYTIC HORIZONS

Psychoanalysis is unique in being at once a theory and a therapy, a method of critical thinking and a form of clinical practice. Now in its second century, this fusion of science and humanism derived from Freud has outlived all predictions of its demise. **Psychoanalytic Horizons** evokes the idea of a convergence between realms as well as the outer limits of a vision. Books in the series test disciplinary boundaries and will appeal to scholars and therapists who are passionate not only about the theory of literature, culture, media, and philosophy but also, above all, about the real life of ideas in the world.

Series Editors
Hilary Neroni, Esther Rashkin, and Peter L. Rudnytsky

Former Series Editor:
Mari Ruti (2018–2023)

Advisory Board
Salman Akhtar, Doris Brothers, Aleksandar Dimitrijevic, Lewis Kirshner, Humphrey Morris, Dany Nobus, Lois Oppenheim, Donna Orange, Peter Redman, Laura Salisbury, and Alenka Zupančič

A list of volumes in the series appears at the end of this book.

Genius After Psychoanalysis

Freud and Lacan

K. Daniel Cho

BLOOMSBURY ACADEMIC
LONDON · NEW YORK · OXFORD · NEW DELHI · SYDNEY

BLOOMSBURY ACADEMIC
Bloomsbury Publishing Inc
50 Bedford Square, London, WC1B 3DP, UK
1385 Broadway, New York, NY 10018, USA
29 Earlsfort Terrace, Dublin 2, Ireland

BLOOMSBURY, BLOOMSBURY ACADEMIC and the Diana logo
are trademarks of Bloomsbury Publishing Plc

First published in the United States of America, 2024

Copyright © K. Daniel Cho, 2024

For legal purposes the Acknowledgments on pp. viii–ix constitute an extension of this copyright page.

Cover design by Daniel Benneworth-Gray
Cover image: Saint Agatha, 1630–1633, by Francisco de Zurbarán (1598–1664)

All rights reserved. No part of this publication may be reproduced or transmitted in any form or by any means, electronic or mechanical, including photocopying, recording, or any information storage or retrieval system, without prior permission in writing from the publishers.

Bloomsbury Publishing Inc does not have any control over, or responsibility for, any third-party websites referred to or in this book. All internet addresses given in this book were correct at the time of going to press. The author and publisher regret any inconvenience caused if addresses have changed or sites have ceased to exist, but can accept no responsibility for any such changes.

Library of Congress Cataloging-in-Publication Data
Names: Cho, K. Daniel, author.
Title: Genius after psychoanalysis : Freud and Lacan / K. Daniel Cho.
Description: New York : Bloomsbury Academic, 2024. | Series: Psychoanalytic horizons; vol 22 | Includes bibliographical references and index.
Identifiers: LCCN 2024010960 (print) | LCCN 2024010961 (ebook) | ISBN 9798765123188 (paperback) | ISBN 9798765123171 (hardback) | ISBN 9798765123164 (pdf) | ISBN 9798765123195 (ebook)
Subjects: LCSH: Psychoanalysis and the arts. | Sublimation (Psychology) | Freud, Sigmund, 1856–1939. | Lacan, Jacques, 1901–1981.
Classification: LCC NX180.P7 C48 2024 (print) | LCC NX180.P7 (ebook) | DDC 700.105–dc23/eng/20240516
LC record available at https://lccn.loc.gov/2024010960
LC ebook record available at https://lccn.loc.gov/2024010961

ISBN:	HB:	979-8-7651-2317-1
	PB:	979-8-7651-2318-8
	ePDF:	979-8-7651-2316-4
	eBook:	979-8-7651-2319-5

Series: Psychoanalytic Horizons

Typeset by Integra Software Services Pvt. Ltd.
Printed and bound in Great Britain

To find out more about our authors and books visit www.bloomsbury.com and sign up for our newsletters.

For Haelyn

Contents

Acknowledgments		viii
Introduction: The Economic Problem of Genius		1
Part One Critique of Pure Pleasure		9
1	Freud's Leonardo	11
2	Sublimation or, On the Sexual Life of Genius	25
3	Finding Satisfaction	41
4	Otherwise than Guilt	53
Part Two The Trouble with Objects		65
5	The Thing about Objects or, Sublimation after Lacan	67
6	Something Missing	87
7	Acute Nostalgia or, The Strange Case of Coca-Cola	97
8	A Problem of Narcissism	107
Part Three Group Psychology and the Analysis of Genius		117
9	The Secret Life of Groups	119
10	The Logic of Debasement	133
11	Toward an Ethics of Subjective Cession	147
12	Life after the Image or, *Cluny Brown*	159
Conclusion: Drive within the Limits of Death Alone		171
Notes		181
Index		205
Volumes in the Series		212

Acknowledgments

On the long journey to Mordor and back, certain people played a crucial role in my life. I want to recognize those people.

I began thinking about genius during graduate school. During that time, my teachers and mentors, Doug Kellner and Ken Reinhard, were instrumental. Rather than discouraging me from taking up this unpopular idea, they provided a nurturing space, where I could cultivate my curiosity. I want to thank Ken especially for the incredible influence he has had on how I read and think about Freud and Lacan. His seminars on the Neighbor were the single most important event to happen in my education. I hope it gratifies him to know that I am still a subject to that event.

Mari Ruti was the first editor of any sort to take my book seriously. During an unspeakably difficult time, she gave me the one thing she didn't have—time. And as someone once said, giving what you don't have is love.

This book would not have been published if it were not for Hilary Neroni. Hilary believed in the book when I didn't. I am eternally grateful to have gone on this journey with Hilary—I could think of no one better—and I only hope that she is happy with the outcome, and that she doesn't regret her decision!

I want to thank Haaris Naqvi at Bloomsbury Academic for being the ideal editor: communicative, generous, and patient. I would also like to thank Hali Han for her consummate professionalism and attention to detail. I also want to thank Peter Rudnytsky and Esther Rashkin of the Psychoanalytic Horizons series for acting as intermediaries at a crucial time in the life of this project. Shamli Priya and her team at Integra worked miracles to make the book presentable.

I also want to thank the two anonymous reviewers whose valuable feedback prompted me to revise significant portions of the book, including even the title. I hope they feel that they've played a critical part in the book's development because they did.

It is not hyperbole to say that this book wouldn't exist without Todd McGowan. Todd played a central role in its existence in at least two ways. First, he suggested that I turn a longish essay I had written on genius in Freud into a book. Second, he used his influence to help me find a publisher (I know he'll hate that I phrased it that way). Yet, while I am extremely thankful for Todd's help with this book, I am more thankful for his friendship. My only complaint is that Todd conned me into joining his fantasy football league by telling me that "fantasy" had something to do with psychoanalysis. It doesn't.

Acknowledgments

I would not be doing justice to Paul Eisenstein if I simply thanked him for the many hours of conversation we've had which, among other things, allowed me to clarify to myself what I was trying to accomplish in this book, for such thanks wouldn't adequately convey the role Paul has played in my life. Simply put, Paul is to me what Samwise Gamgee is to Frodo Baggins. He has been a constant source of friendship and encouragement in an otherwise inhospitable world. Without his presence in my life, I would have shriveled into a raisin on that vine a long time ago.

Jameson, Henry, and Kathryn, you are the detours that are life itself.

Haelyn, you are everything.

Introduction: The Economic Problem of Genius

I

Genius is a concept that receives little philosophical attention these days. Already in Kierkegaard we see philosophy distancing itself from genius. For Kierkegaard, "genius *is born*" and, precisely for this reason, inferior to the apostle, who is not born but called forth by God.[1] However, today, philosophy doesn't criticize the genius. It simply ignores it. To a certain extent, this is understandable given the concept's dodgy history. *Genius* derives from the Latin *gignere*, meaning "to give birth to" or "to beget." This is where the idea of genius as the guardian spirit or "genie" comes from. One receives gifts of intelligence and ability at birth, as if one is being looked after by the family's guardian spirit—this is the idea of genius as innate talent. From here it is barely a step to the idea that hierarchy and inequality are the natural order of things. There are those who are born with natural gifts and talents—we call them geniuses—and those who are not. Those who are exceptional and those who are ordinary. Those who are superior and those who are inferior. Those who deserve more resources and those who don't. Indeed, it appears as if our guardian spirits have left us with more than intelligence and talent; they have left us with hierarchy and inequality as well.

But it gets worse. Not only has genius contributed to the naturalization of inequality—to be sure, an inequality that is socially and historically produced—it has also aided and abetted that engineering of society known as *eugenics*. In his major work *Hereditary Genius*, the father of eugenics, Francis Galton, sets out to prove by quantitative means a "fact" that he finds implicit in the doctrine of heredity: namely, "that genius is hereditary."[2] With Galton, the guardian spirits that give the genius their gifts of intelligence turn out to be the parents. From this, the notion that intellectual abilities "cling to families," as he puts it, Galton discerns a moral imperative.[3] Because genius is hereditary, we owe it to civilization to curate the best and brightest population as possible, a population of only geniuses. Galton writes, "I conclude that each generation has enormous power over the natural gifts of those that follow, and maintain that it is a duty we owe to humanity to investigate the range of that power, and to exercise it in a way that, without being unwise towards ourselves, shall be most advantageous to future inhabitants of the earth."[4] For Galton, the guardian spirits who look after the genius turn out to be none other than ourselves.

Given these unsavory associations, it is no wonder that genius has fallen out of favor with contemporary philosophy. Genius, as Catherine Malabou puts it, contributes to the "collapse of universality," a project that philosophy should want no part of.[5] And yet, it is not as if philosophy itself is innocent. It is not that psychology, in its naïveté, fell for the trap of innatism while philosophy successfully side-stepped it, for philosophy itself has also promoted the idea of genius as innate ability. Here, Kant is exemplary. "Genius," according to Kant, "is the inborn predisposition of the mind (*ingenium*) through which nature gives the rule to art." That is, genius is "an inborn productive faculty," a product of "nature." This is why for Kant genius is "talent" and not "a predisposition of skill."[6] Philosophy's lesson is that genius is born, not made. Could this then be the real reason philosophy ostracizes the genius? It wants to forget its past? If so, this would give philosophy's dismissal of genius an element of repression.

II

What is the outcome of ignoring genius? Does genius simply vanish into nothingness, never to be heard from again? I would argue to the contrary. One of the most basic principles—perhaps, *the* most basic principle—of psychoanalysis is that what is forgotten or ignored is not obliterated as such but, rather, continues to live on in the background until the opportunity for its return arises. So, while philosophy has long ignored the category of genius, it has not gone away; rather, it has set down roots in the popular imagination where it continues to thrive. We see it, for example, in slips of the tongue. A hardened theorist who is absolutely committed to the cause of radical equality will say of the latest book they've read or film they've watched, "It's genius!" Or of a simple task, "It doesn't take a genius!" Of course, when pressed, they'll simply dismiss the statement as an instance of irony or excuse it as a simple colloquialism, an honest mistake—but is it? We also see it on the bookshelves of every library and bookstore. Visit the self-help aisle of your local library, and there you'll find any number of books about unleashing your inner genius. "I don't believe this drivel!" you might protest. But someone does. We see it in our schools where "gifted and talented" programs are the norm. If your child takes a standardized test, you might discover that they exhibit "superior cognition" and therefore qualify for "gifted and talented" services, including entire separate schools where the learning is more free and less standardized. Indeed, the very people who profess to not believe in genius will feel no compunction about enrolling their children in such programs.[7] Speaking of standardized tests, what do we say of the person who receives a perfect score on the SAT, LSAT, MCAT, or GRE? Not simply that they did well but that they must be brilliant and, when our guard is down, that they must be a genius. And of course we still see it in the sciences where psychology and now neuroscience search for genius in intelligence tests, reactions times, and MRIs.

In his popular book *Outliers*, the journalist Malcolm Gladwell sets out to dispel the individualist myth of, among other "outliers," the genius. "I want to convince you that these kinds of personal explanations of success don't work," Gladwell states in a programmatic way. "It's not enough to ask what successful people are like," he continues; "It is only by asking where they are *from* that we can unravel the logic behind who succeeds and who doesn't."[8] So far, so good. Gladwell, like the philosophers, wants us to forget genius. It is an outmoded concept that perpetuates the harmful myth of individual merit.

One outlier that Gladwell considers is Bill Joy, the cofounder of Sun Microsystems. Gladwell wants to convince us that Joy became a silicon success, not because he is a genius but because he had put in over 10,000 hours of computer programming before graduating from university. Gladwell is so certain of this idea that he even gives it a name, the 10,000-hour rule, and he claims, it applies to every success story across the board from Joy to The Beatles.

But here we may ask: what possessed Joy to put in that 10,000 hours of work in the first place? What drove him to try something for 10,000 hours when I imagine he faced periods of difficulty, frustration, and failure? Is there another 10,000 hours of work that he put into the 10,000-hour rule itself? A 10,000-10,000-hour rule? Here is what Gladwell says: "Bill Joy was brilliant. He wanted to learn. That was a big part of it."[9] Wait a minute. So, Joy was able to commit 10,000 hours to computer programming because he was "brilliant"? Well, this brilliance, which Gladwell himself cites as playing a "big part" of Joy's success, is what people would call Joy's genius. That is, people think Joy a genius because he is "brilliant," not because he invented UNIX. He could've invented anything—or nothing at all—and people would still think him a genius because they think he is brilliant. So, did Joy put 10,000 hours into being brilliant? Or was he simply born that way? To find out, Gladwell interviews Joy's father (Is genius hereditary? Galton might ask). And what does the father say? "When Bill was a little kid, he wanted to know everything about everything way before he should've even known he wanted to know." In other words, Joy was *innately* curious, like he was given the desire to learn by a guardian spirit or genie. To this, Gladwell accedes, "He was talent by the truckload."[10] For someone who professes to not believe in genius, Gladwell certainly talks a lot about talent and innate ability. And this goes not only for Joy but for all those that Gladwell claims submitted to the 10,000-hour rule from The Beatles to Bill Gates:

> Joy and Gates and the Beatles are all undeniably talented. Lennon and McCartney had a musical gift of the sort that comes along once in a generation, and Bill Joy, let us not forget, had a mind so quick that he was able to make up a complicated algorithm on the fly that left his professors in awe. That much is obvious.[11]

Undeniably talented? A musical gift? A mind so quick? Forget genius, indeed!

Forgetting or ignoring genius therefore doesn't make it go away. All it does is push it into the background, where it continues to live a second life. What this means is that, although we don't avow it, on some level, we still believe in genius, a belief that is evinced at the most inopportune times, like, say, when we are attempting to expose it as a myth. My view is that philosophy is largely responsible for this situation. Because it has abnegated its responsibilities, genius continues to live this zombie-like existence in which it is simultaneously disavowed and believed. Thus, to truly deal with genius's problematic nature, philosophy must take up its responsibility and confront it head on. That is, to truly negate genius's associations with natural hierarchy and inequality, it is not enough that we ignore it; we must submit genius to what Hegel once called "the labor of the concept."[12] Then, and only then, will we be able to exorcise the guardian spirits that possess genius. *Genius After Psychoanalysis* offers to be a philosophical exorcism of this kind.

III

To exorcise the spirits of elitism and eugenics from genius, I will recruit the help of psychoanalysis, and in particular the work of Sigmund Freud and Jacques Lacan, for it is my view that psychoanalysis gives us the necessary materials to construct an account of genius that doesn't rely on notions of innate ability and inborn talent. There are two concepts in particular that are important here. They are *the drive* and *sublimation*. Let's start with the drive.

In the Standard Edition of Freud's work, the German word for drive— *Trieb*—is rendered into English as "instinct." This is a mistranslation and a particularly unfortunate one at that. It is unfortunate, not simply because German already has a word for *instinct—Instinkt*—but, more importantly, because Freud uses *Trieb* precisely to signify something other than instinct.

Indeed, we might say, Freud uses *Trieb* to signify the exact *opposite* of instinct, something that gets lost in Strachey's translation.[13]

Instinct, in German as in English, indicates a tendency or impulse that is innate to the creature. Often, instinct is tied to biological need. An animal mates with another animal, for example, out of an instinct to procreate. Or an animal eats another animal out of an instinct for nourishment. Instinct, we might say, marks the point of commensurability between the animal and its environment. When a lion eats a zebra, we don't say that it has committed murder because we understand that it has acted out of instinct. The lion and the zebra exist as a complementary pair within the harmonious whole of nature—the circle of life, as Elton John once put it. Instinct is nature.

The drive, however, is not instinct. Indeed, what Freud means to name with the drive is precisely that aspect of the creature which *exceeds* instinct. When the human being engages in sex—or nonprocreative sexual acts—for no reason other than pleasure, they are acting, not out of instinct but out of *drive*. Or when a person eats beyond the point of nourishment or satiation, it is the drive that is at work, not instinct. Unlike instinct, the drive is not aligned to biological need. Indeed, the drive exceeds biological need. The singer Celine Dion possesses over 10,000 pairs of shoes.[14] Jeff Bezos owns a yacht that is 417 feet long. Clearly, something other than biological need is at work. That something is the drive.

Because it is not aligned with biological need, the drive cannot be said to be natural. Rather, it is what falls out with nature. The drive, we might say, marks the point of incommensurability between the human and its environment. While the lion that eats a zebra does not wonder if it has committed murder, the human being who eats an animal may very well ask themselves that question. The reason murder enters the picture is because, for humans, there is some aspect of eating that exceeds the instincts for nourishment and self-preservation, an aspect that has something to do with the pleasure of eating itself—that aspect is the drive. The drive is that thorn in the flesh which prevents the human being and the (eaten) animal from forming a harmonious whole. Not nature but what is at odds with nature. The inhuman within the human.

IV

So, the first concept that we receive from psychoanalysis is *the drive*. The second concept is what psychoanalysis calls *sublimation*, which is a specific relation—or vicissitude, in Strachey's locution—of the drive. To get at this idea of sublimation, let's return to the issue of Strachey's mistranslation.

What makes Strachey's mistranslation of *Trieb* particularly egregious is that, for Freud, human beings are creatures, not of instinct but of drive. This is why Freud argues that our primary experience of the world is one of discontent (*Unbehagen*, in Freud's German). The problem for us humans is that we are inhabited by an unnatural force—the drive—which persists even after every need has been satisfied. Because of this force or drive we feel alienated from nature. We feel that our world lacks what we need to feel truly happy and content. We even feel alienated from ourselves, like our skin doesn't quite fit right. We feel that there is something perpetually missing from our lives, and though we cannot pinpoint exactly what it is, we are certain that it holds the key to our happiness.

This discontent, which, to be sure, is a product of the drive, is the source of envy. We imagine that other people have this missing something. And we think that if we only had what they have, our lives would be complete. Or, better yet, if they didn't have what they have, they'd be miserable like us. But not only is this discontent the source of envy, it is also the source of resentment and grievance. We imagine that we are missing this something because it has been stolen from us. We can't quite put our finger on what exactly was stolen, but we know it was stolen, and thus, we resent those whom we imagine are the thieves. This discontent is also the engine that keeps the gears of capitalism turning. We buy the latest gadget, the newest car, the biggest house, not to fill needs but to get at this missing something in our lives. But no matter how much we take from others, how many imagined thieves we punish, or how many commodities we accumulate, we will never get rid of that nagging feeling of discontent because it is not a contingent feature of our circumstances but, rather, an integral fact of our existence.

I can understand if someone feels that psychoanalysis paints a rather bleak picture of human existence. Our lives appear to be nothing more than envy and resentment with brief interludes of manic consumption. And if this were all that psychoanalysis had to say, then I would agree: it indeed paints a bleak picture. But this is not in fact psychoanalysis's last word. While it insists that we are ineluctably creatures of the drive—and in that way, it is indeed bleak—psychoanalysis also claims that it is possible for us to take up a new relationship to the drive, a relationship that transforms our experience of discontent. While it never suggests that we can ever eliminate our discontent, psychoanalysis proposes that we may nevertheless find a new source of satisfaction right there in our discontent, a satisfaction that leads, not to contentment as such but, rather, to contentment with our discontentment—a satisfaction in dissatisfaction, if you will. The name that psychoanalysis gives this new relationship is *sublimation*.

V

Thus, building on these two concepts—that is, the drive and sublimation—I will argue in these pages that *genius is the sublimation of the drive*. In other words, genius is not innate ability or natural talent. It is not a hereditary trait or "an inborn productive faculty." It has nothing to do with virtuosos or savants, impressive algorithms or generational talent. It is not an inner secret to unlock or unleash. It cannot be earned with 10,000 hours or measured with MRI scans. On the contrary, I will contend, genius is a particular relation of the drive, a relation that finds satisfaction in our inevitable dissatisfaction, a relation that transforms this discontentment into its own form of contentment.

To organize my argument, I have divided *Genius After Psychoanalysis* into three parts. The first two parts—"Critique of Pure Pleasure" and "The Trouble with Objects"—give separate accounts of genius, according to the two principal components of the drive. According to Freud, the drive is made up of two parts. The first part or component is *the aim*. The aim is the particular path that the drive takes. It is an activity or action, like writing. The second part or component of the drive is *the object*. The object is the tool through which the drive achieves its aim. It is the various parts and pieces that go into a particular activity, like this computer, to extend my example.

Part One, "Critique of Pure Pleasure," puts the aim at the center of genius. Beginning with a close reading of Freud's *Leonardo da Vinci and a Memory of His Childhood*, a book that I argue contains a theory of genius, it argues that genius arises from the sublimation of the aim. What this means in Freud is that a transformation takes place in the drive's aim, a transformation that allows the drive to find satisfaction in its own failure to achieve its aim. Part Two, "The Trouble with Objects," puts the object at the center. Through a disquisition on Lacan's seminar, *The Ethics of Psychoanalysis*, it argues that the genius sublimates the object of the drive. For Lacan, this means that genius elevates an ordinary object such that something about it is revealed, something that we don't normally pay any attention to.

The reason why I have given my account of genius in two parts, instead of one, is that, when put together, the aim and the object do not yield a single coherent picture of sublimation. Rather, they form what Slavoj Žižek has called a *parallax*, that is, "two closely linked perspectives between which no neutral common ground is possible."[15] The aim and the object, in other words, are not two halves of a single whole. They are rather two closely linked optics or perspectives that produce proximate yet distinct accounts of sublimation. To join them together into a single account therefore would project a sense of unity that doesn't actually exist. This is why I decided to give the aim and the object their own distinct accounts: I wanted to preserve this parallax.

Part Three, "Group Psychology and the Analysis of Genius," represents something of a departure from the first two parts. Whereas the first two parts are focused squarely on developing an account of genius as sublimation, Part Three uses genius as the occasion to reconsider the theory of groups or, as it is known in psychoanalysis, group psychology. Freud published *Group Psychology and the Analysis of the Ego*, his most systematic account of the group, in 1921, the same year that Hitler took control of the Nazi Party. In it, Freud considers why people seem ineluctably drawn to a leader, how their love for the leader turns them into a group, and why "in the blindness of love remorselessness is carried to the pitch of crime."[16] These are questions that would soon become relevant for Europe, and indeed the world. At the same time, Freud admits that his account of group psychology is incomplete. Among other things, Freud says, he leaves out the question of how "a wish in which a number of people can have a share" might substitute for the leader and become "embodied in the figure of what we might call a secondary leader."[17] A wish like to make America great again? A secondary leader like the 45th president? Clearly, the questions that Freud raises in *Group Psychology* are as relevant now as when they were written. Thus, in Part Three, I use genius as a way to recommence Freud's ongoing inquiry into group psychology and to give it another quarter turn.

The theory of the drive reached its apogee in 1920 with the publication of Freud's *Beyond the Pleasure Principle*. In this, Freud's most speculative book, Freud presents the idea of the death drive as that aspect of the drive which exceeds the impulse toward pleasure. Any account of genius that relies on the notion of the drive must confront this idea of the death drive. This then is how I conclude *Genius After Psychoanalysis*: by briefly considering what the death drive means for genius.

What remains of genius after the notions of innate ability and inborn talent are removed from it? Does anything remain? Some would say no. Genius is nothing more than this idea of natural giftedness, and so, once that disappears, so too does genius itself. There is no denying that innatism has been a part of the story of genius. Indeed, so too have elitism and eugenics. Yet, my wager is that those things—that is, innatism, elitism, and eugenics—are neither the whole of genius's story nor its most crucial part. Something remains of genius after those things have been removed from it, something precious and important. This is the ultimate reason why I have staged this encounter between genius and psychoanalysis: not to grind genius down into nothingness but, rather, to discover what remains of genius after psychoanalysis.

Part One

Critique of Pure Pleasure

There is no denying that Freud believed in genius. In the opening page of *Leonardo da Vinci and a Memory of His Childhood*, Freud openly and unabashedly calls the Renaissance master "a universal genius."[1] He does not mean this ironically. If one doubts this, flip through the pages of *Leonardo* and see all that Freud says about him. He calls Leonardo "one of the greatest men of the Italian renaissance" and one of its "most brilliant examples."[2] He lauds him as an artist, calling his creations "masterpieces of painting."[3] Moreover, he extols him as a scientist, calling him a "prophet and pioneer" in "practically every branch of natural science."[4] At one point, he even calls Leonardo the "forerunner" and "rival" of Bacon and Copernicus![5] So, when Freud calls Leonardo "a universal genius" on the opening page of the book, we can be sure that he means it earnestly and unironically.

Yet, for all the complimentary words he has for Leonardo, Freud does not take any of Leonardo's achievements as the material for his study of Leonardo's genius. He does not examine *Mona Lisa* or *The Last Supper*, nor does he consider Leonardo's flying machine or the anemometer.[6] Rather, he focuses, very oddly, on what was for many of Leonardo's own contemporaries his greatest *failure*: namely, his late turn toward science.

It may seem detrimental—or, at the very least, counterintuitive—for a consideration of genius to give any space to failure. After all, is not success the epitome of genius? Are not geniuses those men of industry, like Bill Gates and Steve Jobs, who have achieved great things and whose vast wealth stands as a testament to that achievement? Is not failure the very opposite of genius, its antithesis? But Freud rebuffs this concern, insisting, "It does not detract from his greatness if we make a study of the sacrifices which his development from childhood must have entailed, and if we bring together the factors which have stamped him with *the tragic mark of failure*."[7] Indeed, as we shall soon see, not only is Freud unafraid of taking on failure when it comes to genius, it is, for him, indispensable.

Thus, from the very beginning, the psychoanalytic idea of genius will be unlike any other. It will not be the prodigy or the virtuoso. It will not be the innately intelligent or the exceptionally talented. It will not be the success story. Indeed, if anything, the psychoanalytic conception of genius will be an intervention into those popular notions of genius. For the psychoanalytic conception of genius will center on a particular relation of the drive. That relation is called *sublimation* or, the drive's capacity "to replace its immediate aim by other aims which may be valued more highly and which are not sexual."[8] I expect this formulation to make little immediate sense—indeed, it is the object of some misunderstanding within psychoanalysis itself. Thus, it will be one of my aims in Part One to break this formulation down so that it is less intimidating and more comprehensible, and therefore more useful and illuminating. But, here, all I want to say about it is that it indicates a kind of failure within the operation of the drive. Whereas the drive ordinarily obtains its aim, the sublimated drive fails, obtaining instead a nonsexual aim. What this means and what it has to do with genius will be the subject of Part One. To get there, however, I will begin somewhere else: namely, with Leonardo's peculiar relationship with love and hate, a relationship that I call *cool indifference*.

1

Freud's Leonardo

I

Toward the latter part of his life, Leonardo became increasingly interested in science. He began taking up studies of the natural world, investigating everything from human anatomy to the mechanics of flight. And he did all of this much to the dismay of his contemporaries. For them, Leonardo's newfound interest in science was troubling. Troubling, not because they found the field of science itself alien or off-putting (although there may have been something of that too), but troubling because Leonardo's newfound interest in science came at the expense of his art. As Leonardo delved deeper into his scientific studies, "he took up his brush with reluctance," writes Freud, "painted less and less, left what he had begun for the most part unfinished and cared little about the ultimate fate of his works."[1]

For Leonardo's contemporaries, the master's behavior was incomprehensible. How could such an inspired artist simply abandon his gift? They found it confounding that a genius such as Leonardo would choose to "fritter away his time when he could have been industriously painting to order and becoming rich."[2] They could not imagine that this newfound interest in science might be the extension of his genius.

There is an apocryphal story told by Giorgio Vasari about Leonardo at the moment of his death, which reveals just how bewildered his contemporaries were. Freud retells it thus: "In the last hour of his life … he reproached himself with having offended God and man by his failure to do his duty in his art." To be sure, there is nothing in the story in terms of truth content. It is a complete work of fiction, a piece of "legend," as Freud puts it.[3] But truth content is not what makes this story interesting. What makes it interesting is that it exists at all. If one were to make up a story—any story—to defame Leonardo, why make up this particular story? Why not make up a story about him being, say, a closet drunk or a sexual pervert? Why make up a story about Leonardo repenting to God on his deathbed for having failed in his art? It is as if the absolute worst thing Leonardo's contemporaries could imagine him doing was not abusing alcohol, engaging in sexually deviant behavior, or even murder. It was abandoning art for science. Though it doesn't contain anything factual, the very fact that this story exists conveys just how difficult it was for Leonardo's contemporaries to conceive of his genius.

The problem for Leonardo's contemporaries is of course that they thought of genius as exceptional talent. For them, Leonardo's art was not a product of his genius. It was his genius. In fact, the association in their minds between art and genius was so strong that when Leonardo turned to science, they saw this turn, not simply as the emergence of a newfound interest but, rather, as the abandonment of genius as such. The image of genius as talent had such a strong grip on their minds that they could not imagine the possibility that Leonardo's burgeoning interest in science was yet another manifestation of his genius. Instead, they took it to mean its complete abandonment. For them, Leonardo was leaving the full potential of his genius unrealized. It was tantamount to betrayal. As they saw it, art was not simply a way for Leonardo's genius to manifest itself; it was that genius, and thus something like a God-given purpose or mission. So, when Leonardo abandoned his art to pursue science full time, they took this act as a sign of betrayal—a dereliction of duty.

II

As one might expect, Freud's own assessment of Leonardo's late turn toward science diverges—and diverges quite widely—from that of Leonardo's contemporaries. Freud does not believe that Leonardo was duty-bound to his art nor does he believe that Leonardo's genius was given to him by God. And yet, the exact manner of Freud's assessment will surprise us, as he does not make any of the obvious arguments. For example, some might want to argue that Leonardo's contemporaries overreacted to his interest in science because they saw that interest in competition with his art. A natural counterargument would then assert that Leonardo's interest in science existed on a continuum with his art. It would argue that art and science do not contradict each other or come at each other's expense but, rather, coexist with one another, complementing each other as a mutually reinforcing pair. It would argue that Leonardo's contemporaries therefore made a false choice between Leonardo, the artist and Leonardo, the scientist. Leonardo was both the artist and the scientist.

As appealing as this argument is, Freud does not make it. In fact—and this will surprise us—Freud actually *agrees* with Leonardo's contemporaries. Science did come at the expense of Leonardo's art. For Freud, as for Leonardo's contemporaries, Leonardo's interest in science was a disruptive force (an event, in Alain Badiou's sense of the word), which cost Leonardo his art; he writes: "[W]hen he made the attempt to return from investigation to his starting point, the exercise of his art, he found himself disturbed by the new direction of his interests and the changed nature of his mental activity."[4] *He found himself disturbed*. Rather than consider science the complement of art, Freud construes it as a disruption, an upheaval that irreparably damages Leonardo's relationship to art.

Another argument that some might want to make—and which Freud also rejects—is that Leonardo's contemporaries too hastily castigated the master. It points out that Leonardo was thought to have abandoned his art only because he left so many artworks unfinished. But were these works truly unfinished? Or were they unfinished only in the eyes of Leonardo? Case in point: *Mona Lisa*. *Mona Lisa* is widely considered to be a masterpiece—perhaps, Leonardo's greatest masterpiece. But according to Vasari, Leonardo himself considered it to be unfinished: "Leonardo undertook the portrait of Mona Lisa ... and after working on it for four years, he left the work unfinished."[5] Surely, if *Mona Lisa* is an unfinished work, it is only so in the mind of the painter himself. For who among us would deny its excellence? What *Mona Lisa* therefore demonstrates is the vast difference that exists between what a genius considers to be finished and what the rest of us consider to be finished. If *Mona Lisa* suffers from anything, it isn't Leonardo's neglect but, rather, his stringency. And if Leonardo's contemporaries understood this, then they wouldn't have been so quick to castigate him.

Just like the first argument, this second argument is very appealing. Yet, as appealing as it is, Freud does not accept it. Indeed, he goes so far as to call it an excuse.[6] Rather than apologize for the state of Leonardo's late artwork, as this argument does, Freud accepts the judgment of Leonardo's contemporaries—and, more importantly, of Leonardo himself—that those works were indeed unfinished. The "struggle with a work, the final flight from it and the indifference to its future fate," all of which were symptoms of Leonardo's waning interest in art, were, Freud insists, real and not the imagined by-products of an impossibly high standard.[7]

In both cases then Freud does the unexpected and sides *with* Leonardo's contemporaries. Freud might not have believed that art was Leonardo's God-given duty, but he nevertheless agrees that science disrupted his relationship with art, causing him to leave many artworks unfinished. So, on the question of whether Leonardo abandoned art, both Freud and Leonardo's contemporaries agree. Where they disagree—and disagree quite widely— is on the significance of that abandonment. For Leonardo's circle, his abandonment of art signified an act of infidelity to his genius. Leonardo was given a gift by God, and so, when he took up science, he betrayed that gift. For Freud, however, Leonardo's abandonment of art signifies something quite different. Indeed, it signifies the exact opposite. For Freud, Leonardo's abandonment of art for science was not a betrayal of his genius but, rather, a direct consequence of his fidelity to it.

III

Freud finds the early signs of Leonardo's eventual abandonment of art already present in what I will call Leonardo's *cool indifference*—the attitude or disposition of "inactivity and indifference," which Freud says, "seemed obvious in him."[8] For an example of this cool indifference, we may look to Leonardo's stance on life. Leonardo did not eat meat because he believed that all life, whether human or animal, has dignity. And yet, he would also attend executions in order to study and sketch the faces of the condemned, "distorted by fear" as they were, as if he were cool or indifferent to their suffering.[9] Another example is Leonardo's stance on war. Leonardo "condemned war and bloodshed," but, as Freud points out, he also did not actively resist war, and even participated in it, as he "accompanied Cesare in a position of authority during the campaign that brought the Romagna into the possession of that most ruthless and faithless of adversaries." Again, Leonardo appears coolly indifferent, this time to the victims of war.

A natural reaction to Leonardo's cool indifference is to think him a hypocrite. After all, in these examples, Leonardo clearly espouses a moral principle at one moment (all life is dignified; war is immoral), and then contradicts that principle in the next moment (sketches at executions; participates in war). And yet, Freud does not reach this conclusion. When Freud considers Leonardo's inconsistent—and even contradictory—behavior, he does not see someone acting hypocritically; rather, he sees someone acting indifferently. That is to say, what Freud finds in Leonardo's cool indifference are not actions that are good or evil but, rather, actions that are "indifferent to good and evil."[10] This is why Freud is not surprised by Leonardo's abandonment of art. Anyone who is able to exhibit cool indifference on such weighty matters as the dignity of life and the morality of war is bound to feel no compunction at all about leaving an artwork unfinished or art itself altogether.

For an explanation of Leonardo's cool indifference, Freud turns to a remark he makes about love and hate. Leonardo claims, "One has no right to love or hate anything if one has not acquired a thorough knowledge of its nature.... For in truth great love springs from great knowledge of the beloved object, and if you know it but little you will be able to love it only a little or not at all."[11] At first glance, nothing stands out about Leonardo's remark.

It appears only to state the obvious. To be significant, love and hate need a warrant, and that warrant is secured by knowledge. To illustrate this point, consider if I told you that I love (or hate) you. Most likely, you wouldn't take my proclamation very seriously. Why? Because, you are probably thinking, I know nothing about you. I don't know anything about your character or your personality. I don't know your political views, whether you smoke, what films you like or if you even like film, whether you like taking long walks along the beach. I don't even know your name! So, how could I possibly love you? Knowledge seems to play a crucial role in love, and without it, love seems impossible or, at the very least, silly, as Leonardo's thesis asserts.

However, upon second reflection, holes begin to appear in Leonardo's thesis. Take, for example, the cultural cliché of love at first sight. What this cliché asserts is that love is impulsive. Love is not based on thought and contemplation. It is based on physical attraction and carnal instinct. And while we might not believe in love at first sight per se, we will agree that we fall in love because we feel it, not because we draw up a spreadsheet. What about conventional romances? Surely, those are based on knowledge. But here too knowledge plays only a minor role. While conventional lovers may know something about each other (at least, more than lovers at first sight), they do not postpone their love until they have learned everything there is to know about each other; they do not wait until they have accumulated "great knowledge of the beloved object," as Leonardo asserts. Rather, they continue to learn about each other even after their love has taken flight. In a way, love here becomes the motive for learning about the other, not its product.[12]

The case against Leonardo's thesis only gets sharper when we consider our love of things, for when we consider our love of things, it becomes clear that knowledge is anathema to love. Take, for example, my love of ice cream. As much as I love ice cream, I must admit, I do not know much about it. I do not know how it is made (presumably, ice and cream are involved), or why it tastes so delicious, or if it is healthy to eat, and yet, I love it. Not only do I love ice cream despite not knowing much about it, but my ignorance seems crucial for that love. That is to say, the reason that I love ice cream as much as I do is precisely because I *do not* know much about it, above all, whether it is good for my health. If I saw the factory in which ice cream is made or learned about its effects on my health, I would start to love ice cream less.

Once, I saw a program on the making of blueberry muffins. I was astonished by how much butter goes into the vat when making a batch. When I tried to relay what I had learned to my friend, he immediately interrupted me, saying, "Stop, I love blueberry muffins." Knowledge was antithetical to his love of blueberry muffins. And it is not just ice cream and blueberry muffins. It's cars, cell phones, hamburgers, batteries, plastic bags, toothbrushes—anything, really. To love these things, there is a certain level of ignorance that we must maintain about them. We must not know the damage our cars' emissions deal to the environment. We must not know that child labor was used to mine the cobalt in our cell phones. We must not think of the dead batteries that are piling up in landfills, poisoning the soil. We must not imagine the cow getting rendered into hamburger meat in the slaughterhouse or plastic bags strangling turtles in the ocean or old toothbrushes washing up on tropical beaches. Indeed, it is as if ignorance is crucial for love, not knowledge.

What about hate? With hate it is even clearer that knowledge is anathema to the passions. The anti-Semite or the xenophobe, for example, feels profound hatred for the Jew and the immigrant despite knowing nothing about them. Of course, it is always possible to hate someone based on what we know about them. For example, we may feel great hatred for a criminal because we know about their crime. But even in this case, our hatred depends on us not knowing certain other facts about them—say, that they were abused as a child, a victim of an exploitative labor system, or a loving father. When making *The Godfather* (1972), Francis Ford Coppola had a conundrum. How to make the audience root for a remorseless murderer? The answer? Begin with a wedding. Once we know that Vito Corleone (Marlon Brando) is a loving father, we will root for him. In other words, to hate Vito Corleone, we must remain ignorant of him as a loving father.

Given these counterexamples, is it possible that Leonardo asserted something false about the passions? Freud certainly thinks so. In strong disagreement with Leonardo, Freud protests, "It is not true that human beings delay loving or hating until they have studied and become familiar with the nature of the object to which these affects apply." "On the contrary," he goes on, "they love impulsively, from emotional motives which have nothing to do with knowledge, and whose operation is at most weakened by reflection and consideration."[13] Freud is adamant: knowledge is inessential to the passions. If knowledge bears any relation to love and hate, it is as its antidote. But if Freud is correct, what about the hypothetical scenario from earlier in which I claimed to love you, the reader? Didn't this hypothetical clearly demonstrate that knowledge plays an indispensable role in love? But this is in fact Freud's exact point. As preposterous as it might sound, we do indeed love crowds of people about whom we know absolutely nothing. It happens all the time. It happens, for example, when a celebrity loves all their fans, when a religious leader serves the entire congregation, when a political leader represents all their supporters, or even when an author appreciates all his readers. Indeed, in 1921, Freud would go so far as to claim that the very possibility of groups and collectives depends on precisely this kind of impartial love.[14]

Thus, Freud roundly rejects Leonardo's remarks on love and hate, for "what they assert," he writes, "is obviously false." We know from experience that the passions are a powerful force against which the intellect can do very little—as Woody Allen once infamously put it, the heart wants what it wants—and "Leonardo must have known this as well as we do." What Freud concludes is that Leonardo must have been commenting, not on the way the passions function in general but, rather, on the way they function in him specifically. That is to say, what makes Leonardo's thesis on love and hate valuable is not that it provides any insight into human beings in general but, rather, that they provide insight into Leonardo himself. What Leonardo wants to do with his remarks, in other words, is to tell us how he loved and hated—not how people in general love and hate—and, in so doing, hold himself up as a model for us to emulate. As Freud puts it, "[H]e wishes to tell us that it happens so in his case, and that it would be worth while for everyone else to treat love and hatred as he does." Thus, when Leonardo writes, *One has no right to love or hate anything if one has not acquired a thorough knowledge of its nature*, we must read him, Freud suggests, as actually meaning, "[O]ne *should* love in such a way as to hold back the affect, subject it to the process of reflection and only let it take its course when it has stood up to the test of thought."[15]

Whatever we may think of Leonardo as an ideal, Freud finds in his peculiar manner of loving and hating the source of his cool indifference. Leonardo could sketch the faces of the condemned and engage in war on the side of the aggressor with cool indifference, not because he loved capital punishment and war or hated condemned criminals and Cesare's enemies but, rather, because he suspended those passions within himself. Leonardo could not love or hate those things—or, as we might say in psychoanalysis, he inhibited love and hate—because he did not possess a "thorough knowledge" about them. And without this knowledge, Leonardo could not bring himself to make those things the objects of his passions. This is why we should not think Leonardo a hypocrite. For Leonardo to be a hypocrite, the moral values of his actions would have had to been decided in advance, and he would have had to know what those values were. But it is precisely those moral values which had not yet been decided. In other words, Leonardo suspended his passions precisely to figure out what those moral values are. Rather than a hypocrite, we should think of Leonardo as an investigator or researcher. That is, someone who is interested in pursuing "thorough knowledge," not in casting moral judgment.

IV

It is this cool indifference that Freud finds at the root of Leonardo's genius. That is to say, genius, for Freud, does not come from inborn talent. It is not Leonardo's art. Rather, it comes from the ability to suspend—or inhibit—the impulse to love and hate. We must be careful not to misunderstand Freud here. He is not suggesting that love and hate are a kind of training ground for cool indifference, that Leonardo built up an immunity to moral ambiguity by repeatedly resisting the impulse to love and hate. Genius is not willpower. Here are Freud's exact words: "His affects were controlled and subjected to the instinct for research; he did not love and hate, but asked himself about the origin and significance of what he was to love and hate. Thus he was bound at first to appear indifferent to good and evil, beauty and ugliness."[16] Notice the move that Freud makes here. He does not present the passions as the precursor to the moral and the aesthetic. He does not claim that Leonardo developed a particular skill or disposition through his control of the passions, which he then applied in the areas of the moral and the aesthetic. Rather, he links Leonardo's suspension of the passions directly to his cool indifference. Leonardo suspended the passions *thus he was bound at first to appear indifferent to good and evil, beauty and ugliness*. The moral and the aesthetic are linked directly to the passions. Thus, Leonardo appeared indifferent to "good and evil, beauty and ugliness" *because* he "did not love and hate."

What this means is that Freud does not conceive of the passions, the moral, and the aesthetic as a sequence. One doesn't follow the other. Rather, they are all simultaneous, intertwined and entangled with one another. The passions are not the training ground for the other spheres of human experience, such as, the moral and the aesthetic, because they overlap, intersect—or, to use a Freudian term, overdetermine—these other spheres. The passions are their animating force. So, when Leonardo struck a coolly indifferent pose toward considerations of "good and evil, beauty and ugliness," he did so precisely by suspending the passions of love and hate within himself. Leonardo's suspension of the passions was his cool indifference to the moral and the aesthetic, not their preceding stage.

Moral and aesthetic questions, for Freud, are therefore never fully independent from the passions. Whether we think something is good or evil, beautiful or ugly, is always, in his mind, connected—wittingly or not—to whether we love or hate that thing. We might say, whether we think something is good or evil, beautiful or ugly is always an answer to the question of whether we love or hate that thing. Those questions are inseparable from one another. For this reason, everything that we said about the passions' imperviousness to intellect and knowledge applies to the moral and the aesthetic as well. That is, moral and aesthetic judgments are never purely rational. There is always an element of the passions involved. No one believes, for example, that a sunset is beautiful based on hearing a convincing argument. Nor does anyone believe in the beauty of their beloved because they've seen the data. Reason may play some role, but it is not alone nor is it primary. The same is true of moral judgments. Nazi resistors did not hide Jews because they had debated the merits of Kant's deontology versus Mill's consequentialism, despite what philosophical thought experiments might lead us to believe. Rather, they did so because they felt it was the right thing to do. Likewise, we believe that a sunset or our beloved is beautiful because we feel it to be true. We call it "gut feeling," "conviction," or even "personal taste," and what it means is that, in both cases, we hold beliefs about what is beautiful or ugly, moral or immoral, *before* we have subjected those beliefs to intellectual scrutiny. We do this, Freud argues, because the moral and the aesthetic are intertwined with the passions, passions that are themselves impulsive and anti-intellectual. Or, at least, that is how it is for most people. For the genius, things are different. The impulse to make moral and aesthetic judgments is suspended or inhibited. It is so, not because they are "open-minded" or "strong-willed" but, rather, because the passions themselves are inhibited.

And so, to describe Leonardo as hypocritical completely misses the mark. For Leonardo to have acted hypocritically, the moral value of his actions—that is, whether they are good or evil—must have been decided at the outset. Their moral value could not have ever been in question, even in his gut. For Leonardo to have been a hypocrite, refusing to eat animals must have been good from the start while sketching the faces of the condemned, evil. Freud's point here is that these judgments are never free of the passions; they always imply—or, better yet, reveal—our passionate impulses about them. Therefore, if I say that the refusal to eat animals is good, I signify that I have already decided, out of impulse, that I love it. And if I say that the sketching of the faces of the condemned is evil, whether I recognize it or not, I signify that I have already decided that I hate it. It is this type of unconsciously impulsive judgment that, Freud claims, was inhibited in Leonardo. Leonardo refused to answer the question of whether some act or thing—or, indeed, person—is good or evil because he refused to decide whether to love or hate that act, thing, or person. Like someone defusing a ticking time bomb, Leonardo forestalled the decision of good and evil by cutting the wires of the passions themselves and, in so doing, allowed something else to emerge, something in place of moral judgment.

V

Clearly, the moral is not the proper framework for grasping the genius's suspension of love and hate. Within a moral framework, this act of suspension always appears as hypocrisy or utter nonsense. Already, we may feel some discomfort with the idea that the genius does not immediately—or impulsively—condemn something like war or capital punishment, but this discomfort, Freud suggests, has more to do with the limitations of the moral framework than with the act of suspension itself. The moral simply does not have the conceptual tools to make this phenomenon comprehensible to us. Thus, rather than force the genius's cool indifference back into that ill-suited framework, Freud looks for a new conceptual framework to house it. That framework is the intellectual.

Freud argues that rather than love or hate, Leonardo engaged in intellectual work. He writes, "During the work of investigation love and hate threw off their positive or negative signs and were both alike transformed into intellectual interest."[17] Freud's view of the genius's suspension of the passions resembles somewhat Kierkegaard's view of the suspension of the ethical insofar as both conceive of an act that cannot be understood from within the perspective of the moral.[18] But rather than open onto the sphere of the religious, as in Kierkegaard, Freud's conception of the genius's act opens onto the sphere of the intellectual. The genius acts by refusing to love or hate something, and in so doing, they throw off the constricting terms of the moral, transforming the passions into "intellectual interest."

If judgments such as good or evil, beautiful or ugly, or even friend or foe are all answers of a sort to the question posed by the passions, as I claimed above, then the intellectual does not so much provide an answer to that question as it poses it itself. That is to say, the intellectual asks the question of whether something should be loved or hated. It does not answer that question itself. Otherwise put, the intellectual is posing problems, asking questions, and exploring them, not answering them and putting them to rest. It is this inclination to pose questions, rather than to answer them, that makes the intellectual supersede the moral. This does not mean that the intellectual is always good or that it can never be used for evil but, rather, that the very terms "good" and "evil" are within the intellectual no longer relevant—they are suspended.

The intellectual is thus the framework through which Freud grasps all of Leonardo's seemingly hypocritical behavior, from his refusal to eat animals to his dissection of horse cadavers. Viewed through its lens, Leonardo's behavior no longer appears as moral contradictions but, rather, as intellectual acts of inquiry—that is, as ways of posing questions in the world. Leonardo refused to eat animals then not because he felt it was wrong. Rather, he did it as a way of experimenting with the morality of eating animals. And he did not dissect horse cadavers because he felt it was right. Rather, he did it in order to test his views on the dignity of life. Indeed, it is precisely the valences carried by the words "right" and "wrong" that were negated when he suspended the passions. For Leonardo, the refusal to eat animals and the dissection of horse cadavers were not moral acts but, rather, intellectual acts. That is, they were part of his quest to learn "the origin and significance of what he was to love and hate," and not the decision to love or hate itself.

Intellectuality—at least, as far as Freud conceives it—is therefore not about the production of information and knowledge. It is not about answering every question in the universe. Nor is it about accumulating data and writing algorithms to control every eventuality in life. Intellectuality is not Barton Keyes (Edward G. Robinson) in *Double Indemnity* (1944) rattling off every category and subcategory of suicide known to humankind. Indeed, it is the very opposite of those things. Intellectuality, for Freud, is about asking questions, posing problems, and embracing ambiguity. It is about living with the discomfort that comes from tarrying with the negative and wrestling with the noumenal—not from solving it. Finally, intellectuality is about curiosity, about sparking it and, more importantly, about keeping it alive, even when—or, rather, especially when—one cannot predict where it will lead or how it will end, if it will at all.

VI

All of this then gives us insight into Leonardo's ambivalent relationship with art. Art for Leonardo was not mimesis or creative expression. It was not even about creating beauty or, if you wish, ugliness. Art was, for him, an intellectual endeavor, a mode of inquiry—an extension of his curiosity— defined by the suspension of the binary terms "beauty" and "ugliness." As Freud writes, "What interested him in a picture was above all a problem."[19] Thus, in art, what Leonardo was after was not the creation of a beautiful object but, rather, the solution to a problem. That problem, on some surface level, was the aesthetic problem of beauty or ugliness. But, on a more fundamental level, it was the passionate problem of love or hate. As such, when Leonardo completed an artwork, it meant that he had found the solution to his problem.

Already, we can appreciate why Leonardo would abandon an artwork. If completing an artwork simply meant creating a beautiful object, then it wouldn't have been a problem for him. Clearly, he had the skill to create a beautiful object. But completing an artwork was not just that. It meant something more. It meant answering the fundamental question of whether an object deserves to be loved or hated. To answer that question, Leonardo needed to know more about his object. For this knowledge, he turned to science. He studied the physical properties of his object: "[H]e directed his efforts to the properties and laws of light, colours, shadows and perspective in order to ensure mastery in the imitation of nature and to point the same way to others."[20] Yet, having learned all he could about the physical properties of his object, Leonardo found that he now had more questions than when he started: "[B]ehind the first one he saw countless other problems arising."[21] But instead of hastily returning to his artwork, he continued to suspend his passions and extend his investigations, this time expanding their parameters to include "animals and plants, and the proportions of the human body," and then "passing from their exterior, to proceed to gain a knowledge of their internal structure and their vital functions, which indeed also find expression in their appearance and have a claim to be depicted in art."[22]

Early on, the accumulation of this type of knowledge was enough to give Leonardo his answer, and thus, he was able to complete his artwork. However, as he matured as an artist, he began to find this type of knowledge insufficient. He began to see the object, not as an isolated monad but, rather, as a part of an entire world. Thus, "He was no longer able to limit his demands, to see the work of art in isolation and to tear it from the wide context to which he knew it belonged." Leonardo needed to know about this "wide context." But how could one know an entire world? That would take an infinite amount of inquiry. Leonardo was therefore faced with a decision. Either he could complete the artwork by imposing limits on his knowledge, limits that he knew would be arbitrary and artificial, or he could continue his investigations, maintaining fidelity to his curiosity. Leonardo chose the latter. "After the most exhausting efforts to bring to expression in [the artwork] everything which was connected with it in his thoughts," writes Freud, "he was forced to abandon it in an unfinished state or to declare that it was incomplete."[23] This fidelity to the infinitude of inquiry, and to the suspension of the passions that underwrites it, is, for Freud, Leonardo's genius. Not an innate talent for art but, rather, a fidelity to the infinite demands of curiosity.

Leonardo's genius therefore had nothing to do with the production of *Mona Lisa*, *The Last Supper*, or any other artwork. This is because genius, on Freud's view, has nothing to do with the production of beautiful artwork or with any other kind of achievement. Genius, for Freud, is not spending one's time "industriously painting to order and becoming rich," but, rather, recognizing the impossibility of knowing it all and suspending the passions— indefinitely—to engage in inquiry anyways. Yet, as Leonardo's abandonment of his artwork and of art altogether demonstrates, this commitment is not without its consequences. Genius indeed costs something. It costs the sense of mastery that one holds over the unknown when one believes one knows it all, a mastery that is to be sure illusory, but satisfying all the same. At the same time, this sacrifice of the illusion of mastery, and the satisfaction that it affords, does not mean that genius is bereft of enjoyment—the genius is not an ascetic—for, as I will show in the next two chapters, genius indeed comes with its own strange pleasure, a strange pleasure that substitutes for the lost satisfaction that comes when the illusion of mastery is given up. This peculiar pleasure—the pleasure that is enjoyed by the genius—is the pleasure that issues from the sublimation of the drive.

2

Sublimation or, On the Sexual Life of Genius

I

According to psychoanalysis, human beings possess—or, perhaps, more accurately, are possessed by—*Trieb* or, drive. In *Three Essays on the Theory of Sexuality*, Freud describes it this way: "By an 'instinct' is provisionally to be understood the psychical representative of an endosomatic, continuously flowing source of stimulation."[1] The keyword here is *continuously*. That is, the drive is the body's own constant innervation or excitation. What we call "pleasure" then is, for psychoanalysis, nothing more than the decrease or expenditure of that excitation, and what we call "pain," nothing more than its increase or accumulation.[2] To illustrate the point, think of the tension and release you feel while watching a horror film. The tension you feel rising within you when you don't know what is behind that door or underneath that bed is what psychoanalysis calls *pain*. And the relief you feel when the camera reveals that there is indeed nothing behind that door or underneath that bed? That is called *pleasure*.

Based on these admittedly quantitative understandings of pleasure and pain, psychoanalysis then asserts that human beings always "strive towards gaining pleasure" and always avoid "any event which might arouse unpleasure."[3] Otherwise put, human beings always seek decreases in the flow of stimulus and avoid increases. This law—or principle—of human behavior is what psychoanalysis calls *the pleasure principle*:

> In the theory of psycho-analysis we have no hesitation in assuming that the course taken by mental events is automatically regulated by the pleasure principle. We believe, that is to say, that the course of those events is invariably set in motion by an unpleasurable tension, that it takes a direction such that its final outcome coincides with a lowering of that tension—that is, with an avoidance of unpleasure or a production of pleasure.[4]

In various places in his writings, Freud argues that the affects of love and hate serve the pleasure principle. They do this by acting as signals of a kind, alerting the ego to the possibility of either pleasure, in the case of love, or pain, in the case of hate. As the ego encounters objects in the world, it learns that certain objects facilitate expenditure, lowering the amount of tension within the body, thereby producing pleasure, while other objects cause accumulation, increasing the amount of tension, thereby producing pain. As Freud explains, when the ego encounters an object that facilitates expenditure, "a motor urge is set up which seeks to bring the object closer to the ego and to incorporate it into the ego." "We then speak of that 'attraction' exercised by the pleasure-giving object, and say that we 'love' that object," he writes. Conversely, when the ego encounters an object that causes accumulation, "there is an urge which endeavours to increase the distance between the object and the ego." When this happens, he continues, "We feel the 'repulsion' of the object, and hate it."[5] The words *love* and *hate* then are, for Freud, simply ways of signifying whether or not an object is compatible with the overall aim of expenditure. "Love" signifying compatibility while "hate" signifying incongruity.

Later, Freud extends this account of hate in a fascinating direction. He suggests that in some cases hate can actually serve the pleasure principle, not simply as a signal but, rather, as a source of pleasure in itself. He explains that in situations where the path of love is blocked—like, between two rivals, an employer and their employee, the noir detective and the femme fatale, or Rick and Jesse's girl—hate can replace love, not to steer the ego away from the object, as it normally would, but, rather, "to bring the object closer to the ego" in the same manner as love itself. Hate, in this way, functions as a kind of compromise. Because the ego cannot incorporate the forbidden object as it would like, it does the next best thing and preserves its proximity to the object by hating it instead.

It may be tempting to read Freud here as meaning that hate serves as a cover for love, like when a child teases their crush. But Freud doesn't doubt the sincerity of the hate at stake in these types of situations. He takes it at face value. And yet, he argues, it gives rise to feelings of pleasure. In other words, hating can be as pleasurable as loving. Sports fans who hate a bitter rival will understand this. There is something profoundly—some may say, disturbingly—pleasurable in throwing popcorn at the TV screen when they score, getting on a message board and writing a tirade when they win, or reveling in their misfortune when their players get injured. Indeed, hating a rival may be even more pleasurable than loving one's own team. Putting this type of hate in the language of the pleasure principle, we could say that hate, in this case, facilitates the expenditure of stimulus and, as such, produces pleasure. In this way, "[H]ate acquires an erotic character and the continuity of a love-relation is ensured."[6]

Because hate too can function as a means of expenditure—that is, because hate too can produce pleasure—it makes no difference from the perspective of the pleasure principle whether one loves or hates. Either way, one still obeys it. The one who loves obeys by decreasing the flow of stimulation through a facilitating object while the one who hates obeys by decreasing the flow of stimulation through a repulsing object. But what about the one who neither loves nor hates? What about the one who suspends both love and hate? That is, what about the genius? If both love and hate are experiences of pleasure, insofar as both ultimately facilitate the expenditure of stimulus, then doesn't the suspension of love and hate lead to pain? If this is true, then why does genius exist?

Here, we can appreciate just how counterintuitive Freud's theory of genius is. It is counterintuitive, not only from the perspective of the popular imagination, insofar as it defies the image of savants and prodigies, but also from the perspective of psychoanalysis itself, insofar as it directly contradicts the doctrine of the pleasure principle. According to the pleasure principle, genius, as it is conceived by Freud, should not exist. No human being would ever suspend the impulses of love and hate. It would be tantamount to choosing pain, and no human being, it believes, would ever choose pain. The notion is absurd. And yet, Freud insists, against the momentum of psychoanalytic theory itself, that genius exists. The only question is how?

II

In the seminal paper "Instincts and Their Vicissitudes"—the first of Freud's major papers on metapsychology—Freud sets out to give the definitive account of the drive. Written ten years after *Three Essays on the Theory of Sexuality*, Freud modifies his definition of the drive slightly. The drive, he now writes, "never operates as a force giving a *momentary* impact but always as a *constant* one."[7] Notice the change? It is subtle. What was once described in *Three Essays* as a "continuously flowing source of stimulation" is now described simply as a "force."

Though this change from "continuously flowing source of stimulation" to "force" is indeed subtle, it has a significant theoretical implication. Namely, it allows Freud to distinguish between the drive and other forms of mental stimulation. He writes, "There is nothing to prevent our subsuming the concept of 'instinct' under that of 'stimulus' and saying that an instinct is a stimulus applied to the mind." "But," he goes on, "we are immediately set on our guard against *equating* instinct and mental stimulus."[8] In other words, the drive may be like other forms of mental stimulus, but they are not the same. The difference, Freud says, is in their respective places of origin. Whereas ordinary mental stimulus originates from outside the body in the external world, the drive originates from within the body.

This difference in origins has a profound practical consequence for us. Because it originates from outside the body, ordinary mental stimulus can be dealt with relatively easily, and therefore, it does not present much of a problem at all, all things being equal. If, for example, the sun overstimulates my eyes, thereby causing me pain, I can simply block it with my hand or go stand under a shady tree. When my first son was young, I once sang him a song about Cheerios, which had the effect of overstimulating him. Once this was brought to my attention—as I was unaware of the effect my song was having on him—I stopped singing, and he immediately calmed down. In this way, the pain caused by ordinary mental stimulus is "momentary," that is, "it can be disposed of by a single expedient action," like standing under a tree or stopping dad's singing.[9]

The same, however, cannot be said of the drive. Because the stimulus that emanates from the drive emanates from within the body, "no flight can avail against it."[10] If I stand under the bright sun, the drive is there, and if I stand under a shady tree, the drive is still there. To paraphrase the psalmist: if I ascend up into heaven, the drive art there; if I make my bed in Sheol, behold the drive art there. There is nowhere we can go to escape from the force of the drive. It is always with us. Indeed, it is always within us. This is why Freud describes the drive as a force giving *constant* impact. Because it emanates from within, no amount of change in our external circumstances can put an end to its stimulation. What is needed instead is a change in our internal situation or, as Freud puts it, to effect "an appropriate ... alteration of the internal source of stimulation."[11]

For Freud, the primary means for changing one's internal situation is mental activity. A year before "Instincts and Their Vicissitudes," in the 1914 paper, "On Narcissism," Freud writes the following:

> We have recognized our mental apparatus as being first and foremost a device designed for mastering excitations which would otherwise be felt as distressing or would have pathogenic effects. Working them over in the mind helps remarkably towards an internal draining away of excitations which are incapable of direct discharge outwards, or for which such a discharge is for the moment undesirable.[12]

The key phrase here is *internal draining away of excitations*. By utilizing the mind—"mental apparatus," in Freud's locution—we are able to expend stimulus without having to change our external circumstances. The mind is unique in this regard. Only the mind has the ability to metabolize stimulus through its own operation. Every other bodily "apparatus" requires some sort of external change. Standing under a shady tree, for example, requires that I move my body from its present location to its new location under a tree. It also requires the presence of a shady tree. Thus, standing under a shady tree requires that I change my external circumstances. Thinking, on the other hand, is different. It is solipsistic. That is to say, it takes place entirely within the mind. As such, I do not need to change my external circumstances to think. Whether I am standing under a shady tree or under the bright sun makes no difference to the mind. I am able to think either way.

So, while Freud makes no mention of the drive in the quote from Narcissism, by theorizing the mind as a "device" capable of internal expenditure, he identifies a way for us to deal with the constant force of the drive. Unable to satisfy the drive by changing our external circumstances—such as by standing under a tree or getting dad to stop singing—we can turn inward, "draining away" the drive's excitations by "working them over" in the mind.

This is a very active picture of the mind indeed.[13] The mind here is presented not simply as a passive bystander, assisting the process of expenditure only by storing up ever-accumulating stimulus. Rather, it is as an active participant in that process. Indeed, it is that process itself. In *Leonardo*, Freud elaborates on how so. There, he claims that the pleasure produced by the mind—he calls it "the intellectual feeling," but elsewhere, he calls it "intellectual pleasure"—derives from the mind "having found a solution."[14] That is, we do not experience intellectual pleasure simply by mulling problems over in our heads. Rather, we experience it by figuring out their solutions.

In the language of Freud's metapsychology, the mind—or, more precisely, the mind's various processes, like thinking and reflecting—is the *aim* of the drive. That is, "the act toward which the instinct tends."[15] What is needed for the mind to achieve its aim—what the mind's various processes are missing, in other words—is *the object* or, "the thing in regard to which or through which the instinct is able to achieve its aim."[16] I will return to this issue of the missing object in Chapter 6, but here I only want to point out that when Freud introduces the solution into the matrix of intellectual pleasure, he is identifying the solution as the object to the mind's aim. Otherwise put, intellectual pleasure is not derived from the mind engaging in thinking and reflecting alone. Nor is it derived from the fact of the solution alone. Rather, it is derived from the mind, through thought and reflection, *finding* the solution.

As an illustration of this idea, think of the crossword puzzle. While I was an undergraduate in university, I would do the daily crossword puzzle featured in the school newspaper. I always found the exercise pleasurable. But where did my pleasure come from? It didn't come from doing the crossword puzzle itself. I know this because if the clues were too hard to solve, I would simply toss out the newspaper, hoping to find an easier puzzle the next day. At the same time, it didn't come from the answers themselves. I know this because the school always published the answers in the next day's paper, but I never waited until the next day and simply copied down all the answers. There was nothing satisfying in simply having the answers. I had to find them. That is, "the intellectual feeling" of doing the crossword puzzle came entirely from *finding* the answers. The Eureka! or Ah ha! moment, we might call it. The best crossword puzzles then were the ones that were not too hard but also not too easy, so that I could struggle a little bit on a clue and then find the answer.

What is so striking about Freud's account of intellectual pleasure is how at odds it is with his theory of genius. Recall that when faced with the question of whether to love or hate, the genius chooses neither, opting to investigate instead. *One has no right to love or hate anything if one has not acquired a thorough knowledge of its nature* is the genius's motto. What this means is that the genius postpones finding the solution—the very source of intellectual pleasure itself—in order to engage in the mental processes themselves. They would rather ruminate on the problem than find the solution. Indeed, this is precisely what makes someone a genius in Freud. Not that they arrive at answers quickly but, rather, that they engage in the long process of inquiry. And yet, doesn't this mean that the mind of the genius is a "device" designed for producing *pain*, and not pleasure? If the genius postpones finding the solution in order to investigate, are they not postponing the feeling of intellectual pleasure at the risk of experiencing pain?

Thus, on two important counts—the suspension of love and hate and the postponement of the solution—Freud's account of genius directly contradicts the psychoanalytic doctrine of the pleasure principle. Indeed, the contradiction is so stark that it appears as though one must choose between the two. Either Freud's theory of genius is right and the pleasure principle is wrong or the pleasure principle is right and Freud's theory of genius is wrong. Both cannot be correct at the same time.

To address this contradiction, Freud introduces a third concept into his account: the concept of sublimation. Sublimation, Freud writes, is the drive's "power to replace its immediate aim by other aims which may be valued more highly and which are not sexual."[17] I will elaborate on what Freud means by this formulation in what follows, as I admit, it is not immediately obvious. But we should know this at the outset: it is not a synthesis. Sublimation does not reconcile Freud's theory of genius with the doctrine of the pleasure principle by bringing the two together in some kind of synthesis or third way.

Rather, sublimation theorizes the very limit of the pleasure principle itself, the place where the distinction between pleasure and pain itself breaks down and the two become intertwined and implicated with one another. That is to say, sublimation, as I will argue, is not the reconciliation of a contradiction but, rather, the name of one.[18]

III

In *Leonardo da Vinci and a Memory of His Childhood*, sublimation enters the picture as one of three possible orientations—or vicissitudes, in Freud's locution—that we can take in response to the failure of our earliest intellectual experiences, what Freud calls the infantile sexual researches. Our earliest intellectual experiences, Freud observes, occur while we are still children, typically around questions of a sexual nature, such as, "where babies come from."[19] However, as Freud also observes, these "infantile sexual researches" invariably end in failure—that is, insofar as we define success as the discovery of scientifically valid answers. They end in failure, Freud argues, because of the incongruity that exists between the sexual nature of the question at hand and our own sexual constitution at the time. For example, a child does not yet see the penis as a sexual organ, equipped with the capacity to inseminate, and therefore, they cannot figure out what the father has to do with procreation. Or a child does not yet conceive of the vagina as a sexual organ, and therefore, they think the mother simply excretes babies like feces. The child, we might say, is constitutionally or structurally prevented from discovering the solution to childbirth.

For Freud, the failure of these infantile sexual researches is not something reserved for some and not others. For him, the failure is universal. That is, the infantile sexual researches end in failure for everyone *without exception*. And that includes even the genius. Understandably, for some, this assertion may be difficult to accept, especially those who imagine the genius as some sort of silicon success, like Bill Gates or Steve Jobs. But on this point, Freud is absolutely firm. The failure of the infantile sexual researches is universal. However, we need not find this fact discouraging. There is a positive upshot to it. It means that failure is not an impediment to genius. What makes someone a genius is not whether or not they experience failure while doing intellectual work, for we have all failed at some point in our lives. What matters instead is the relationship or orientation which we take toward that failure.

The first orientation or vicissitude that Freud identifies is *neurotic inhibition*. In neurotic inhibition, "research shares the fate of sexuality; thenceforward curiosity remains inhibited and the free activity of intelligence may be limited for the whole of the subject's lifetime."[20] That is to say, with neurotic inhibition, everything that the pleasure principle predicts comes to pass. The infantile sexual researches end in failure. All future intellectual endeavors recall the painful memory of that initial failure. Thus, instead of engaging in intellectual work, and reliving that painful memory, the neurotic simply forgoes intellectual work altogether in favor of more pleasurable activities. Freud calls this shunning of intellectual work "neurotic inhibition," but a more common name for it is anti-intellectualism.

The second vicissitude that Freud identifies is *compulsive brooding*. With compulsive brooding, a complete repudiation of intellectual work is avoided. Freud writes, "Sometime after the infantile sexual researches have come to an end, the intelligence, having grown stronger, recalls the old association and offers its help in evading sexual repression." With compulsive brooding, thinking becomes a legitimate aim of the drive. The trouble, however, is that it often becomes the *exclusive* aim of the drive. So, while the compulsive brooder avoids the fate of anti-intellectualism, thinking, for them, becomes "a sexual activity" in its own right, imbued with all "the pleasure and anxiety that belong to sexual processes proper."[21]

Another name for the compulsive brooder might be the know-it-all. They are the ones that have all the answers. It must be this way because pleasure for them is wrapped up in knowing the answer. But there is a problem. A different problem from that of anti-intellectualism, but a problem all the same. Recall that the mind produces pleasure not purely in itself but, rather, through its ability to find solutions. What this means is that there is no pleasure in *having* the answers. All the pleasure that comes from thinking comes from *finding* the answers. To have the answers is always to have them too long. This is why no one saves their crossword puzzles once they are done. Once solved, the crossword puzzle has already outlived its usefulness. For this reason, there is always a bittersweet taste mixed into the know-it-all's pleasure, for what they truly know is that pleasure is fleeting. Discovered knowledge is for them like a stack of old completed crossword puzzles—useless. What they need is to find new answers. This is why the know-it-all loves to show off their knowledge. In showing it off, they hope to relive its discovery vicariously through the other. They live for the other's Ah ha! moment, since theirs is gone. Yet, the only way to truly experience new pleasure is to find new knowledge. And so, the know-it-all embarks on an incessant search for new knowledge, hoping to experience fresh pleasures, until "this brooding never ends and that intellectual feeling, so much desired, of having found a solution recedes more and more into the distance."[22]

The third and final vicissitude that Freud names is *sublimation*. Freud writes of it this:

In virtue of a special disposition, the third type, which is the rarest and most perfect, escapes both inhibition of thought and neurotic compulsive thinking. It is true that here too sexual repression comes about, but it does not succeed in relegating a component instinct of sexual desire to the unconscious. Instead, the libido evades the fate of repression by being sublimated from the very beginning into curiosity and by becoming attached to the powerful instinct for research as a reinforcement.[23]

In this vicissitude, the infantile sexual researches importantly still end in failure, but the pain of that failure does not cause the child to abandon intellectual pursuits altogether, like the anti-intellectual. Rather, the child continues to take them up. They do this by sublimating their infantile curiosity with the drive. Another name for the child who sublimates their curiosity with the drive is the genius. In other words, the genius suspends the passions and embraces inquiry by sublimating their curiosity with the drive.

In sublimation, as in compulsive brooding, "research becomes to some extent compulsive and a substitute for sexual activity." But genius is different from compulsive brooding insofar as "the quality of neurosis is absent." Unlike the compulsive brooder, the genius does not become obsessed with the original failure of the infantile sexual researches, and so, the genius does not use inquiry as a way of righting that initial failure. As a result, the genius does not become fixated on the idea of finding a solution in the way that the know-it-all does. Instead, the genius decouples the drive from the object of the solution, thereby allowing it to "operate freely in the service of intellectual interest."[24]

IV

Sublimation is something of a mystery in Freud. It appears from time to time throughout his work, but it is never thoroughly elaborated. There is no paper or book dedicated to its topic.[25] What one finds instead are fragments and allusions. In fact, the most developed account of sublimation we have is from *Leonardo da Vinci and a Memory of His Childhood*. For this reason, sublimation has been the object of some misunderstanding, not only for those outside of psychoanalysis but even—or, I should say, especially— for those inside of it. Take, for instance, the definition of sublimation that Freud gives in *Leonardo* as the drive's "power to replace its immediate aim by other aims which may be valued more highly and which are not sexual." The standard way of interpreting this definition is to read it as meaning that the drive substitutes sex with other activities like art, sports, or research. On this view, the erotic energy that would have gone into sex gets diverted into these other activities, giving them the same passionate character as sex itself. Thus, the artist creates and the scientist researches instead of having sex. But we should reject this interpretation—call it, the standard interpretation—as it suffers from two significant problems.

The first problem with the standard interpretation is that it confuses sublimation with compulsive brooding. Recall that in compulsive brooding, thinking becomes a substitute for sex. The "pleasure and anxiety that belong to sexual processes proper," Freud says, are felt through thinking, and the pleasure that belongs to thinking is felt in place of sex. As Freud himself puts it, in compulsive brooding, the drive imbues thinking with its constant supply of stimulus, which is "sufficiently powerful to sexualize thinking itself."[26] The compulsive brooder literally thinks instead of having sex. In all these ways, Freud describes compulsive brooding as the replacement of sex with thinking. Or, to put it another way, he describes compulsive brooding in exactly the same terms that the standard interpretation describes sublimation.

The second problem with the standard interpretation is that it conflates what are in Freud two separate concepts: *sex* and *the sexual aim*. When the standard interpretation takes "the power to replace its immediate aim by other aims which may be valued more highly and which are *not sexual*" to mean that sublimation replaces sex with activities such as art and sports, the standard interpretation treats sex as the sole aim of the drive, completely missing how things like art and sports can also be legitimate aims of the drive. Indeed, if films like *Ghost* (1990) and *Bull Durham* (1988) have taught us anything, it is that art and sports are as sexual as sex itself.

What is particularly unfortunate about the standard interpretation's conflation of sex and the sexual aim is that one of Freud's earliest, and most important, interventions into our understanding of sexuality was the introduction of this exact distinction. On the very first page of *Three Essays on the Theory of Sexuality*, Freud calls out the common view of sex, saying that it promotes "a very false picture," full of "errors, inaccuracies and hasty conclusions."[27] The reason Freud takes the common view to task is because it assumes sex to be a single entity, the copulative act itself. But this is not at all the case, contends Freud. Sex is not a single thing. It is, rather, a composite act, made up of multiple smaller parts called *sexual aims*. As Freud puts it, "[T]here are certain intermediate relations to the sexual object, such as touching and looking at it, which lie on the road towards copulation and are recognized as being preliminary sexual aims."[28]

To illustrate Freud's point, take what is for many people the narrowest definition of sex possible: heterosexual, procreative sex. To say that sex is a single entity would be to say that the libido aims solely at the penetration of the vagina by the penis for the purpose of insemination, to put it bluntly. But, as Freud points out, when we examine even this narrow conception of sex, we find the presence of all sorts of minor acts, which are not in themselves "the union of the genitals," but which nevertheless have a claim on sex.[29] We find, for example, partners kissing one another, touching one another, and gazing at one another. We find them dressing in certain kinds of clothes, saying specific kinds of statements, and making particular kinds of gestures. And we find them doing all these things—and more—in addition to the copulative act itself. In fact, it would be very difficult, even for the most narrow-minded individual, to imagine sex without any of these intervening acts. After all, what would sex be if it involved only the penetration of the vagina by the penis—and only for the purpose of procreation—and nothing else? Would we even call it sex at that point? Or would we think of it as some sort of strange clinical procedure? Like something from a dystopian science-fiction film? Freud's argument is that these intervening acts play a vital role in this thing called sex and that sex would not be what it is without them. For that reason, he insists, we must recognize the sexuality of seemingly nonsexual things, like looking and touching or indeed making pottery and playing baseball. Designating them as "sexual aims" is Freud's way of giving them that recognition. It is his way of saying that the libido aims at those things as much as it aims at "the union of the genitals" itself. Thus, to interpret "the power to replace its immediate aim by other aims which may be valued more highly and which are not sexual" to mean the substitution of sex with art and sports, as the standard interpretation does, amounts to saying that sublimation is the substitution of one sexual aim with another sexual aim—a nonsensical statement.

What then is a *nonsexual* aim, if it is not something like art or sports? The simplest answer is: the opposite of a sexual aim. And what is a *sexual* aim? A sexual aim, Freud writes, in *Three Essays*, "consists in replacing the projected sensation of stimulation in the erotogenic zone by an external stimulus which removes that sensation by producing a feeling of satisfaction."[30] That is, a sexual aim is an act that produces "a feeling of satisfaction" by removing or expending the stimulation occurring at an "erotogenic zone" of the body. It does not matter what the act is, if it is sex itself or an act that is normally unassociated with sex, such as, looking, touching, or even simply talking.[31] All that matters is if the act removes stimulation from the body. If it does, then it counts as a sexual aim.

Here, Freud relates the work of the sexual aim to the presence of "external stimulus," but later, in "Instincts and Their Vicissitudes," he extends that work to include the drive, writing, "The aim of an instinct is in every instance satisfaction, which can only be obtained by removing the state of stimulation at the source of the instinct."[32] A sexual aim then is an act that produces satisfaction by lowering or removing excitations occurring within the body, whether those excitations owe to the presence of external stimulus or the drive. What those aims might be in practice vary. For one person, it is exercising at the gym. For a second, it is having drinks with friends. For a third, it is sex. Indeed, as Freud points out, there may even be "various nearer or intermediate aims" embedded within a single aim.[33] Thus, for someone, the ritual of getting dressed up to have drinks with friends is in itself satisfying. Regardless of what it is, a sexual aim produces satisfaction by reducing stimulation.

Turning now to the nonsexual aim: if a *sexual* aim is an act that produces satisfaction by removing "the projected sensation of stimulation in the erotogenic zone," whether that "projected sensation" is caused by external stimulants, like the sun or dad's singing, or by the drive itself, then a *nonsexual* aim is an act that does *not* produce satisfaction because it does *not* remove that "projected sensation of stimulation" caused by either external stimulants or the drive. To put it in positive terms, a nonsexual aim is any act that produces *dissatisfaction*. That is to say, for an act to be considered a nonsexual aim in the psychoanalytic sense, it must be an act that produces the feeling of dissatisfaction—and that is it. It does not matter if the act in question is normally considered nonsexual, like making pottery or playing baseball, or sexual, like masturbation. What matters is if the act in question produces satisfaction by removing stimulus or not. If it does, then it is a sexual aim, and if it does not, then it is a nonsexual aim, no matter what it is. It doesn't even matter if the act in question is sex itself. If there is someone for whom sex does not produce feelings of satisfaction—perhaps, for them, it produces feelings of anxiety instead—then, as strange as it might sound, from a psychoanalytic perspective, sex would be for them a *nonsexual* aim. No wonder Freud says of the psychoanalytic view of sexuality that "it goes lower and also higher than its popular sense"![34]

Now, if we return to Freud's definition of sublimation as the drive's "power to replace its immediate aim by other aims which may be valued more highly and which are not sexual," and we plug in this properly psychoanalytic definition of the nonsexual aim, this is what we get: sublimation is not the substitution of sex with thinking as the standard interpretation has it, but, much rather, the replacement of the aim of satisfaction with the aim of dissatisfaction. Otherwise put, sublimation is the act of aiming the drive at a target that is "other than, and remote from, that of sexual satisfaction."[35] Thus, the genius—as the exemplary figure of sublimation—is not someone who simply investigates instead of having sex, as the standard interpretation has it. They are rather someone who has turned their curiosity into a nonsexual aim by "renouncing libidinal satisfaction" itself as the ultimate aim of the drive.[36]

V

For the pleasure principle, sublimation is an odd phenomenon indeed. From its perspective, sublimation appears to be an aim without an object. What do I mean by this? Recall that to obtain satisfaction, the aim by itself is not enough. There must also be an object through which the drive can achieve its aim. To exercise at the gym, there must be a gym. To drink with friends, there must be drinks and friends. And to have sex with a partner, there must be a partner. But sublimation does not aim at satisfaction. It aims at dissatisfaction. So, what need is there for an object? All that is needed for sublimation to obtain its aim is the aim itself. That is to say, if the *sexual* drive wants to exercise at the gym with a gym, to drink with friends with drinks and friends, and to have sex with a partner with a partner, then the *sublimated* drive wants to exercise at the gym without the gym, to drink with friends without either drinks or friends, and to have sex with a partner without a partner. The sublimated drive is like Voltaire's quip about the Holy Roman Empire being neither Holy nor Roman nor an Empire. It is an aim without any of the objects needed to achieve that aim. As Kant might have put it, it is purposiveness without purpose.[37]

I will return to the issue of the object in Part Two. Here, I only want to consider what effect the lack of an object has on the genius's relationship with the aim of inquiry, as I believe this way of looking at genius will clarify two important aspects of it. The first of these aspects is the genius's relationship with the infantile sexual researches.

As we learned, the genius avoids the fate of both the anti-intellectual and the know-it-all, despite having also experienced failure as an emergent intellectual. As we also learned, the genius avoids the fate of both through the help of sublimation. But what we did not know was exactly why sublimation helps the genius avoid those two fates. But now we know. By aiming the drive away from sexual satisfaction, sublimation deemphasizes the role of the object in intellectual work. It makes no difference to the genius if they are unable to find the solution to the problem of birth. For them, what is important is the process of inquiry itself. This is not the case with either the anti-intellectual or the know-it-all. For them, finding the answer is paramount. Indeed, they cannot imagine doing intellectual work otherwise; it makes no sense. For the genius, however, joy comes from doing intellectual work itself, not from finding answers—inquiry without solutions.

To be sure, this doesn't mean that the genius has no appreciation for accuracy and facticity or that they love falsity and factitiousness. The genius is not a science denier. All it means is that inquiry for them is a creative act. It is meant to create new thoughts and ideas, not to arrive at predetermined answers and solutions.

We find an example of this creativity in one of Leonardo's sketches: *Coition of a Hemisected Man and Woman*. This sketch depicts the cross-section of a man and woman during the act of copulation. It possesses a number of strange features. Rudof Reitler enumerates nearly all of them. The man is depicted in full while the woman lacks a head. This is made up for by the androgynous identity of the man. Indeed, for Reitler, his head resembles more that of a woman than that of a man. The breast is depicted as having only a single lactiferous duct, which is connected internally to the female sex organs. The two figures are standing in a position that would make coitus uncomfortable, if not impossible. The detail that Reitler overlooks is the depiction of the penis.[38] It possesses, not one but two ducts, one connected to the testes and the other connected to the spine. But "the clumsiest blunder" of all, according to Reitler, is the transposition of the figures' legs.[39] The feet are reversed, making it impossible for the legs to belong to the figures to which they are assigned. Indeed, given the situation of the legs, it almost appears as though Leonardo's *Hemisected Man and Woman* is not in fact two figures at all but, rather, a single figure, conjoined through the genitals. In this regard, the figure is reminiscent of Aristophanes' myth of the origins of human beings from Plato's *Symposium*. In that myth, human beings were originally conjoined creatures which were split apart by Zeus as a punishment. *Hemisected Man and Woman* appears to be just such a creature.

Freud is well aware of the "remarkable errors" contained within Leonardo's sketch. Indeed, they cause him to openly question whether "Leonardo ever embraced a woman in passion."[40] And yet, his assessment of these errors—and by extension the sketch itself—differs quite widely from that of Reitler. For Reitler, the errors are a clear indication that Leonardo's "excessive instinct for research has totally failed."[41] For Freud, however, they are the auspicious signs of Leonardo's genius.

The core of Freud's contention with Reitler has to do with the status of the sketch itself. When Reitler considers the sketch, he sees an attempt to solve the mystery of human sexuality. For this reason, he is disappointed to discover the presence of many gross errors. For as far as Reitler is concerned, the sketch only has value insofar as it conveys scientifically accurate information about human sexuality. And so, the fact that it contains many "remarkable errors" means that Leonard's "instinct for research" has run amok. To put this another way, for Reitler, inquiry is what psychology calls a convergent process, a process meant to close in on or converge upon a single predetermined answer. Thus, the fact that Leonardo's sketch presents so many divergent ideas about human sexuality—a lactiferous duct connected with the ovaries, the differentiation of the nervous and sexual systems in the penis, the ambiguity of sexual identity itself, and so on—indicates to Reitler that the research process for Leonardo has gone awry.

When Freud considers the sketch, on the other hand, what he sees is not an attempt to solve the mystery of human sexuality but, rather, an "endless and inexhaustible investigation of nature."[42] Thus, for Freud, it is not at all surprising that the sketch would contain errors. In fact, it is expected. For the sketch is not in search of an answer that already exists. Rather, it wants to ask questions which push us beyond what we already know. So, of course, it contains errors! In this regard, Leonardo's sketch is like the theories of childbirth which children create through their research. Children will conjecture that babies are excreted from the anus like excrement or that mothers spontaneously generate them when they feel love. These theories, Freud says, "go astray in a grotesque fashion," but they also exhibit remarkable imagination and ingenuity, and so, for that reason, they deserve to be called "strokes of genius."[43] Likewise, Leonardo's *Hemisected Man and Woman*, from a scientific perspective, gets it incredibly wrong. The breast doesn't possess only one duct for milk; the penis doesn't have separate ducts for insemination and micturition. In this way, Leonardo's sketch goes grotesquely astray. But it also dares to invent ideas where knowledge is lacking at the risk of being wrong. And for that reason, it deserves to be called a true work of genius.

What gives Leonardo's sketch value then is not that it conveys scientifically valid information about human sexuality but, rather, that it presents an array of "suggestive ideas," ideas that push the boundaries of our preconceived notions about sexuality.[44] That is to say, if inquiry for Reitler is a convergent process, then, for Freud, it is a divergent one; a process for creating new ideas, for diverging from a single correct answer. Thus, for Freud, the many "remarkable errors" contained within *Coition of a Hemisected Man and Woman* are not the indicators of research gone awry but, rather, research at its creative best.

The relationship with the infantile sexual researches—and inquiry, more generally—is then the first aspect of genius that is clarified by the formulation *aim without an object*. The second aspect is the fidelity to inquiry. According to the pleasure principle, human beings will gravitate toward aims that produce satisfaction and stay away from aims that produce pain. This is why the anti-intellectual shuns intellectual activities. These activities fail to bring them satisfaction. At the root of the anti-intellectual's particular difficulty with intellectual processes is, as we know, the inability to find answers. The answer or the solution, as we also know, is the object through which an intellectual aim achieves the goal of satisfaction. Thus, failing to find answers is for the anti-intellectual tantamount to pain.

The genius, however, rejects the aim of satisfaction itself. For them, the aim of the drive is dissatisfaction. For this reason, answers play only an incidental role in the intellectual activities of the genius. Of primary importance are the activities themselves. What the genius finds so enjoyable about doing crossword puzzles, in other words, is doing the puzzles themselves, not finding the answers. It is not the discovery of the answer, after a long struggle with a problem, that the genius finds enjoyable. It is the long struggle itself. For this reason, it is no problem at all for the genius that the pleasure principle makes finding answers the precondition for experiencing intellectual pleasure. The genius is not after intellectual pleasure in the first place, so what difference does it make if pleasure depends on finding the answer?

This is why the genius is able to engage in inquiry infinitely. The genius has refused the aim of satisfaction as such, which means they are not in it for the answers. Where they find joy is in the process of inquiry itself. So, when the answers do not appear, and the inquiry keeps going, this is not a problem for the genius like it is for the anti-intellectual and the know-it-all. Indeed, the genius is right at home. In fact, we may go so far as to suggest that the genius is not only unfazed by the lack of answers but actively desires it, since it prolongs inquiry, the very source of the genius's joy. Thus, if the genius aims the drive at something "other than, and remote from, that of sexual satisfaction," then it is not too much to say that they aim their intellectual work at something "other than, and remote from" the answer.

Yet, while the pleasure principle clarifies why the genius would survive the failure of the infantile sexual researches and engage in the process of inquiry infinitely, it raises a very important question about the origin of genius itself. If, as I have said multiple times, the pleasure principle dictates that we strive after pleasure and avoid pain, then why does the genius exist in the first place? If finding answers produces intellectual pleasure, and if the genius refuses to find answers, then why does genius exist at all? As I have suggested, it would be tantamount to choosing pain. And no human being, according to the pleasure principle, would choose pain. Freud's answer to this question may surprise us. He argues that the genius exists, not because they defy the pleasure principle like some kind of ascetic. Rather, they exist because sublimation affords its own unique satisfaction. A strange sort of satisfaction that comes, not from the expenditure of stimulus but, rather, from its accumulation. A satisfaction in dissatisfaction or a pleasure in pain, which issues from the innervations of the drive itself. Freud calls this strange satisfaction *forepleasure*.

3

Finding Satisfaction

I

According to the terms set by Freud's metapsychology, pleasure is the decrease of stimulus and pain its increase. Based on these terms—terms set by Freud himself—one should conclude that genius is the experience of pain. After all, sublimation replaces the aim of satisfaction with the aim of dissatisfaction, causing stimulus to accrue within the body. And the accrual of stimulus is pain. And yet, amazingly, this is not what Freud concludes.

In a small encyclopedia article on libido theory, Freud writes the following: "The most important vicissitude which an instinct can undergo seems to be sublimation; here both object and aim are changed, so that what was originally a sexual instinct finds satisfaction in some achievement which is no longer sexual but has a higher social or ethical valuation."[1] Much of this sentence should be familiar by now. Sublimation is a rare and highly regarded vicissitude; it transforms the drive; it replaces a sexual aim with a nonsexual aim. But it also contains something new. It also asserts that sublimation "finds satisfaction." *What was originally a sexual instinct finds satisfaction.* But how can this be? Is not every experience of satisfaction at bottom an expenditure of stimulus? So, how can sublimation, which according to Freud himself is the repudiation of libidinal satisfaction, still be an experience of satisfaction? What does Freud mean when he says that sublimation "finds satisfaction"?

What is so counterintuitive about Freud's assertion is that it thinks together two opposing claims at the same time. On one hand, it thinks the claim of sublimation. That is, the claim that sublimation is the renunciation of satisfaction. And on the other hand, it thinks the claim of the pleasure principle. That is, the claim that all human beings pursue pleasure and avoid pain. And yet, instead of drawing the conclusion to which these two opposing claims seem to logically and naturally lead—namely, the conclusion that sublimation is the experience of pain—Freud draws the opposite conclusion: sublimation "finds satisfaction." It is as if these two claims were conspiring to hide a truth, and Freud plucked that truth from obscurity. But if this is the case and Freud was indeed rescuing a truth from oblivion, it is not a truth that comes from the synthesis of opposites. Freud does not assert something like: sublimation is the expenditure of stimulus through nonsexual aims. Rather, it is the truth that emerges when the moment of truth in opposing claims confront each other in a contradiction. For what Freud asserts is that sublimation is the pleasure that comes from the nonexpenditure of stimulus. Or, otherwise put, a satisfaction in dissatisfaction.

II

The idea that dissatisfaction affords its own kind of strange satisfaction is a challenging one to grasp. Part of the issue, it seems to me, are the words themselves. "Satisfaction" and "dissatisfaction" convey opposition, and so, as words, they make it difficult for us to appreciate how satisfaction and dissatisfaction, as phenomena, might be entangled with one another. For this reason, I suggest that we find a new word, one capable of capturing the contradictory nature of sublimation. In that case, the term "masochism" suggests itself. After all, is not masochism—at least, as it is popularly understood—pleasure in pain? Could "masochism" then name the odd pleasure in nonexpenditure which inheres in sublimation?

As tempting as it might be to put masochism together with sublimation, we must reject the term. We must reject it, however, not because the idea of masochism itself is off-putting. We must reject it rather because, according to Freud, the pain at stake in masochism does not arise from the quantitative situation of the drive. That is to say, it is not the pain that arises from the accumulation of stimulus. Rather, it is the qualitative correlate of a different underlying economic reality, which must be called pleasurable. As Freud puts it in his 1924 paper on masochism, "Pleasure and unpleasure ... cannot be referred to an increase or decrease of a quantity." He goes on: "It appears that they depend, not on this quantitative factor, but on some characteristic of it which we can only describe as a qualitative one."[2] The reason the masochist is able to derive pleasure from pain is because pain, in this case, does not have to do with accumulation. It is merely the way the masochist experiences the expenditure of stimulus—that is, pleasure. This is why pleasure and pain are intertwined for the masochist. Pain is simply the qualitative experience of what is, from an economic point of view, pleasure. Or, to put it another way, for the masochist, pain is a sexual aim. This is why there is nothing contradictory about masochism. The pleasure at stake in it is still the pleasure of reduction—the pleasure of the pleasure principle—and not the pleasure of nonexpenditure, which we find in sublimation.

With "masochism" off the table, I am tempted to volunteer the term "enjoyment"—*jouissance*, in Lacan's locution. The advantage of the word "enjoyment" is that it conveys a sense of insatiability—a sense of more— which gets at the economic dimension of the drive. For example, compare the statements, "Coffee *gratifies* me" and "I *enjoy* coffee." As statements, both convey the idea that I find coffee pleasing. In that sense, they are equivalent. But only one—"Coffee gratifies me"—conveys a sense of contentment. If I say, "Coffee gratifies me," I give the sense that with coffee I have enough. I may lack bread and water, but if I have coffee, I have all that I need. Gratification fulfills my desires. It sates me. The statement "I enjoy coffee," on the other hand, lacks this dimension of contentment. If I say, "I enjoy coffee," I give the sense that I like coffee on top of everything else I have. It doesn't matter if I've just eaten a full meal or if I'm about to go to sleep. It doesn't even matter if I've just had a cup. "I enjoy coffee" means that I can always go for another cup. In fact, you could imagine me responding to my colleague's shock at seeing me pour my tenth cup of the day with a laconic, "I enjoy coffee." Enjoyment exceeds gratification. It always says "more" or, as Lacan puts it, "encore."[3]

It is this sense of insatiability—of excess or encore—that makes "enjoyment," as a word, particularly evocative in this context. All that is needed to make "enjoyment" work as our term is to connect this sense of insatiability to the nonexpenditure of stimulus. In that case, what if enjoyment does not bring contentment because it does not expend stimulus? What if enjoyment is the particular experience of nonexpenditure itself? That is, what if enjoyment does not bring contentment precisely because it is the pleasure that issues from the nonexpenditure of the drive? But here I will break off this line of thought because Freud in fact already has a term to name this peculiar satisfaction in dissatisfaction which is at stake in sublimation. *Forepleasure.*

III

Recall that in *Three Essays on the Theory of Sexuality*, Freud finds in sex the presence of numerous intermediate acts accompanying the copulatory act itself. Acts, such as, hugging, kissing, looking, and touching, for instance. Freud calls these intermediate acts "preparatory acts," and he argues that they are indispensable for the intensity of pleasure which is felt through sex.[4] Here is the idea. If pleasure is the expenditure of stimulus, then the more stimulus there is to expend, the more pleasure there is to experience. For intense pleasures, such as, sex, there must be an extraordinarily large amount of stimulus to expend. The copulatory act itself cannot be responsible for creating this quantity because its job is to expend stimulus. Something else must therefore increase that quantity. That something else is the preparatory act.

Whereas copulation is responsible for reducing stimulus, the preparatory acts are responsible for "introducing sexual excitations." Using the example of looking, Freud describes the work of the preparatory act this way: "The eye is perhaps the zone most remote from the sexual object, but it is the one which, in the situation of wooing an object, is liable to be the most frequently stimulated by the particular quality of excitation whose cause, when it occurs in a sexual object, we describe as beauty." So, the preparatory act of looking—like all preparatory acts—introduces sexual excitations by stimulating the "erotogenic zones" of the body (in this case, the eye).[5] And the introduction of this sexual excitation is what increases the overall potential for pleasure through sex. Or, in other words, looking at one's beautiful partner increases the pleasurability of sex with them.

But now Freud is faced with a problem. The increase of sexual excitation is the precise definition of pain. And yet, who can deny the fact that the preparatory acts themselves have a pleasure all their own? Touching the other's skin, for example, is an act that Freud says is "better calculated than anything to arouse a sexual excitation," but it also comes with "a feeling of pleasure" of its own.[6] Is this not why people commit preparatory acts in the first place? Because they are pleasurable? People don't hug one another, touch one another, and kiss one another simply as a means to an end. They don't simply tolerate the preparatory acts because it is the prerequisite to sexual pleasure. Rather, people do those things because they find them pleasurable in themselves. They have a sexual pleasure all their own. In this way, the preparatory acts serve as a kind of "incentive bonus" to copulatory pleasure.[7] A pleasure along the way to experiencing pleasure. And yet, there is no denying that they play a part in the introduction of sexual excitations to the body. "How, then," Freud asks, "are this unpleasurable tension and this feeling of pleasure to be reconciled"?[8]

Freud's answer to this question is quite ingenious. He claims that pleasure itself is split. It is split between, what he calls, on one hand, *endpleasure*, and, on the other hand, *forepleasure*. Endpleasure is the pleasure that is experienced through the copulatory act itself while forepleasure is the pleasure that is experienced through the preparatory acts. With endpleasure, Freud introduces nothing new except nomenclature. Underneath the new moniker is the same old idea of pleasure as the expenditure of stimulus. That is, endpleasure is the pleasure of the pleasure principle. The innovation comes with forepleasure.

Unlike endpleasure, which is derived from all the normal mechanisms of the pleasure principle—reduction, expenditure, removal, and so on—forepleasure, Freud claims, issues from "an increase in tension."[9] Pleasure from *an increase of tension*? Now, that is a truly radical idea in terms of Freud's metapsychology, and it shouldn't be overlooked. To be sure, it is not the qualitative pleasure that Freud associates with masochism. Freud's point here is not that forepleasure is simply another way of experiencing expenditure. As the juxtaposition with endpleasure makes clear, forepleasure is a pleasure that derives directly from the economic situation of the drive. That is, forepleasure is a pleasure that comes from the accumulation of stimulus. This doesn't negate the idea that the accumulation of stimulus is unpleasurable. What it means is that there is a strange pleasure in excess of this unpleasure. A pleasure in pain or, as Lacan puts it, "the pleasure of experiencing unpleasure."[10]

To grasp what Freud means by forepleasure, think of the horror film example that I used in the previous chapter to illustrate the psychoanalytic definitions of pleasure and pain. The tension that we feel when we don't know whether or not the killer will pop out from behind the door or a monster will jump out from underneath the bed is in one sense unpleasurable. We grip the armrests of the chair we are sitting in, hold our breath, and cover our eyes, as ways of dealing with the discomfort that we feel with the mounting tension. However, in another sense, this tension is intensely pleasurable. It is the whole reason people love (or hate) horror films. Indeed, horror film aficionados live for it. To be sure, it is not the same type of pleasure that we feel when we learn that there is nothing behind the door or underneath the bed. That type of pleasure feels more like relief. This type of pleasure feels more like agitation or excitation. A pleasure in anticipation which can only be felt when we are held in suspense.

Or think of the rollercoaster. One of the great pleasures of riding a rollercoaster are the big drops. They are exhilarating. But as anyone who has ever ridden a rollercoaster can tell you, for every big drop, there is a big climb. And when you are on that big climb, leaning back at a 45-degree angle and watching the people down below shrink into dots, you feel fear, yes, but you also feel great pleasure as you anticipate the drop to come. That strange cocktail of excitement and tension is what Freud calls *forepleasure*.

So, now, Freud is able to solve his problem. The preparatory acts are pleasurable, despite the fact that they introduce stimulus to the body, because the stimulation of the body itself is strangely pleasurable. Speaking to the erotogenic zones of the body—that is, areas of the body that bear excitation—Freud explains it this way: "They are all used to provide a certain amount of pleasure by being stimulated in the way appropriate to them."[11] Did you catch it? *By being stimulated*. Stimulation is presented here, not as the obstacle to pleasure but, rather, as its source. In no way does this suggest that Freud was wrong to define pleasure and pain as the decrease and increase of stimulus, for there is certainly something painful in the innervations of the body. Just think again of the horror film or the rollercoaster. What it means, rather, is that pleasure and pain, as phenomena, are not as exclusive as the words themselves lead us to believe. There is indeed a point where pleasure and pain, even in the quantitative terms that Freud understands them, touch and intermingle, and that point is forepleasure.

IV

Let us now return to Freud's claim that in sublimation "what was originally a sexual instinct finds satisfaction in some achievement which is no longer sexual." The reason this claim appeared so mysterious to us in the first place was because we knew of only one way for the drive to find satisfaction: the expenditure of stimulus. When the drive expends its stimulus through a sexual aim, the quantity of tension within the body is lowered, and this produces pleasure. Finding satisfaction, we believed, meant finding satisfaction in that pleasure—the pleasure of expenditure or, endpleasure, as we now know it. The issue with this form of pleasure is of course that it is fleeting. The drive, as we will recall, is a force giving *constant* impact. Therefore, to find satisfaction, the drive must constantly produce pleasure. To fail in this endeavor, in any way, even for a moment, is to fail satisfaction itself.

However, thanks to Freud's account of forepleasure, we now know of another path to satisfaction, a path that is provided by the innervations of the body. When we engage in nonsexual aims, such as, the preparatory acts, we excite the drive, inducing it to produce more stimulus, which are then stored within the body, thereby increasing the amount of tension within it. We once looked at this increase of tension as the definition of pain itself, which to be sure it still is. But we now know that along with causing pain, this tension within the body affords its own unique form of pleasure—the pleasure of tension or, in other words, forepleasure. To find satisfaction then all the drive must do is find satisfaction in this forepleasure, which is precisely what happens in sublimation.

Under sublimation, the drive no longer finds satisfaction in the pleasure that is produced with finding an object—that is, through endpleasure. Rather, it finds satisfaction in innervation, which it finds in abundance within itself, since it is itself a constant supply of stimulation. We may therefore think of sublimation as the drive turning back on itself and finding satisfaction in its own innervating movement. So, when Freud writes, "what was originally a sexual instinct finds satisfaction in some achievement which is no longer sexual," we should not understand "achievement" here to mean some product in the world. Sublimation is not the production of masterpieces of art or the making of scientific discoveries. It is not the invention of gadgets or the solving of math problems. To find satisfaction in any of those "achievements" is to find satisfaction in endpleasure, which is precisely what sublimation abandons. Rather, we must understand "achievement" here to mean the drive itself. The achievement of sublimation then is none other than the drive finding satisfaction in the forepleasure afforded by its own innervating movement.

The implication here is that the drive can always find satisfaction. It need not wait for a facilitating object or amenable external circumstances. It has everything it needs within itself. Thus, even when the drive fails to complete the path to expenditure, it can still find satisfaction in itself. Or, to put it another way, even when the drive fails to complete the path to expenditure, it can still find satisfaction by turning itself into an aim. Indeed, this is one of the ways in which we may understand Freud's definition of sublimation as the drive's "power to replace its immediate aim by other aims which may be valued more highly and which are not sexual." If a nonsexual aim is an aim that doesn't satisfy, as I argued it is in Chapter 2, then the drive itself is the original nonsexual aim, since its constant supply of stimulation is the primary source of dissatisfaction—indeed, the first dissatisfaction. Sublimation, we may then say, is the drive's power to replace its immediate aim with itself.

But we may push this idea even further. Since forepleasure and endpleasure derive from opposing economic dynamics, we shouldn't think of them as complements. Forepleasure is not simply what we feel when we are not experiencing endpleasure. Keep in mind that nonexpenditure is also pain. Rather, we should think of them as antagonists, one coming at the expense of the other. When we expend the drive, we loosen the tension within the body, thereby diminishing our capacity to experience forepleasure. And when we withhold the drive, we prevent expenditure, completely eliminating the possibility of endpleasure. Because of this, we should not envisage sublimation as a passive power. It isn't a second gear or an alternative setting which the drive can shift into when the path to expenditure is blocked. Again, keep in mind, nonexpenditure is also pain. Rather, we should think of it as an active power, a choice, or a decision. The decision to pursue forepleasure, to seek it out. The choice to look at the pain of innervation and find the kernel of forepleasure lodged within it. Sublimation, on this view, then is not simply the peaceful exchange of sexual and nonsexual aims. It is much rather the violent cut that severs the drive from the sexual aim and welds it to the nonsexual aim. Or, if you like, it is the rewiring of the drive such that it no longer considers its constant innervation as a problem to be solved but, rather, a feature in itself. Thus, when the sublimated drive fails to obtain its ultimate aim of expenditure, we must think of that failure as an active failure, a decision to fail or a making fail.

V

We are now finally ready to answer the question that has been lingering in the background since last chapter. Why does genius exist? When the genius suspends the impulse to love and hate, they refuse the satisfaction made available through the passions, and when the genius commits to inquiry, they refuse the satisfaction offered in the solution. For the pleasure principle, this behavior is incomprehensible. Refusing satisfaction is tantamount to inviting pain, and no human being, it believes, would ever do that. Either we are wrong about genius or the genius violates its principle. Either way, genius shouldn't exist. So, why does genius exist?

The answer to this question is of course forepleasure. Genius exists because forepleasure exists. This is why it is wrong to think of the genius as an ascetic figure. They do in fact pursue pleasure. It is just that they do not pursue endpleasure. For the genius, the pleasure that comes from doing inquiry comes entirely from the tension it creates within the body, not from its release. To put it simply, the genius enjoys how doing research makes them feel. They enjoy the feeling that comes from the investigation of an inscrutable problem—that mixture of frustration, suspense, and wonder. They find that feeling satisfying in itself. For them, it is the whole point of doing research in the first place, not finding the solution. This is not the case with the anti-intellectual or the know-it-all. For those two, the only pleasure that exists is endpleasure. Thus, the only thing they find enjoyable about doing inquiry is finding the answers. The research itself is something they can do without.

The tragedy is of course that forepleasure is as available to the anti-intellectual and the know-it-all as it is to the genius. This is because forepleasure derives, not from the success of finding the answer—which, it is true, varies from person to person—but, rather, from the constancy of the drive, which is universal. In that sense, forepleasure is something that the anti-intellectual and the know-it-all experience every day but do not recognize. When they consider the innervations of the drive, all they find is pain. As such, they are unable to appreciate the forepleasure that is afforded by those innervations. To put it another way, both the anti-intellectual and the know-it-all experience genius as well. The only difference is that for them genius is a problem to be solved, not something to be enjoyed. Thus, to experience genius, all the anti-intellectual and the know-it-all must do is reorient themselves to what is an everyday experience. They do not need to obtain advanced degrees from Harvard or receive a MacArthur Fellowship (the so-called "Genius Grant"). They do not need high scores on IQ tests. They do not need better genes or good luck. All they need is to experience the innervations of the drive in a new way: no longer as the impediment to pleasure but, rather, as its impetus.

The reason that the genius is incomprehensible to the pleasure principle then is because the pleasure principle lacks any notion of forepleasure. Viewed from the perspective of the pleasure principle, forepleasure is simply pain. For this reason, when the pleasure principle considers the genius's pursuit of forepleasure, all it sees is a violation of its principle, a kind of perversion. It cannot comprehend the idea that the genius might actually be obeying it. Of course, from a certain point of view, the pleasure principle is right. The genius is indeed violating the pleasure principle insofar as they are pursuing pain. The issue, however, is that pain—and here I want to be very clear that I mean the accumulation of stimulus and not the qualitative feeling—is the very form in which the genius's pleasure appears. For the genius, pleasure is pain. So, from another point of view, the pleasure principle is wrong. The genius indeed obeys the pleasure principle insofar as they pursue pleasure precisely by pursuing pain.

What the phenomenon of genius points to then is a contradiction at the very heart of the pleasure principle itself. The reason the pleasure principle has no conception of forepleasure is because pleasure and pain, from its perspective, are completely extricable from one another. They exist on opposite sides of the conceptual border, never to intermingle with one another. But what the genius emphatically demonstrates is that pleasure and pain cannot be finally extricated from each other. Pleasure and pain may very well exist on opposite sides of the conceptual border, but there is a chainlink fence on that border, not a concrete wall. As such, there is a point at which pleasure and pain finally meet and touch, becoming indistinguishable from one another. That point of interaction is forepleasure.

For this reason, it is impossible to obey the pleasure principle without at once disobeying it. There is a way in which the very pursuit of pleasure already exceeds the terms that have been carefully laid out by the pleasure principle, that is, a way in which the very pursuit of pleasure is itself already the pursuit of pain. This is why the genius appears to violate the pleasure principle. To pursue their pleasure, they must allow the agitation of the drive, which, from the perspective of the pleasure principle, can only appear as pain. In this way, the genius's obedience to the pleasure principle is an obedience that is at once a disobedience, an obedience in disobedience. What this paradoxical form of obedience demonstrates is that the pleasure principle is ultimately a nonsensical principle, a principle that doesn't work. To properly function as a principle for human behavior, the pleasure principle must excise from itself the contradictory point where pleasure and pain meet. It must plaster over the holes in that chainlink fence, so to speak. This is why the pleasure principle has no concept of forepleasure. As a contradiction, it must fall out of the picture in order for the dual mandates of pursuing pleasure and avoiding pain to take effect. In that case, we might think of genius as the safety net that catches this contradiction as it falls out from the pleasure principle.

VI

Interestingly enough, "The Economic Problem of Masochism" makes no mention of forepleasure, despite its obvious relevance for its subject matter.[12] Indeed, forepleasure only makes a few appearances in Freud's vast body of work, and then mostly in his writings on jokes and aesthetics.[13] The motive for this omission, I believe, is found on the opening pages of the Masochism paper. After arguing that the pleasure and pain at stake in masochism are qualitative experiences, disconnected from the economic realities of the drive, Freud writes, almost in relief, the following: "The conclusion to be drawn from these considerations is that the description of the pleasure principle as the watchman over our life cannot be rejected."[14]

What Freud wants is an ultimate governing principle for human behavior, a principle that is able to regulate that behavior even when it defies rationality—what he describes as "the watchman over our life." For Freud, that "watchman" is the pleasure principle. And yet, he must have also known, on some level, what is abundantly clear to us by now. Forepleasure is a stumbling block to the pleasure principle. Forepleasure reveals that one cannot pursue pleasure without simultaneously pursuing pain, which calls into question the ability of the pleasure principle to serve as that watchman over our lives. Or, to put it in terms that Freud himself would have understood, forepleasure is that "drug" which puts the pleasure principle to sleep.[15] No wonder Freud makes no mention of forepleasure in Masochism!

In 1920, Freud would finally take up the question of the absolutism of the pleasure principle. He would ask if that principle is indeed the ultimate horizon of human behavior or if there is something else, some other principle, operating just beyond the horizon. He would indeed find something beyond the pleasure principle. He would call it *the death drive*.

I will revisit the notion of the death drive at the conclusion of this book, but here I only want to point out that fifteen years prior to *Beyond the Pleasure Principle*, at the very beginnings of psychoanalysis itself, in *Three Essays on the Theory of Sexuality*, Freud already discovered something beyond the pleasure principle, thereby evincing a remarkable continuity between 1905 and 1920. That something is forepleasure. It is not a "beyond" that exists outside the boundaries of the pleasure principle. Rather, it is a "beyond" that is lodged within its very core, a stain or leftover that prevents the dual mandates of pursuing pleasure and avoiding pain from adding up to a single coherent principle. Indeed, it is because of this beyond—the beyond that lies within—that the pleasure principle is ultimately powerless to prevent us from seeking pain and avoiding pleasure (for as it turns out, they are the same thing). But it is also because of this beyond that we are able to make something out of our pain, that we are able to turn our pain into its own kind of strange pleasure. The name for this act of finding satisfaction in the pain of the drive is sublimation, and its subject is the genius.

4

Otherwise than Guilt

I

To conclude Part One, I want to consider the place renunciation has in Freud's account of sublimation. Here is a clear example of it; Freud writes:

> There are only two possibilities for remaining healthy when there is a persistent frustration of satisfaction in the real world. The first is by transforming the psychical tension into active energy which remains directed towards the external world and eventually extorts a real satisfaction of the libido from it. The second is by renouncing libidinal satisfaction, sublimating the dammed-up libido and turning it to the attainment of aims which are no longer erotic and which escape frustration.[1]

Renunciation, as it appears in this passage, is one of two possible responses to the inability to find satisfaction in the world. The first response is either to comport ourselves to the stringency of the world by modifying the type of aims we pursue in it or to make the world fit our needs by transforming it. In either case, we remain attached to the world—in dialogue with it—so that we may "extort" a satisfaction from it. The second response is to renounce the aim of libidinal satisfaction altogether and to find satisfaction by sublimating "the dammed-up libido." In this response, we free ourselves from the world such that our satisfaction no longer depends on it.

In this account, renunciation is shown in very positive tones. It presents absolutely no threat to our psychic life. More than that, it functions as the source of our freedom. Through the renunciation of libidinal satisfaction, the possibility of satisfaction no longer depends on finding favourable conditions in a capricious world. We are free to find satisfaction at any moment from "the dammed-up libido," which constantly wells up inside us. But this is not why I want to reexamine renunciation. My worry has nothing to do with renunciation receiving a positive showing in Freud's account of sublimation. Rather, it has to do with the role renunciation plays in a different account of Freud's: namely, his account of guilt.

Guilt, Freud argues, also results from renunciation. As he puts it, "Every renunciation of instinct now becomes a dynamic source of conscience and every fresh renunciation increases the latter's severity and intolerance."[2] If it were possible to satisfy the drive without restriction, we would not experience guilt, so Freud's logic goes. The trouble is of course that unrestricted satisfaction is impossible. The path to satisfaction intersects the lives and interests of other people, and as such, out of pure self-interest, those people place restrictions on our satisfaction, thereby forcing us to renounce a portion of it. So, parents, for example, tell their children not to touch their genitals, which forces these children to give up the satisfaction which is possible through the genitals. Or we pass any number of laws—such as, laws on alcohol consumption, murder, gambling, drug use, rape—which (thankfully) limits the field of satisfaction.

As Freud develops this narrative further, the exact temporal sequence of these events comes into question, as he suggests that it may be the other's restriction that comes first, not our satisfaction: "A considerable amount of aggressiveness must be developed in the child against the authority which prevents him from having his first, but none the less his most important, satisfactions."[3] Note here that Freud calls the renounced satisfaction our *first* satisfaction, suggesting that others restrict our satisfaction even before we've experienced it. In any case, whether it is the satisfaction or the restriction that comes first, when we renounce our satisfaction, we develop "a considerable amount of aggressiveness" toward others.

Crucially, however, this newfound aggressiveness is not new at all but simply the renounced drive transformed. Thus, we would like nothing more than to satisfy our aggressiveness on others as a form of revenge, but since we depend on them for love and protection, we cannot satisfy this aggressiveness against them. So, instead, we compromise by turning this aggressiveness on ourselves in the shape of conscience or, as it is known in psychoanalysis, the superego. Guilt then is nothing more than renounced drive turned against the ego in the form of the superego. For this reason, the more we renounce satisfaction, the stronger the superego becomes, as there is more renounced drive to turn into conscience. "The effect of instinctual renunciation on the conscience," Freud writes, "then is that every piece of aggression whose satisfaction the subject gives up is taken over by the superego and increases the latter's aggressiveness."[4] To wit, the more we obey, the guiltier we feel.

There is much in this strange and complicated account of guilt that one could comment on—not least of all is its plausibility, which the first-time reader might feel is the most pressing matter of all—but my only concern is with the place that renunciation has in it. For, it seems to me, if renunciation leads to guilt, as Freud argues it does, then it cannot serve as the basis of our freedom. Rather, it serves as the basis of our bondage, as it binds us to the superego. And if renunciation serves as the basis of our bondage, and not our freedom, then does this mean that sublimation also leads to our bondage, given the role that the renunciation of sexual satisfaction plays in it? Does this mean then that the genius is a figure of guilt? A figure of the superego? These then are the questions that I want to consider as I bring Part One to a close.

To find answers to these questions, however, we will have to look outside of Freud, as the relationship between sublimation and guilt remains unthought in him. There are of course good reasons for this. As I have already mentioned, Freud's thoughts on sublimation are idiosyncratic, not systematic. Therefore, it is likely that Freud simply didn't grasp the implications his account of guilt would have for his account of sublimation. However, more to the point, Freud's major work on the superego and guilt came after *Leonardo da Vinci and a Memory of His Childhood*, that is, after he had already developed his most significant account of sublimation.[5] Yet, as legitimate as these reasons are, the fact still remains that sublimation's relationship with guilt remains unthought in Freud.

For this reason, I will look to Lacan and, in particular, to the account of guilt as "having given ground relative to one's desire," which he develops in his seminar, *The Ethics of Psychoanalysis*.[6] What makes Lacan's account of guilt particularly evocative in this context is that it touches on a dimension of guilt which is otherwise overlooked in Freud. Namely, the possibility of guilt arising, not from the renunciation of the drive but, rather, from its satisfaction. In this way, Lacan turns Freud's account of guilt on its head. Rather than construing renunciation as the source of guilt, Lacan presents it as an ethical stance in its own right, a faithful maintaining of the drive's constancy, a stance which is embodied in the refusal to give ground on one's desire. Thus, with Lacan's help, I will advance the following response to the questions that I posed above. Far from implicated in guilt, sublimation presents an alternative to guilt, a way of being that is otherwise than guilt.

II

On its face, Lacan's formulation "having given ground relative to one's desire" appears to be nothing more than a reiteration of Freud's thesis "Every renunciation of instinct now becomes a dynamic source of conscience." On this view, giving ground on desire is simply renouncing a satisfaction of the drive. I have a desire, say, for cake, but I give ground on that desire by refraining from eating a slice, and thus, I have renounced a satisfaction of the drive. On this interpretation, giving ground on desire creates surplus excitations, which are then internalized within the psyche in the shape of the superego, which, in turn, produces guilt. If this is in fact what Lacan means by this formulation, then sublimation is indeed implicated in guilt, as this rendition of Lacan's formulation aligns with Freud's account of guilt. However, there is something that prevents me from proffering this conclusion, a subtle yet crucial difference between the two formulations: Lacan's formulation concerns *desire* while Freud's formulation concerns *the drive*.

Though they may appear equivalent, to Lacan's way of thinking, desire and drive are radically different from one another. In *Desire and Its Interpretation*, Lacan makes the following statement: "[D]esire, far from being equatable with the feeling of an obscure and radical pressure"—*obscure and radical pressure*, meaning the drive—"is situated beyond it." *Situated beyond it*, keep that phrase in mind. He continues: "This drive, call, or pressure is only of interest, exists, is defined, and is theorized by Freud inasmuch as it is caught up in the unusual temporal sequence that we call the signifying chain …. Desire is not this sequence."[7] Otherwise put, the drive is an irresistible force—a *call* or *radical pressure*—which compels us to seek satisfaction. In pursuit of satisfaction, we name the missing objects of our satisfaction in language—*the signifying chain*—which creates for us a sense of time, a *temporal sequence*, a before and after satisfaction. Desire, on the other hand, is something not represented in that "sequence" but, rather, is *situated beyond it*.

To put this difference another way, the drive, as we know from Freud, is a constant force—a "radical pressure," in Lacan's locution—while desire, as Lacan puts it, is "the central lack in which the subject experiences" itself.[8] That is, the drive is a constant force which I must satisfy in order to avoid the pain of its accumulating tension while desire is what I experience when I *lack* that satisfaction. The drive compels me to run to the point of self-injury, to feed my addiction to Fabergé eggs, to eat an entire carton of ice cream all by myself while desire is what I experience when I am out those satisfactions: when I cannot run, buy Fabergé eggs, or eat ice cream. Or, to put it yet another way, desire is what I experience when the drive lacks satisfaction.

Put in these terms, something becomes apparent about desire. Because desire only exists when satisfaction is lacking, desire is a kind of sign or signal that a renunciation has *already* taken place. That is, we desire precisely because we have already renounced the drive, not because we have satisfied it. If I say that I desire cake, it is because I lack cake, and this deprivation, from a Freudian point of view, means that I have renounced the satisfaction made possible by cake. Or, to put it in terms of genius, if the genius desires to know, it is because they have renounced the satisfaction that is offered to them in the solution. In this way, desire is a sign that a satisfaction has already been renounced—renunciation's leftover, if you will.

With all this in mind, if we now return to Freud's notion of guilt, as resulting from the renunciation of the drive, and try to square it with Lacan's definition of guilt, as giving ground relative to one's desire, we find that they are incongruous with each other. *Having given ground relative to one's desire* cannot be a simple reiteration of *every renunciation of instinct now becomes a dynamic source of conscience* because desire is itself the sign that a renunciation has already taken place. What this means is that giving ground on desire is giving ground on a renunciation, not a satisfaction as we originally thought. If desire is itself the sign that a renunciation has already taken place, then *giving ground relative to one's desire* means giving ground on that renunciation. Or, put in positive terms, *giving ground relative to one's desire* means satisfying the drive.

Thus, for Lacan, guilt exists, not when we lack satisfaction—since desire is already the lack of satisfaction—but when we give ground on this lack of satisfaction, when we back off of it. Put in Freudian terms, guilt arises, not when we renounce the satisfaction of the drive, but when we give ground on this renunciation, that is, when we give into the urge to satisfy it. When do I, as a parent, feel guilty? Not when I put down my beer to help my daughter with her homework—that is, not when I desire to drink my beer. But when I say No! to my daughter and Yes! to my beer—that is, when I give into my desire to drink beer. For Freud, it is the exact opposite. According to Freud, I should feel guilty when I've obeyed the superego's injunction to renounce the satisfaction offered in my beer.

Hopefully, this makes it clear that Lacan doesn't simply reiterate Freud. If Lacan had wanted to simply reiterate Freud, then he would have said something like: guilt is *having* desire, since having desire means we have renounced a satisfaction. But this is not what he says. Lacan does not say that we feel guilty when we have desire but, rather, when we give ground on that desire. Not a simple reiteration of Freud, Lacan's formulation of guilt identifies a completely different source of guilt: not the renunciation of satisfaction but, rather, the renunciation of the renunciation of satisfaction.

III

It should now be clear—or at least clearer—that Lacan conceptualizes guilt differently from Freud. For Freud, guilt arises when we renounce satisfaction while, for Lacan, it arises when we go in for satisfaction. That is, for Freud, we feel guilty when we put down that slice of cake—when we obey the superego's

No!—while, for Lacan, we feel guilty when we gobble it up, when we obey the superego's Yes! What is less clear in all this is *why*. Why does Lacan think giving ground on desire causes guilt, and not desire itself, as Freud might have thought? The answer to this question has to do with the cause of desire itself.

When Lacan says that desire is "the central lack in which the subject experiences" itself, he does not mean that desire is the lack of a phenomenal object like cake. Of course, we may feel that our desire for cake has something to do with our lack of cake, but Lacan disagrees. For him, there is something more fundamental at stake in our desire, something *situated beyond* cake, something noumenal. That something, he insists, is a lack in our ontology, that is, a lack in our being. This is why he calls it "the *central lack*." It is a constitutive or structural lack. In other words, for Lacan, we do not desire simply because we lack something like cake. Rather, we desire something like cake because we lack something essential in our makeup as human beings, because we are as creatures lacking beings.

For this reason, when we recognize our desire for cake as a desire for cake as such, we are missing something fundamental about it. To Lacan's way of thinking, it would be more appropriate to recognize our desire for cake as a hunger or a demand for cake, but never a desire. This is because our desire is not really about the cake itself but, rather, about this lack in our being. This is why eating cake is ultimately so disappointing. The cake is at best a temporary fix for this lack in our ontology. Thus, when we finally eat it, we continue to desire, since our desire never had anything to do with the cake in the first place.

Because for Lacan our lack is ontological in nature, there is no object that can fill it. Not cake, not anything. And yet, our capitalist culture wants us to believe that such an object exists.[9] When we turn on the TV or flip through a magazine, we are constantly bombarded by advertisements which tell us that the missing piece of our ontology can be purchased on the market—at a discount no less! Indeed, the entire capitalist economy is predicated on this very possibility. For capitalism, demand can supply desire. As Lacan observes, "All kinds of tempting goods offer themselves to the subject" as the objects of our desire. It is, he insists, "the American way."[10] Thus, a car is not advertised simply as a mode of transportation but, rather, as the very thing that gives the driver their identity, whether as a classy entrepreneur, an independent spirit, or an environmentally responsible consumer—and sometimes all three! Medicine, we are told, is not temporary relief but a miracle cure, such that no ailment—including stage four metastatic cancer—can stop us from living the good life. Dating services claim to have, in their vast inventory of others, our missing other half, the salve for our existential loneliness. And the list goes on.

But buyer beware! When we go in for one of these objects, we are not receiving the missing object of our desire because that object doesn't exist as such. Thus, we must ask ourselves, when we purchase one of these self-advertised objects of desire, we do so "for the good of whom?"[11] For our good? Or for the other's good? When advertisement after advertisement tells us that this particular deodorant will make us sexually irresistible, that this brand of liquor will make us prestigious in the eyes of others, that this degree program will ensure our employment, that this retirement fund will secure our future, we must ask ourselves: whose goods are being peddled? Our goods? Or the other's goods? Are these the goods that will truly satisfy our desire? Or are these simply the goods that the other wants us to have?

If Lacan is right—if desire arises from a lack in our being—then the goods that are peddled to us can never be our goods. They must always be the other's goods. So, when we go in for one of those goods, we are like Cypher (Joe Pantoliano) from *The Matrix* (1999), trading in his freedom for a taste of steak. We are betraying our desire for a taste of the other's good. Or, to put it another way, we are *giving ground on our desire* for the other's good.

IV

So, here we are again at Lacan's formulation of guilt as giving ground on desire, only this time with a bit more context around its ethical implications. Giving ground on desire is the attempt to satisfy our desire with the other's good. The reason Lacan frames this move in ethical terms, however, is because desire is for him essential—or, as he puts it, "central"—to who we are as human beings. It is what makes us singular, unique. Therefore, when we buy into the other's pitch and purchase one of its goods, we are making a compromise. We are giving up something central about ourselves for the sake of the other's good. We are betraying our singularity—our desire—in order to fit in better with the other's ideas about what we should be and what we should desire. In essence, we are saying: "Well, if that's how things are, we should abandon our position; neither of us is worth that much, and especially me, so we should just return to the common path."[12] But why guilt? Why isn't compromising our desire simply a matter of ethical standing? Why does it lead to the subjective experience of guilt? To understand this link between betraying desire and guilt, we need to appreciate the utter inadequacy of—or the lack in—the other's good.

As I have already pointed out, the other's good cannot satisfy our desire despite what the advertisers and marketers promise. Perhaps, it can satisfy a need or a demand, but never a desire because desire is not correlated with a particular object. So, even if we compromise our desire by acquiring the other's good—indeed, even if we acquire a whole warehouse full of the other's goods—our desire will not be satisfied. We will simply desire the next good and the next one after that. At this point, we are faced with a choice. We must decide if we continue desiring because the other's good is insufficient or because there is something deficient in us, in our desire.

Though it may not appear so at first blush, the stakes of this decision are of the highest order. If the problem is the other's good, then, Lacan states, "the Other is wanting, and the signifier is that of his death."[13] That is, if the problem has to do with the other's good, it is because the other itself doesn't know how to satisfy our desire. The omniscient other is dead, and the ignorant other is alive. And if the other doesn't know how to satisfy our desire, then we must confront the possibility that there is no satisfying desire.

This is not an easy truth to accept, for desire is pain. How so? If desire signals that a renunciation has taken place, as I argued it does, then desire from a metapsychological standpoint is the nonexpenditure of stimulus, and the nonexpenditure of stimulus is, as we know, the psychoanalytic definition of pain. Is this not why we are so quick to give ground on our desire in the first place? We want to avoid the pain of desire? If so, then the idea that the other cannot satisfy desire is extremely unsettling, since it implies that no one knows how to end the pain of desire.

To avoid this uncomfortable thought, we uphold the belief in a full and potent other—the other who knows—even though such an other doesn't exist, which raises a question: if the other in my imagination knows all about desire, then why does its good fail to satisfy? When I compromise my desire by eating that slice of cake, I imagine that I am receiving from the other the good which will satisfy my desire, the good which will put an end to the pain of desire once and for all. I imagine that I am entering into a kind of pact or agreement with the other. I give up my desire, and the other gives me the goods. And while the cake does indeed satisfy my demand, it leaves my desire unaffected. Oriented around the lack in my being as it is, my desire continues to persist, even as I eat the slice of cake. And so, I eat another slice, and another, and still another, believing that the satisfaction of desire is simply a matter of quantity, a matter of a little bit more. The problem is of course that desire is not a matter of quantity. So, no matter how many slices of cake I eat, no matter if I eat the whole entire thing, my desire will persist since my desire was never really about the cake in the first place. And yet, because I believed that the other and I had a deal—that I would give it my desire, and it would give me the goods—I am left wondering why I still desire. The problem couldn't be the cake, I think to myself. It was delicious, just as advertised. The problem couldn't be the other itself, since the other, I continue to believe, is a knowledgeable other. The problem must be me! I am responsible! I am the reason I still desire! There is something wrong with *me*, with *my* desire! And thus, guilt enters the picture.

V

If I continue to desire, it must be because there is something deficient in me, something odd in my desire, I think to myself. I must be the reason that the other's good failed to satisfy, not the other itself. I must be one of those malcontents who is never satisfied with anything in life—always restless, always critical, always looking elsewhere. Unlike other people, who I imagine are satisfied by the standard goods, I have this strange—and, I can only presume, perverse—desire which cannot be satisfied. And it never once occurs to me that what might be perverse in this situation is not my desire, which is perfectly neurotic, but my belief in this other who knows all about my desire and how to satisfy it.[14]

By this account, the superego is neither a moral agency nor unexpended drive turned back against the ego. Rather, it is a remnant of this belief in the knowledgeable other. This is why, for Lacan, "the superego is the imperative of jouissance—Enjoy!"[15] If the other is to be a truly knowledgeable other, the superego cannot be an agency that only tells us No!, an agency that only knows how to prohibit. To be truly knowledgeable, the other must also be an agency that tells us Yes!, an agency that also knows what is good and what must be enjoyed.

As an illustration of Lacan's point, take the so-called American Dream—the fantasy that with enough hard work one can achieve the good life.[16] Many Americans find this dream a burden, as it causes us to put in long hours at jobs we often find stultifying and unrewarding, even as the dream itself recedes into the distance. And yet, strangely enough, we pursue it all the same. Why? What gives the American Dream its power over us? What makes it so compelling? It is not because it prohibits us from the good. Indeed, the American Dream is not a list of prohibitions at all but, rather, a list of goods: a well-paying job, a house in the suburbs, a spouse and two and a half children, and so on. But therein lies its power. That is, the American Dream is so compelling precisely because it's a list of goods, because it enjoins us to Enjoy! By encouraging us to enjoy, rather than prohibiting us from enjoying, the American Dream gives us the impression that the American Other truly knows what makes for the fulfilled life. After all, if such goods as vacation homes, cars, spouses, widescreen TVs, and so on, cannot satisfy us, then why would it endorse them? It must be that these goods truly do make for the good life.

Thus, if the American Dream is a figure of the superego—and indeed it is—it is precisely because it operates through enjoyments, not prohibitions. It relentlessly commands us to Enjoy! Enjoy that penthouse apartment in the city! Enjoy that beautiful spouse! Enjoy those honor-roll children! Enjoy that vacation in the Bahamas! Enjoy! Enjoy! Enjoy! That the superego lies behind those injunctions, and not our desire, becomes abundantly clear when we fail to enjoy, for it is then that we hear the other's voice chide, *What is wrong with you? You have everything that you could ever dream of, so why aren't you enjoying?*

Of course, the goods of the American Dream will never satisfy our desire because our desire is not about those goods. In this sense, the Freudian superego—that is, the superego which imposes renunciation—is a last-ditch effort, on our part, to preserve the belief in the knowledgeable other. That is, because the other's good leaves us unsatisfied, we imagine that the superego has restricted the properly satisfying goods, which preserves the appearance that the other still knows. So, while one can hardly live with a harsh and cruel superego, which punishes us even as we obey it, the alternative is that much worse. For what is worse? A cruel other or an ignorant other? A capricious and petty other who punishes us for pursuing the good or a stupid and ignorant other who doesn't know what the good is? Indeed, the ignorant other is always worse because it means that no one knows how to end the pain of desire.

So, while it is far from ideal to live under a cruel and sadistic superego, we do it anyways because it is easier to live with this cruelty than it is to accept the reality that there is no such thing as a satisfied desire. We would rather have a cruel superego impose upon us prohibition after prohibition—even as we fail to obey them—than accept the idea that there may be something irreducibly discontented about existence itself. Guilt then, in this way, is integral to the operation of the superego, not so much because it demarcates the boundary between what is permissible and what is impermissible but, rather, because it covers over the lack in the other's good. Because we feel guilty, we do not investigate why the other's good fails to satisfy. We simply accept it as our fault. But if we were to push aside our guilt and press a little further, we would quickly realize that the other's good fails to satisfy because it is not in fact what we desire at all, a realization that would put us face to face with the uncomfortable truth that the other doesn't know one iota about satisfying desire—that the stern, finger-wagging other is dead, and the clueless, shoulder-shrugging other is alive—which is of course why we don't ask questions in the first place.

VI

Let's now return to Freud's account of sublimation and consider the place renunciation has in it. If we approach Freud's claim that sublimation is "renouncing libidinal satisfaction" directly, it elicits all sorts of associations with guilt, given the close link guilt and renunciation have in his thought. However, if we approach Freud's claim by way of Lacan, all those associations with guilt disappear, as the words *renouncing libidinal satisfaction* become simply another way of writing *desire*. Lacan, in other words, changes the status of renunciation itself, taking what was once associated with the superego and guilt and raising it to the level of the ethical by turning it into the subject's stance against the other's good. Thus, when Freud claims that sublimation is "renouncing libidinal satisfaction," he now appears to be claiming that sublimation is holding true to one's desire against the temptation of the other's good.

For this reason, we must never think of the genius as a figure of the superego. Rather, we must think of the genius as a subject of desire insofar as their commitment to the renunciation of libidinal satisfaction is a commitment to desire itself. In this way, the genius exemplifies what it means to answer affirmatively to Lacan's ethical question: "Have you acted in conformity with the desire that is in you?"[17]

Acting in conformity with desire is not, as some think, giving into every temptation, every impulse, and every whim that we have. It is not about gobbling up every slice of cake in sight, hoarding as much money as possible, and having as much sex as we can bear. If it were indeed about these things, then *acting in conformity with desire* would be nothing more than another formulation of the superego, as the superego is always what commands us to Enjoy! But *acting in conformity with desire* cannot be about any of those things because desire, as we know, is about lack—the lack of the good, we might say. Thus, when Lacan asks, "Have you acted in conformity with the desire that is in you?" he is asking, not if we've given into every urge or impulse, as if psychoanalysis were some kind of bankrupt hedonism, but, rather, if we've remained true to the lack that is within us. Have we kept our lack lacking or have we attempted to fill it up with the other's good? That is Lacan's question.

If we were to put Lacan's ethical maxim in terms of the drive, it would read thus: *acting in conformity with desire* is living faithfully with the constancy of the drive. It is remaining with the tension that comes from the drive's constant accumulation rather than seeking to end it by finding the mythical object that it lacks. For this reason, I want to suggest that Lacan's ethic of acting in conformity with desire is incomplete without a supplementary ethic of relinquishing the object, as we must give up this belief in that mythical object. I will return to this question of relinquishing and the ethics that it opens up—what we might call, the ethics of subjective cession—in Chapter 11, but here, I only want to point out that to live faithfully with one's desire, one must be able to relinquish or cede the other's good, since, as Lacan states, "The sphere of the good erects a strong wall across the path of our desire."[18]

But we must also take care that we do not think of the genius's commitment to desire as an act of willpower. It is not that the genius is constantly drawn toward the other's good and that they simply resist its gravitational pull through a sheer act of the will like some kind of ascetic. If this were the case, then the genius would indeed be a figure of guilt, as there is nothing incompatible between this image of the ascetic and Freud's account of guilt. Rather, we must think of the genius's fidelity as something pleasurable in itself. The reason the genius is able to renounce the other's good is not because they have a stronger will than others but, rather, because sublimation turns the pain of desire into its own kind of pleasure—what Lacan describes as "the pleasure of desiring, or, more precisely, the pleasure of experiencing unpleasure."[19] For the genius, the jouissance—or, in Freud's locution, forepleasure—that comes from desire is simply more satisfying than any good that the other has to offer. And if Lacan is right that only "sublimation-love allows jouissance to condescend to desire," then we might say that the genius is simply someone who loves their desire.[20]

Part Two

The Trouble with Objects

Much has been made of the genius's particular mode of pleasure—or, rather, forepleasure—in this book. Yet, I would be negligent if I did not acknowledge that considerations of genius rarely, if ever, center on the genius's particular form of pleasure. What they focus on instead are the objects they produce. We think Leonardo a genius, not because he found satisfaction in inquiry but, rather, because he created great works of art, like *Mona Lisa* and *The Last Supper*, which are of course objects. Similarly, we think Einstein and Woolf geniuses, not because they took forepleasure in the innervations of the drive but, rather, because they developed paradigm-shifting ideas and wrote great works of literature—once again, objects. This is why we think people like Elon Musk geniuses. We associate them with a great object, like the Tesla car, even if they've made no material contribution to its existence.

Naturally, then, one will want an account of sublimation and genius from the standpoint of the object. Lacan even says, "One cannot characterize the sublimated form of the instinct without reference to the object, whatever one does."[1] It is here then that the idea of the masterpiece—and its modern-day counterparts, the invention and the gadget—enters our imaginations. What distinguishes the masterpiece as an object, in our minds, it seems to me, is a kind of superiority or well nigh perfection that we imagine it possessing—what in psychoanalysis is called "original narcissism," a kind of preverbal wholeness or unity that lends certain objects their "charm."[2] In that case, the genius is the one who produces a masterpiece.

What is crucial in psychoanalysis, however, is that original narcissism does not exist as such. It is an illusion or lure. A lost wholeness that exists only insofar as it has always been lost. A product of our "overvaluation" of the object, a perfection that we confer upon the object in order to uphold its possibility for ourselves.[3] Consequently, from a psychoanalytic standpoint, the masterpiece is a myth, a fantasy of our own making. It does not exist as such. Indeed, what talent and innate ability are for the genius, the masterpiece is for the object: a form of mystification. Thus, whatever account of the object we will find in psychoanalysis, we shouldn't expect it to be about the masterpiece.

"But what does the object mean at that level?" asks Lacan. His answer: "sublimation is characterized by a change of objects, or in the libido, a change that doesn't occur through the intermediary of a return of the repressed nor symptomatically, indirectly, but directly, in a way that satisfies directly."[4] There are many interesting things being said in this statement, but the phrase that should grab our attention here is *a change of objects*. What characterizes sublimation, in part, is that it changes the object. And what change could that be? Sublimation, Lacan famously, if enigmatically, answers, "raises the object ... to the dignity of the Thing."[5] As was the case with Freud's formulation of sublimation, I do not expect Lacan's formulation *raising the object to the dignity of the thing* to make much immediate sense, and so, it will be one of my tasks in Part Two to offer an account of it—a presentation that is hopefully both illuminating and convincing—which I will do in the next chapter. But here I only want to point out that there is a world of difference between the idea of changing an object and the masterpiece. What psychoanalysis proposes then is not that the genius creates the perfect object but, rather, that they change something about an object, sometimes one as ordinary and mundane as a matchbox or an apple, which, in turn, changes our relationship to it—no longer as the bearer of original narcissism but now as a thing.

5

The Thing about Objects or, Sublimation after Lacan

I

What is an object to the genius? As we know from Freud, the object is "the thing in regard to which or through which the instinct is able to achieve its aim," which "in every instance is satisfaction."[1] The object is a mere means, in other words—a vehicle through which we obtain satisfaction. Like those cartoons in which a person morphs into a piece of steak or a bag of money, thereby revealing what they truly are for the other, the object represents satisfaction for us—it is the signifier of satisfaction, we might say. But as we also know from Freud, the genius sublimates the drive, which "consists in the instinct's directing itself towards an aim other than, and remote from, that of sexual satisfaction."[2] The genius emphatically does not aim at satisfaction; rather, they aim at something *other than and remote from* satisfaction. So, what is the genius aiming at then when they aim at the object?

The simplest answer is of course nothing. The object is nothing to the genius, and the genius has nothing to do with the object. The genius lives in a world without objects, a world that is decidedly different from the one we live in. This would indeed suit a certain stereotype we have of the genius as the absentminded professor—usually of mathematics or physics—who evinces no concern for anything other than their designated field of study. But this is not in fact what Freud claims. Freud claims, not that the genius abandons the object but, rather, that they *change* the object.[3] Recall that in the encyclopedia article on libido theory, Freud writes, "The most important vicissitude which an instinct can undergo seems to be *sublimation*; here both object and aim are changed."[4] Freud is very clear: sublimation changes the object. What that change exactly is, however, Freud unfortunately does not elaborate, not in this encyclopedia article, not anywhere in his extensive corpus. Lacan comments, "It is remarkable that the object in question is nowhere articulated by Freud"—another artifact of Freud's idiosyncratic approach to sublimation.[5]

It is in this vacuum left by Freud's silence that Lacan, in *The Ethics of Psychoanalysis*, submits the claim that sublimation "raises an object ... to the dignity of the Thing."[6] What Lacan means by this formulation—and, above all, what he means by *the thing*—will of course have to be elucidated. But what we can already discern about it, even at this preliminary stage, is that it responds to the Freudian question of what changes in the object after sublimation. We might state it like this: sublimation changes the object by giving it the same stature as the thing. In this way, we may grasp Lacan's project in the *Ethics*, at least in part, as offering a kind of supplement to Freud's idiosyncratic thoughts on sublimation. Supplement, not in the sense that it fills in its gaps and aporias, like the missing piece of a puzzle, but, rather, in the sense that it "presents itself as excessive to, or unthought by" Freud himself.[7]

Here, I am reminded of a small footnote from *Three Essays on the Theory of Sexuality*; it reads:

> The most striking distinction between the erotic life of antiquity and our own no doubt lies in the fact that the ancients laid the stress upon the instinct itself, whereas we emphasize its object. The ancients glorified the instinct and were prepared on its account to honour even an inferior object; while we despise the instinctual activity in itself, and find excuses for it only in the merits of the object.[8]

The ancients stressed the aim of the drive—*the instinctual activity in itself*—while the moderns *emphasize its object*. Does this not make Freud's account of genius an Ancient or Classical theory of genius insofar as it lays stress on the change in the drive's aim? Indeed, it does. In that case, Lacan's account of sublimation, emphasizing the object as it does, forms its Modern supplement.

II

The place to begin with Lacan's formulation *sublimation raises an object to the dignity of the thing* is to focus on the distinction it makes between the object, on one hand, and the thing, on the other. Though it may appear obscure or even frivolous, this distinction is rooted in a similar—and important—distinction made by Freud in his unpublished *Project for a Scientific Psychology*, a text that is as fascinating as it is bizarre. In the section on "Remembering and Judging," Freud considers what happens in the mind when we encounter difference. He writes, "Let us suppose that the object which furnishes the perception resembles the subject—a *fellow human-being*." That is, let us suppose that the subject encounters an object which bears both some resemblance to it and some difference. In that case, Freud explains, the subject will form a cognition of the object by differentiating—or judging—between the aspects of the object that appear familiar to it because they "coincide" with some aspect of itself or its experience, and the aspects that appear alien or unfamiliar to it because they are "new and non-comparable."[9]

What Freud wants to demonstrate in this discussion is how the human mind can be explained without resorting to psychologistic models of human nature. That is, we do not need to envisage the human mind, for example, as a robust computational machine to understand where cognition comes from.[10] We may grasp it instead as the consequence of our inevitable encounter with difference. For example, the child wishes for the breast but instead finds the mother. The child can then form a cognition of the mother—say, that she is a helpful object—by finding aspects of her that are like the breast, such as the fact that they both provide nourishment, and separating those aspects from aspects that are "new and non-comparable." Based on this cognition, the child can then form feelings of affection for the mother, as they recognize the mother as an object that provides for their needs just like the breast. Therein lies the origin of the mother-child bond. Children are bonded to their mothers, not because that bond is "preprogrammed" in their minds by nature or evolution but, rather, because the mother, through her metonymic similarities with the breast, comes to signify nourishment—or satisfaction, more generally—to the child.

"Thus," Freud writes, "the complex of the fellow human-being falls apart into two components." The first component is comprised of all the qualities of the object that are familiar to the subject because they "can be traced back to information from [the subject's] own body." While the second component is comprised of "a constant structure," which is radically alien—*new and non-comparable*—to anything found in the subject, a component that "stays together as a *thing*."[11] There it is! *The thing*. The thing is the second of the two components which Freud claims compose the object. The first component, he tells us, is everything that is familiar about the object because it bears some resemblance to the subject or its experience, and the second component, *the thing*, is something in the object—"an unassimilable component," as Freud also describes it—that resists understanding and knowledge because it is radically different to anything having to do with the subject or its experience, a component of radical otherness.[12] "As a consequence," Freud writes in summary, "the perceptual complexes are divided into a constant, non-understood, part—the *thing*—and a changing, understandable, one—the attribute or movement of the thing."[13]

Thanks to the first of Freud's two components—that is, the familiar or traceable component—we are able to relate to objects. For example, when I encounter someone of the same ethnicity, nationality, religious or political affiliation as me, I feel an instant bond with them, like we share the same mind or subjectivity. I feel that we must've had similar experiences growing up, that we share the same worldview, and that we hold identical political beliefs. I feel that I can predict their behavior, that I know what jokes will make them laugh. And so, I feel that I know how to behave around them, which emboldens me to tell my jokes. Even in the case of minor differences, I feel that I have some sort of purchase on the other, as I am still able to trace their differences to something familiar in me. So, when I encounter someone with a different ethnicity, nationality, religious or political affiliation as me, I still feel that I can understand them, since I feel that I can draw some sort of parallel between their experiences and mine. I may not have had *that* childhood experience, but I have had a childhood; and so, I feel that with some work we can come to understand each other. In other words, while on some manifest level we are different, on some deep, underlying level, we are, I reassure myself, still the same, even if that sameness is just the mere fact of our humanity.

The object in question need not even be "the fellow human-being;" it may be an animal, an inanimate object like an orange, or even an idea like my dream job. While my neighbor's dog is an object that is other than myself, when I look into his beautiful glassy eyes, I see the same bright spirit that I see in my own eyes. And so, I feel that I understand how he feels when I see him limping on his aging legs. His whimpers are definitively not the sounds of springs and gears coming undone like a broken clock. They are the painful expressions of a living, breathing being like me. And while this orange that I hold in my hand has no eyes at all, it is a phenomenal entity like me—it extends into space, endures through time, has mass, color, density, etc.—and so, it is governed by all the same physical laws of nature as I myself am. As such, I know that I can put this orange down on my desk, and it will not float away into space or spontaneously combust, a predictability that I can plan my future around, even if that future is simply to eat it at snack time. And this dream job, though exists only in my mind, still bears some resemblance to me insofar as I myself am also an idea, and therefore, it has the capacity to bear meaning in the world—such as the meaning of life itself—just as I myself do.

And yet, if this were all that objects are—if objects were nothing but the first of Freud's two components—then they would be no trouble at all. Total mastery of the object would be possible because total knowledge of the object would be possible. We may not have the requisite knowledge now, but the point is: total knowledge would be within the horizon of possibility. With enough time and energy, we could know absolutely everything there is to know about an object such that nothing about it would ever surprise us. We would always know exactly how much enjoyment could be gotten from the object, and no object on earth would ever over- or undershoot that expectation. Objects would be completely predictable, and Ava (Alicia Vikander) would not have killed Nathan (Oscar Isaac) in *Ex Machina* (2014).

But as anyone who has ever eaten an orange and been disappointed—not because it was under- or overripe but, rather, because for some inexplicable reason it failed to satisfy—or looked into a dog's eyes and saw nothing but nature's brute indifference, or failed to suss the reasons for their parents' cruelty toward them, or been disappointed by a child, vexed by a lover, or unfulfilled by their dream job, or experienced buyer's remorse at any point in their life, or built an android that ended up murdering them could tell you: objects are unpredictable. Try as we might, we cannot control them. Objects retain a modicum of autonomy, which makes the idea of mastering them the ultimate fantasy—a fantasy that many of us seem to possess—the product of our narcissistic self-belief. The reason is that there is something in the object, some irreducible otherness, that cannot be "traced back" to anything having to do with us or our experience and, therefore, cannot be understood full stop. It is not a minor difference like phenomenal appearance or personal history, which with work we can eventually link to some "information" in ourselves, but, rather, a radical difference, which marks the point of noncoincidence between us and the object. Freud's name for this radical difference is *the thing*.

We should therefore understand the distinction that Lacan makes between *the object* and *the thing* in his formulation of sublimation in terms of the two components of the Freudian object. On one hand, there is the component that we recognize because it bears some resemblance to ourselves and our experience—Lacan calls this component *the object* proper because it comes to represent what the object is to us as such. And, on the other hand, there is the piece that we are unable to recognize, try as we might, because it is completely foreign or alien to anything associated with us—Lacan, following Freud, calls this piece *the thing*. Based on these understandings of *the object* and *the thing*, we may then grasp Lacan's formulation *sublimation raises an object to the dignity of the thing* as meaning that sublimation changes an object by giving it the same stature—or "dignity"—as the radical otherness contained within it.

III

What the genius aims at when they aim at the object, we may then say, is the thing in the object, the unassimilable component that makes the object "the absolute Other of the subject."[14] Genius, in other words, is a kind of receptivity or alertness to the radical otherness in the object, an orientation toward that part of the object which is irreducible to the subject, that part which remains pure object. To paraphrase Walter Benjamin, the genius is like a sunflower who shows its face to the sun and bends its stem as it follows it across the sky—a heliotropism of the thing, so to speak.[15] Genius as a form of attention or listening that picks up on the faint signals of the thing through the background noise of the object.

Put this way, genius sounds incredibly easy. It doesn't require that one write a great symphony or unite general relativity with quantum mechanics. All it requires is that one change one's orientation toward the object ever so slightly, to construe it no longer as something traceable to oneself but now as something strange, something that is "by its very nature alien, *Fremde*."[16] But as simple as that may sound, there is nothing easy about genius because, as it turns out, orienting oneself toward the object in this way is incredibly difficult. The reason is because the object and the thing do not form a complementary pair but, rather, an antagonism. That is, the object and the thing do not sit happily side by side, providing what the other is lacking. Rather, they come at each other's expense. It is because of this antagonism that the object seems to resist our attempts to master it. It is what makes the other with whom I believed I shared something in common defy my expectations, the reason why my jokes fall flat with them. It is what makes the beloved resistant to my attempts to mold them into my ideal lover, the final residue that I cannot scrub from their image. It is what makes the child impossible for the parents to control, a remnant of obstinacy that thwarts their carefully laid out plans.

We find an excellent example of the thing's antagonism with the object in the clinical work of Bruce Fink. Fink discusses the case of an analysand he refers to as Patrick. "[Patrick's] work with me," he explains, "was not his first foray into therapy, for he had gone some years before to a therapist with whom he vehemently criticized his Catholic upbringing and Catholic school education for about six months. At that point, the therapist told Patrick she was Catholic, leading Patrick to feel so guilty he never went back to see her."[17] It appears from Fink's presentation of the story that the therapist disclosed her Catholicism to Patrick as a defensive reaction to his execrations of Catholicism, but it is important to note that we do not actually know the full context of this exchange—and nor does Fink. It may very well be the case that the therapist acted defensively—and Patrick may very well have conveyed the anecdote to Fink in this light—but it is also possible that the therapist disclosed her Catholicism in an effort to make a connection with him, that she told him of her Catholicism in order to find something in common with him, something familiar. We could imagine her saying, for example, "Yeah, I know how that goes. I'm Catholic too," or even "Yeah, I agree with you—and I'm Catholic!"

But this is where the anecdote becomes interesting because the therapist did not in fact build a bridge to Patrick but drove him away. One way to interpret this situation is to construe Catholicism as the therapist's thing, the strange component that repels Patrick, causing him to end the therapy. But this interpretation wouldn't make much sense, since Patrick could "trace back" the therapist's Catholicism to himself. This then leads to a second interpretation, which places the thing, not *with* Catholicism—that is, not on the same level as Catholicism—but, rather, *inside* Catholicism. On this interpretation, the thing is not Catholicism itself but, rather, something inside Catholicism, a strangeness or antagonism, that prevents it from functioning as a bridge between Patrick and the therapist, despite the fact that they share it in common.

The antagonism between the thing and the object is therefore what makes the other defy my expectations, even when we share something in common. But not only does this antagonism make the other defiant of our expectations; it also makes *ourselves* defiant of our own expectations, lest we forget that we ourselves are objects as well. We find an excellent example of this in Freud's essay "The Uncanny." In a footnote, Freud recounts an experience he had while on a train. "I was sitting alone in my *wagon-lit* compartment," he writes, "when a more than violent jolt of the train swung back the door of the adjoining washing-cabinet, and an elderly gentleman in a dressing-gown and a travelling cap came in." When Freud went to redirect the man, he continues, "I at once realized to my dismay that the intruder was nothing more but my own reflection in the looking-glass on the open door." Adding insult to injury, Freud adds, "I can still recollect that I thoroughly disliked his appearance."[18] What causes Freud to misrecognize his own image—or, to put it another way, what causes Freud to recognize himself as something strange and unfamiliar—is, we can now say with Lacan, "a vestigial trace" of the thing within him.[19] This is why Lacan describes the thing as "something strange to me, although it is at the heart of me."[20] It is that alienated part of me—the otherness within me—which makes me an intruder to myself.

Because the thing presents a constant threat to our relations with the object, we regularly attempt to negate it. Rather than receive the other's thing as something dignified in itself, we pathologize it. We treat it as a problem requiring a cure. Or we demand that the other give it up or otherwise change it. Or we simply ignore it, hoping that our ignorance will mean it doesn't exist. At times in history, we have dealt with the strange thing by sequestering those who bear it in camps and ghettos, and too many times, we have eradicated the lives of those people. But most commonly, we mute the thing by imagining the object in our own image. Once again, Fink provides the example:

In the early days of my psychoanalytic practice, a woman in her fifties came to see me and tearfully told me a story about how she had gotten married, divorced, and later remarried the same man. I was quite incredulous, thinking at the time that this sort of thing only happened in Hollywood, and must have had a surprised or bewildered look on my face. Needless to say, the woman felt I was being judgmental and never came back. She was right, of course: I was trying to imagine myself in her shoes and found it quite impossible or at least unpalatable.[21]

Caught up in the implausibility of the woman's story, Fink fails to consider the possibility that this repetition might be the woman's particular form of enjoyment—her thing. In other words, he fails to be receptive to the thing that is announcing itself to him through the woman's repetition. But what causes Fink to be incredulous in the first place? What prevents him from recognizing the woman's repetition as a potential site for encountering the thing? He tells us: *I was trying to imagine myself in her shoes*. Fink was attempting to relate to the woman's repetition, to build a bridge to it—or, using Freudian terms, to trace her repetition back to information from his own experience—and found that he could not do it, that the woman's repetition was simply too "unpalatable" for him. To put it another way, the woman's repetition was the thing in her shoes that didn't quite fit his feet.

What Fink had done in this anecdote is not unusual. In fact, it is something that we all do on an everyday basis. He listened to the woman's story through the filter of his own experience. "Our usual way of listening," Fink observes, "is highly narcissistic and self-centered, for in it we relate everything other people tell us to ourselves." He continues: "We compare ourselves to them, we assess whether we have had better or worse experiences than they have, and we evaluate how their stories reflect upon us and their relationship with us, whether good or bad, loving or hateful."[22] As Fink's anecdote demonstrates, he is no exception. When listening to the woman's story, rather than listening carefully for the elements of it that are singular to her—the elements that bear what Fink so elegantly calls "the otherness of the other"—he listened for the elements that were familiar to him, that he could comprehend through his previous experience.[23] And when he heard something that he couldn't assimilate into his understanding, something strange or *Fremde*, he simply stopped listening, becoming incredulous instead.

We find another example of this muting of the other's thing in the final shot of Alfred Hitchcock's classic *Rear Window* (1954). In one long take, the camera tracks across the courtyard, visiting all the neighbors we've been living with for the past two hours—Miss Lonelyhearts, the Songwriter, the Couple on the Fire Escape, Miss Torso, the Newlyweds—until finally revealing L.B. "Jeff" Jefferies (James Stewart), asleep in his wheelchair with a self-satisfied look on his face, and Lisa Fremont (Grace Kelly), lounging on the bed next to him, reading. This long take has the effect of quilting Jeff's world together into one single happy whole, complete with matching broken legs. It says, *Nothing can cut into Jeff's happiness*. Then, Lisa looks at Jeff, and seeing that he is fast asleep, she puts down her book—*Beyond the High Himalayas* by William O. Douglas—and with a hint of defiance, picks up her issue of *Bazaar* magazine.

The standard way of interpreting this scene is to see it as emphasizing Lisa's resilience as a character. The whole ordeal with Lars Thorwald (Raymond Burr) has changed Lisa, along with all the neighbors, in profound ways—a change that is emphasized by her costuming, as she wears pants for the first time in the film (Jeff, on the other hand, has not changed at all—literally—as he wears the same old pajamas he's worn throughout the film)—but when she picks up her magazine, she reassures us that, on some fundamental level, she is still the same Lisa … Carol … Fremont.

The question that I think we should ask of this scene is this: why must Lisa wait until Jeff has fallen asleep before she can read her magazine? Why must she hide the fact that, deep down, she is still the same Lisa? The answer is obvious. Because Jeff has made it a precondition of their relationship that she give up her love of fashion and high society—in other words, that she give up her thing. It is not enough that she has helped catch a murderer, risking her own life in the process. For Jeff to accept Lisa, she must give up her thing. Throughout the film, Lisa's "perfection," as he refers to it, is the one thing that cuts into his world, the one thing that disrupts and mars it. Thus, for Jeff's world to be quilted together into a single happy whole, Lisa's thing must be cut from it. There is simply no room for her thing in his world. Indeed, when the film fades out on Lisa reading her magazine, it has the effect of suggesting that the reintroduction of her thing puts an end to Jeff's short-lived happiness. And what if Jeff wakes up to catch her reading that magazine? Will they argue again? Will he leave her? Or worse? Thus, when we watch this scene, yes, we should absolutely see it as a testament to the steadfastness of Lisa's character, but we should also see it as a testament to the narcissism of Jeff's love.

Objects therefore are not perfectly flat screens on which we may unproblematically project our image. They are not passive entities that simply drift in and out of our world. There is an otherness to them, "an unassimilable component," that we must mute or otherwise negate in order to enter into relations with them. Indeed, to the extent that we think of objects as flat screens, we have already negated what is other about them. This is why Lacan says that objects relations "emerge in a narcissistic relation." "At this level," he comments, "the object introduces itself only insofar as it is perpetually interchangeable with the love that the subject has for its own image."[24] *The love that the subject has for its own image*: what an indictment! What it means is that there is no negating the object's thing which is not already narcissistic. Whenever we convince the other to get rid of their thing, or whenever we take it upon ourselves to blot it out, we are always boiling them down to what is traceable to ourselves, to what is familiar—hence, narcissism. And this is true even when we believe we are doing it for the other's good. As Lacan stingingly states, "What I want is the good of others provided that it remain in the image of my own."[25] So, while Jeff may believe that he is simply improving Lisa by getting her to give up her fashion magazines, all that he is really doing is making her more familiar, making her more like himself. To put it in Lacan's words, Jeff is all about Lisa's good only insofar as it remains in his image. Thus, whatever love Jeff has for Lisa, so long as it is predicated on her giving up her Park Avenue lifestyle, it is the love he has for his own image.

This is why genius is so difficult. There is no neutral site or ground on which we may encounter the object. Either we will force the object to meet us on our side of the field by muting the thing within it or we will forgo our narcissism and enter "the field of *das Ding*." There is no in between. "With this field that I call the field of *das Ding*," explains Lacan, "we are projected into something that is far beyond the domain of affectivity, something moving, obscure and without reference points owning to the lack of a sufficient organization of its register."[26] That is, if I leave the familiarity of my narcissism and cross the border into the unfamiliar territory of the thing, I will no longer be the one in control of the object, as I will have encountered something that I cannot trace back to myself or my knowledge, something for which I am *without reference points* because it is radically alien to anything in me. Within the confines of my narcissism, I am safe. The object is entirely predictable to me, and reciprocally, I know exactly how to behave toward it. In narcissism, the object relation poses no threat to me. But once I step outside the safety of my narcissism, I enter into a field where I no longer write the other's narrative. A field in which my prior knowledge and experience have no currency. A field where the missing signifiers that might overwrite the other's thing, thereby transforming it into something familiar, something controllable, "doesn't stop not being written."[27] This radically obscure place is what Lacan calls "the field of *das Ding*," and it is the field where the genius pitches their tent.

IV

When the genius aims at the thing in the object, they change the symbolic status of the object as a whole. What do I mean by this? To start, we must appreciate that for Lacan the field of human-object relations is one that is mediated by symbolic structures, language being foremost among them. He comments, "it is obvious that the things of the human world are things in a universe structured by words, that language, symbolic processes, dominate and govern all."[28] Lacan's point here is that "symbolic processes"—such as, language—afford us our only access to objects. There is no accessing objects outside of those "processes," no jettisoning the prosthetic of symbols and touching objects directly. A dog is a carnivorous animal from the Canidae family or man's best friend because those are the notions of *dog* that language and culture have handed down to us. Even if I say that a dog is a wild beast of nature to signify something as far away from culture as I can imagine, I immediately recognize that *wild nature* is itself a construct developed by culture to designate what is outside of itself. Indeed, the very fact that I must use the signifier *dog* to indicate what is at stake in this example demonstrates the extent to which the object is shot through with the word—"they form a couple," as Lacan states.[29] For this reason, words and symbols, for Lacan, are not simply tools for human communication; they are the building blocks of reality itself.

The point that Lacan is making here is of course a Kantian one. Kant famously claimed that objects are known to us only insofar as they are objects given to our senses—that is, as mere appearances. "What may be the case with objects in themselves and abstracted from all this receptivity of our sensibility," Kant maintains, "remains entirely unknown to us."[30] But the point that Lacan is making here is not only a Kantian one; it is also a sociolinguistic one. Since objects are mediated by words and symbols, they are not stuck being what they are in themselves. They are able to take on a variety of meanings for us. Thus, money, for example, beyond what it might be in itself, is not merely paper with colorful images printed on it. It is also the expression of a commodity's value. In many societies, including ours, it is the symbol of power and prestige. For many of us, it represents the pathway to a better life—and much more.

But as we know, Lacan maintains that objects are not entirely meaningful. He insists that there is some aspect of the object—the thing—which resists our attempts to make meaning out of them. A thing that disrupts our narcissism. What place does this thing have in the symbolic? What is its symbolic status? "You will not be surprised," Lacan answers, "if I tell you that at the level of the *Vorstellungen*," that is, at the level of mental representations, "the Thing is not nothing, but literally is not."[31] What Lacan is suggesting here with this distinction between *nothing* and *not* is that the thing is a negativity within the symbolic, but crucially, it is not a negativity in the same way that words like *nothing* and *zero* are negativities. This is because words like *nothing* and *zero* have meaning in symbolic terms. They mean *no value* or *the absence of something*. If I say, "I have *nothing* in my bank account" or "I have a *zero* balance," I signify a value. It is the value of no value—that is, no money—but a value nonetheless. In that sense, words like *nothing* and *zero* aren't negativities at all but, rather, positivities—values or signifiers—with a negative meaning.

Not, on the other hand, is a true negativity in the sense that it lacks symbolic meaning altogether. Whereas *nothing* signifies the absence of meaning, *not* is the absence of meaning as such. Otherwise stated, *not* is a placeholder for the place within the symbolic where meaning or value fails to materialize, the place where no signifiers can be found—a void or an abyss.

A way to understand this distinction between *nothing* and *not* is to understand it in terms of the distinction computer scientists make between *zero* and *null*. For computer scientists, *zero* is a value, the value of nothing—exactly like the word *nothing*. *Null*, however, is a non-value. It simply indicates that no values have been given. In other words, it is the placeholder for the absence of values. If a computer scientist says that a null response has been given, what they mean is that the place within the computer's memory where the software went to retrieve data was missing data, no values were inputted—not the value of nothing, like zero, but, rather, no value itself. No computer scientist would ever say, "I have *null* in my bank account," but if they did, what they would be signifying isn't that they have a zero balance in their bank account but, rather, that they couldn't find a value in the first place, not even zero. Lacan's *not* is a non-value of this kind. When Lacan says that the thing is *not*, we can read him as meaning that it has the same status within the symbolic that *null* has in computer science. That is, the thing designates the place within the symbolic where symbols are missing, a knot or void within the symbolic where symbolization itself fails.

By aiming at the thing within the object, the genius then changes the symbolic status of the object by giving it the same status as the not or null. That is, the genius turns the object, which was once full of meaning and significance, into something, not so much unmeaningful as non-meaningful, the placeholder for the lack of meaning. Or, to put it another way, the genius doesn't simply empty the object of its meaning, thereby turning it into the zero of the symbolic. Rather, they place the object in the place within the symbolic where meaning itself cannot be found, thereby turning it into the null of the symbolic. This is then one way to understand Lacan's formulation *sublimation raises an object to the dignity of the thing*. When the genius sublimates the object, they put that object in the place within the symbolic where the words and symbols that might make it meaningful are missing—that is, the genius turns the object into something for which there are, literally, no words—which changes how we see that object: no longer as something we understand because it traces back to something we know but now as something that points to the hole in what we know.

Lacan finds an example of this type of transformation in his friend, the poet and screenwriter Jacques Prévert. Lacan recalls visiting Prévert at his home and seeing his friend's extensive matchbox collection. The "match boxes appeared as follows," recollects Lacan:

> [T]hey were all the same and were laid out in an extremely agreeable way that involved each one being so close to the one next to it that the little drawer was slightly displaced. As a result, they were all threaded together so as to form a continuous ribbon that ran along the mantlepiece, climbed the wall, extended to the molding, and climbed down again next to a door.

What is at issue in this collection for Lacan is not the pleasure that Prévert got from putting it together, whatever that might have been. Rather, it is the excessive uselessness of the matchboxes themselves, which the collection seems to bring out or underline. This excessive uselessness, Lacan argues, serves as a reminder that there is something in the matchbox—a "thingness as match box"—that is irreducible to its utility or perfection as an object, a reminder that "the match box all by itself is a thing with all of its coherence of being."[32]

What I find particularly evocative in Lacan's example is the way Prévert's sublimation changes the way Lacan looks at a matchbox. Lacan describes the change this way: "I believe that the shock of novelty of the effect realized by this collection of empty match boxes … was to reveal something that we do not perhaps pay enough attention to, namely, that a box of matches is not simply an object, but that … it may be a Thing." What Lacan describes here is something on the order of a revelation—he calls it "the revelation of the Thing beyond the object."[33] By amassing a large collection of matchboxes, Prévert reveals something about the matchbox to Lacan, *something that we do not perhaps pay enough attention to*. Prévert did not put that certain something in the matchbox. It was already there for anyone to see. And yet, it took an act from Prévert for Lacan to see it.

To illustrate this revelation, let us imagine Lacan in his daily life. He regularly sees matchboxes. In fact, he sees them every day. He sees them in the store; he sees them in the restroom of a cafe; he sees people sharing them with each other on the streets; indeed, he sees one in his own hand. But there is something about seeing matchboxes in isolation like this that hides an important aspect of the matchbox from him. Because he sees them only one by one, he sees them strictly as an object with a particular use—namely, holding matches—and nothing more. Then, one day, Lacan visits his friend Prévert, and he sees an enormous mass of interconnected matchboxes sprawling all over his friend's abode, and this sight makes him realize that the matchbox is not simply an object which holds matches. There is something additional in the matchbox—the thing—that outlives its existence as a container for matches. And from that day forward, Lacan appreciates that there is a certain use for the matchbox beyond its use as a container for matches, a use that serves no use, a surplus or *"jouissance* use."[34]

Or imagine this: you are walking along a beautiful beach, when you suddenly see a massive amount of toothbrushes—let's say 3.5 billion or, the approximate number sold in one year—washed up on the shore. The encounter would no doubt be shocking. It would be shocking, at least in part, because the sight of 3.5 billion toothbrushes together in one place reveals to us, in ways that seeing a single toothbrush every day in our bathrooms doesn't, that a toothbrush is not simply an object with a particular use— namely, cleaning teeth—but, also, a thing that outlives its life as an object. Or, to put it another way, upon seeing the sight of the toothbrushes, we wouldn't immediately think of all the teeth that will go uncleaned as a result of the spill. That is, we wouldn't think of the spill merely as a waste of toothbrushes. This is because the sight of 3.5 billion toothbrushes so far exceeds any notion we have of waste that such thoughts become unthinkable. Rather, it would make us think of how we lack the proper conceptual framework to even begin thinking about how we, as a society, have uncritically mass produced a disposable object which is effectively indestructible. There is no place within the symbolic where that kind of "data" exists. The sight, in other words, would raise the toothbrush to the place within the symbolic where we would expect to find the concepts and signifiers to comprehend such a phenomenon but which do not exist—the place of the null.

The genius, I want to claim, effects exactly this kind of transformation of the object. When the genius raises an object to the dignity of the thing, they change how we look at that object, sometimes an object as ordinary and mundane as a matchbox or toothbrush. What makes someone a genius therefore is not that they create the perfect object or the masterpiece. Rather, it is that they reveal something about the object, *something that we do not perhaps pay enough attention to*, a thing that outlives its life as an object. Indeed, there could be no better motto for the genius than that. *To reveal something that we do not perhaps pay enough attention to.*

V

Some accounts of Lacan's theory of sublimation take on an antisocial or even a nihilistic bent. On these accounts, *raising an object to the dignity of the thing* is to introduce something into the social field which is so traumatic, so explosive that it causes the entire field to collapse—something like the opening of the Ark of the Covenant in *Raiders of the Lost Ark* (1981), but on a grand scale. To a certain extent, I understand where this idea comes from. The thing, as I have emphasized, is the place within the symbolic where symbolization itself is missing, and this sounds a lot like a sore spot within the symbolic which, if pressed, would cause it to implode. But I would caution against such interpretations. I would caution against them, not because I think we should be wary of the so-called revolutionary consequences of those interpretations. In any case, to me, they sound more nihilistic than revolutionary. Rather, I would caution against them for reasons having to do with Lacan himself.

For Lacan, the fact that we are symbolic creatures—that is, the fact that "symbolic processes" mediate our relationship with objects—means that we are also creative creatures. Lacan reminds his audience of this very fact, stating, "For many years now I have habituated you to the notion, the primary and dominant notion, that the signifier as such is constituted of oppositional structures whose emergence profoundly modifies the human world." To this, he adds: "It is furthermore the case that those signifiers in their individuality are fashioned by man, and probably more by his hands than by his spirit." In other words, language is a human invention. It was not sent to us from the heavens by the gods. Rather, it was *fashioned* by human beings—by human *hands*, Lacan emphasizes—to organize and structure the chaotic sensations and intensities into which we are thrown, to make a world out of that chaos. For this reason, to Lacan's way of thinking, any discussion of language—including sublimation—must take into account our capacity as creative beings: "We must now, therefore, consider the notion of creation with all it implies, a knowledge of the creature and of the creator, because it is central, not only for our theme of the motive of sublimation, but also that of ethics in its broadest sense."[35]

So, what do we human beings create? "I posit the following," Lacan answers, "an object, insofar as it is a created object, may fill the function that enables it not to avoid the Thing as signifier, but to represent it."[36] Lacan's claim here is that human beings have the capacity to create objects that do not circumvent the thing but, rather, convey it in some fashion. We will look at a few examples of such objects in a moment, but, first, we should take a second to appreciate what Lacan does *not* say in this quote. He does not say, for example, that we create objects that make the thing meaningful or significant. He does not say that we create objects that fill in the symbolic void with signifiers or "data." And he does not say that we create objects that integrate the thing into the symbolic, thereby tempering or normalizing it. Rather, he only says that we create objects that *represent* the thing. This is why we must avoid all those nihilistic interpretations of Lacan's formulation.

While it is absolutely the case that we have a tendency to mute the thing, to overwrite or blot it out, the alternative is not to destroy the entire social field in its name. There is a third option. Along with the capacities to negate the thing and to destroy the symbolic, we human beings also have the capacity to create objects that represent the thing, that bring it to light or discourse—or, to paraphrase Lacan himself, we have the capacity to make the thing suffer the signifier.[37] That capacity is sublimation.

So, we now have a complete picture of what an object is to the genius. For the genius, the object is definitively not the image of perfection or the masterpiece. Rather, it is an object that not only points to the thing in the symbolic but, also, represents that thing to us, brings it into discourse— what we might call, the signifier of the thing. This is then how I understand Lacan's formulation *sublimation raises an object to the dignity of the thing*. Sublimation is the creation of an object that signifies or represents the thing, a signifier that brings the thing into discourse. I know that this may sound like a contradiction because it is a contradiction—and Lacan knows it too. "The fact is," Lacan states, "man fashions this signifier and introduces it into the world," clarifying, "in other words, we need to know what he does when he fashions it in the image of the Thing, whereas the Thing is characterized by the fact that it is impossible for us to imagine it." "The problem of sublimation," he sums up, "is located on this level."[38] Lacan thus recognizes that it is a contradiction to say, on one hand, the thing is the absence of symbolization as such, *it is impossible for us to imagine it*, and, on the other hand, sublimation creates an object which signifies the thing, *he fashions it in the image of the Thing*. And yet, in a series of remarkable examples, Lacan demonstrates that precisely this happens.

The first of Lacan's examples is the vase. What interests Lacan in the vase is that it contains an emptiness. "Emptiness and fullness are introduced into a world that by itself knows not of them," Lacan explains. "It is on the basis of this fabricated signifier, this vase," he adds, "that emptiness and fullness as such enter the world, neither more nor less, and with the same sense."[39] When we think of a potter molding and shaping clay into the form of a vase, we always focus on the substance of the clay itself. That is, we think of the potter manipulating the clay into a particular shape. What Lacan draws our attention to here is the void or emptiness at the center of the vase—that is, the space that holds the flowers and the water. For Lacan, this space is as much a part of the vase as the material that surrounds it. If one wants proof of this claim, try imagining a vase with no void space inside—it is impossible. Such an object, whatever it might be, is by definition not a vase. Thus, for Lacan, when we think of the potter forming the vase, we should not only think of them as manipulating the substance of the clay. We should also think of them as manipulating this void space itself. We should think of them, in other words, as starting out with a certain amount of empty space and turning that empty space into a vase by surrounding it with clay.

In this way, the vase becomes the representation of emptiness as such. This is what Lacan means when he says that the vase introduces emptiness and fullness into the world. Through the vase, we come to understand what it means for something to be empty and, consequently, what it means for something to be full. Or, otherwise put, the vase signifies emptiness to us. Crucially, however, the vase does not present emptiness to us as meaningful. It does not, for example, add predicates to emptiness: emptiness is good, emptiness is bad, emptiness is loneliness, emptiness is happiness, or whatever. All it does is present emptiness itself as emptiness, *neither more nor less*. That is, it turns emptiness itself into an object so that we may grasp it as a concept. Or, as I have been putting it, the vase brings emptiness into discourse.

The vase then is the first of Lacan's examples. The second example is like the first insofar as it too is a negativity wrapped in a positivity: macaroni (yes, the pasta). Macaroni, Lacan observes, "is a hole with something around it." We might find this observation of Lacan's somewhat humorous—indeed, its humor lies precisely in its truth—but he is not being facetious; he means this example earnestly and uni-ironically. "The fact that we laugh," Lacan warns, "doesn't change the situation." Macaroni demonstrates that "the fashioning of the signifier and the introduction of a gap or a hole in the real is identical."[40] What is crucial in macaroni is that it demonstrates that one cannot point to a gap without making an object, and vice versa. So, while we may think of the genius's transformation of the object into the null as a separate act from the creation of the signifier of the thing, they are in fact one in the same act. When one creates the signifier of the thing, one already points to the void within the symbolic, and when one points to the void within the symbolic, one creates its signifier. Such is the lesson of macaroni.

Lacan's third example operates according to a slightly different logic than the first two. It is the example of Paul Cézanne's various paintings of apples. There is something in Cézanne's art, and in particular his depiction of apples, that captures Lacan's attention, and yet, it is clear from reading his comments on these paintings that Lacan himself has difficulty articulating exactly what it is. He states, as a commonsense, "Everyone knows that there is a mystery in the way Cézanne paints apples, for the relationship to the real as it is renewed in art at that moment makes the object appear purified." He adds, "it involves a renewal of its dignity by means of which these imaginary insertions are, one might say, repetitively restated."[41] Mari Ruti helpfully discerns in these comments a fascination on Lacan's part with Cézanne's singular ability "to capture something about the enigma ... of the Thing in its representation of an utterly banal object."[42] In this way, Cézanne's apple functions much like the matchbox in Lacan's discourse. That is, it points our attention to something in the apple that we normally do not pay much attention to. And yet, while I fully concur with Ruti's insight, I would also contend that there is something else at stake in Lacan's intrigue, something having to do with the way Cézanne both succeeds and *fails* in his imitation of apples.

Works of art, Lacan acknowledges, "imitate the objects they represent."[43] In this, Lacan admits, Plato was right.[44] And yet, at the same time, art also fails to fully imitate their objects insofar as "they make something different out of that object." This is what Plato didn't grasp, contends Lacan. A work of art is never fully what it depicts. It is always simultaneously imitating its subject matter as well as exceeding or overshooting that imitation in some fashion—"Thus," Lacan argues, "they only pretend to imitate."[45] From these comments, we may then say that what fascinates Lacan apropos of Cézanne's apples is the way they imitate real apples, *works of art imitate the objects they represent*, as well as deviate from or overshoot that imitation through Cézanne's signature post-Impressionistic style, *they make something different out of that object*. In other words, there is something realistic and yet unrealistic in Cézanne's depiction of apples.

Accounting for this, what Alenka Zupančič calls, *minimal difference* between imitation and failed or excessive imitation is the thing. "Thus we see the difference between the object and the Thing," Zupančič explains, "without ever seeing the Thing." She elaborates: "[W]hat we are *shown* are just two semblances, yet what we *see* is nothing less than the Thing itself, becoming visible in the minimal difference between the two semblances."[46] That is, what we are "shown" are Cézanne's attempt to imitate apples (semblance one) and Cézanne's failed attempt to imitate apples (semblance two), and what we "see" in the minimal difference between those two semblances—which to be sure are parts of a single painting—is the thing. So, while I wholeheartedly endorse Ruti's claim that Lacan's intrigue has to do with Cézanne's uncanny ability to capture, through painting, the thing in the apple, I will add to it that this ability comes through the "double affirmation" of Cézanne's imitation and over-imitation of the apple.[47]

These three objects—the vase, macaroni, and Cézanne's apples—then are all examples of what I will call, following Lacan, *promoted signifiers*. In his seminar *Transference*, which takes place the year following *The Ethics of Psychoanalysis*, Lacan, while discussing the Socratic notion of *epistémé*—what he translates as *science*—makes the following comment:

> The best formulation you can give for the instating of this science—in what? in consciousness—in a position, in an absolute dignity, or more

precisely in a position of absolute dignity, is to say that it involves nothing other than what we can express in our vocabulary as the promotion of the signifier itself to a position of absolute dignity.[48]

Now, there is a lot going on in this quote, but all I want to focus on here is the phrase *the promotion of the signifier itself to a position of absolute dignity*. Is there not a striking resemblance between that phrase and Lacan's formulation of sublimation as *raising an object to the dignity of the thing*? Indeed, not only does the phrase *the promotion of the signifier itself to a position of absolute dignity* resonate with Lacan's formulation of sublimation, it also resonates with my description of the sublimated object as the signifier of the thing. What I therefore want to suggest is that the genius, insofar as they sublimate the object, promotes a signifier, which allows the social field to register the thing, a registration that might possibly lead to its transformation—and not its disintegration—for the ultimate goal of the genius is to form a better symbolic, not to destroy it.

I want to end this chapter by adding two more examples of promoted signifiers to the three we already have from Lacan. One is a joke and the other is political. First, the joke. After a long day of work, a group of coworkers decide to get some drinks together. One of the coworkers excitedly announces, "I know a bar where everything is $1.99. And I mean *everything*! You want a glass of beer? $1.99. A shot of whiskey? $1.99. A glass of wine? $1.99. It doesn't matter what it is. Everything is $1.99 all day, every day." Skeptical, the coworkers go to this bar. Once there, the first coworker demonstrates for the rest, "Give me a tall glass of beer." The bartender promptly pours the man the tallest glass of beer there is and tells him, "That'll be $1.99." Stunned, the next coworker jumps in, "Give me a double shot of whiskey!" The bartender promptly pours her a double shot of whiskey and says, "That'll be a $1.99." The third coworker goes next, "I'll have a glass of your best wine," to which the bartender pours the finest vintage of red wines and replies, "That'll be a $1.99." Then, noticing that the last coworker still hasn't ordered anything, the bartender asks them, "What'll you have?" The coworker replies, "Oh, nothing for me, thanks. I'm the designated driver," to which the bartender says, "That'll be a $1.99." The joke, of course, is not that the bartender misunderstands "Nothing" to be the name of a drink. Rather, it is that in this bar, everything, including nothingness itself, is a thing that costs a $1.99. In this way, *$1.99* is a promoted signifier.

The political example. When Russia, unprovoked, invaded Ukraine in 2022, thousands of Russian citizens took to the streets to protest their government. Their cry was: *NO WAR!* To quell the unrest, the Russian government not only deployed thousands of police to intimidate, beat, and arrest the protesters, it went so far as to ban the signifier "No war" itself. Despite the threat posed to their lives by their own government, the Russian citizens took to the streets again. At one protest, a woman held up a sign. The sign didn't read *No war*. Rather, it bore no inscription at all. It was completely blank. She was promptly arrested by the police. While the woman showed the police a blank sign, the police were nevertheless able to see the signifier *No war* through a minimal difference contained within it. Or, to put it another way, the woman's genius was her ability raise the lack of inscription to the dignified place of the banned signifier *No war*. In this way, she turned a blank sign into a promoted signifier.

All these examples, whether big or small, lighthearted or serious, comic or political, demonstrate the same crucial point. While genius is a contradiction, it is not for all that impossible. Miracles do happen. Genius does happen.

6

Something Missing

I

During the lockdowns of 2020, I took up biking, as it was one of the few outdoor activities that were permissible at the time. But something strange happened. I started becoming obsessed with bikes. I started watching videos about bikes, following social media about bikes, subscribing to newsletters about bikes—I got "into" bikes, as they say. Soon, I decided that I needed a bike that was better suited for long commutes, as I started using the bike as my primary mode of transportation, so I traded in my aluminum performance bike (a perfectly fine commuter) for a steel bike. I made this trade believing that the steel bike was the only bike I needed, but no sooner had I acquired it than I felt the need for another bike. This time it was a mountain bike, which I eventually purchased. But the mountain bike I purchased had full suspension, which I felt was excessive, so I dreamed of getting a "hardtail" mountain bike, never once realizing that my desire for a new bike was the excess. So, I sold my "full-squish" and purchased the hardtail. But no sooner had I got the hardtail than I began fantasizing about getting yet another bike. This time a bike from a particular maker. But it didn't stop there. I began fantasizing about getting all sorts of bikes, as if the lid on the jar containing all my bike fantasies had been blown off: a step-through bike for riding around town, a bike for getting groceries, a retro-style nostalgia bike, a bike for hauling cargo, a bike for this and a bike for that. There was no end to this saga.[1]

This story, for me, perfectly illustrates the trouble we have with objects. While we have a deep longing for objects, we also find them profoundly disappointing, such that finding a new object brings the desire for another object rather than satisfaction. We pursue the object, believing it will supply what has been missing from our lives, but once we acquire it, we feel that there is something missing in the object instead. And so, we pursue the next object.

Beginning with this chapter and continuing for the next two, I want to reflect on this trouble we have with objects. What causes our deep longing for objects? And why do objects, even long sought after ones, disappoint?

Why do we feel objects are strangely familiar, even when they are brand new? What do we want from objects; how do they serve us? And lastly, what might we learn about our trouble with objects if we approached it from the standpoint of the genius? These are the questions that I want to explore over the next three chapters. To start, however, I will consider the origin of this trouble, an origin that takes us to what I believe is psychoanalysis's greatest insight into our ontology. Namely, that there is always something missing in the drive.

II

In *Project for a Scientific Psychology*, Freud introduces the concept of the *spezifische Aktion* or specific action, which will turn out to be the concept of the aim in his mature metapsychology (although the language of the specific action itself will never completely disappear from his vocabulary). The idea behind the specific action is quite simple. As stimulus accrues within the organism, discharging that stimulus becomes imperative. The problem, however, for the organism is that the world is indifferent to its need for expenditure. For this reason, discharge always requires "an alteration in the external world (supply of nourishment, proximity of the sexual object) which, as a *specific action*, can only be brought about in definite ways."[2]

Thus, a specific action is a particular act, which facilitates the discharge of stimulus by affecting changes in the external world. In *Civilization and Its Discontents*, Freud gives an example. Early in life, an infant learns to distinguish between objects that are always present, like "his own bodily organs," which "can provide him with sensations at any moment," and objects that "evade him" and therefore must be "forced to appear by a special action." Freud's example of this second, evasive kind of object is the mother's breast. When the infant hungers, it seeks satisfaction—that is, the expenditure of stimulus—by sating itself on the mother's breast. And yet, the breast is not always assuredly available. When the breast is not available, Freud claims, it is made to "reappear as a result of his screaming for help."[3] Screaming is therefore a *specific*—or, as he calls it here, *special*—*action*, which causes the mother to provide the breast, thereby turning a hostile world into an amenable world.

On its face, the idea of the specific action is simple, even elegant. It offers a perfect solution to the problem of a hostile and unabiding world. If the world is inhospitable to our need for expenditure, then it makes perfect sense that we would develop actions specifically designed to subdue and comport it to our need. And yet, for Lacan, there is something in this idea that doesn't quite add up, something that Freud himself, in the *Project*, seems to overlook or at least take for granted. The "specific action will always be missing something," Lacan remarks.[4]

With this comment, Lacan calls our attention to the insurmountable distance that exists between the specific action's ostensible purpose (i.e., to make the world amenable to expenditure), on one hand, and the actual conditions needed for expenditure—in particular, the existence of a facilitating object (e.g., "supply of nourishment, proximity of the sexual object," mother's breast, etc.)—on the other hand. For it is not enough to simply possess the ability to alter our conditions. An object must also exist, and not only exist but given in such a way that we can appropriate and exploit it for our needs. And therein lies the problem. For no action, no matter how specific, has that kind of authority over the object. Because it is also a thing, the object will always retain a modicum of independence or autonomy from the specific action, which, no matter how minimal, can never be fully eliminated. Or, to put it in a Freudian key, all objects are ultimately evasive objects.

Take Freud's own example of the screaming infant for instance. As a specific action, the infant's screaming, as Freud theorizes it, facilitates discharge because it brings the mother and her breast ("they aren't the same thing," Lacan reminds).[5] But as any child could tell you, there is no guarantee that their screaming will in fact bring the mother. What if she is not there to hear the screams? Or worse, what if they bring the father instead? And even if their screaming succeeds in bringing the mother, there is still no guarantee that she will offer the breast. What if she misinterprets the screams as a request for a loving cuddle? Or worse, what if she responds with an angry spanking? Despite what Jesus presumes is possible, the mother could just as well give the infant a stone or a snake.[6]

Any mastery that the infant's screaming seems to have over the mother's breast is strictly imaginary. Even Freud himself recognizes this fact when he writes: "At first, the human organism is incapable of bringing about the specific action. It takes place by *extraneous help*, when the attention of an experienced person is drawn to the child's state by discharge along the path of internal change."[7] Freud's mistake, however, is that he attributes the impotence of the specific action to the infant's own physical limitations—*At first, the human organism is incapable of bringing about the specific action*—and not to the efficacy of the specific action itself. But if there is no food to be found, then it does not matter if it is the infant or the "experienced person" who is doing the finding; the infant simply will not be fed. The problem is not the infant's lack of physical maturity, as Freud believes; it is, rather, the specific action itself. The specific action simply does not have the type of absolute authority over the object that it needs to accomplish its own purpose. In this way, the specific action is a mechanism that is, by its very nature, lacking or inadequate—to quote Lacan again, the "specific action will always be missing something."

III

The inability of the specific action to master the object provides our first insight into the origin of our trouble with objects. Because we need objects to satisfy the drive, we imagine that they exist exclusively for our purposes. Thus, the child imagines that the mother exists purely to provide for their every wish. Or the man imagines that the woman exists purely to provide him with sexual pleasure. Or the capitalist imagines that nature exists purely for the extraction of raw materials. The psychoanalytic word for this imagining is of course *narcissism*. And yet, what we find with the failure of the specific action is that the object does not exist purely for our needs. It has its own existence outside of our narcissism. To put it in the language of the previous chapter, the object is a thing that exists beyond our narcissism. And this confounds us about the object. *Why doesn't the object submit to my will?* we wonder. *Why is it so obstinate? It is as if there is something deficient in the object*, we think to ourselves, never once considering that it might be the specific action that is defective.

As Freud's metapsychology develops, the idea of the specific action all but disappears, and in its place, we get the concept of the aim, which is not an alteration of the external world per se but, rather, "the act towards which the instinct tends."[8] But while Freud's metapsychology shifts away from the specific action and toward the aim, the idea that the object is always missing remains. Indeed, by *Three Essays on the Theory of Sexuality*, the missing object becomes formally understood as inherent to the drive's structure.

To help his readers better grasp the drive—a concept with which they might not be familiar—Freud begins *Three Essays* by comparing it to hunger, which he assumes they will find more familiar and intuitive. Hunger, Freud notes, is like the drive in many respects. Both are kinds of felt pressure or *Drang*, both call for the elimination of that pressure through the performance of an act and the use of an object, and both produce the feeling of pleasure upon the elimination of that pressure. But for all of their similarities, the drive and hunger are radically dissimilar in one very important respect. Only hunger possesses an essential relationship with its object.

When someone hungers, the only way they can eliminate that hunger is by eating food. They could not, say, buy a car or a tennis racket and expect their hunger to disappear. Indeed, they could not even drink water and expect to sate their hunger, even though food and water are similar in many respects (e.g., both are consumable, both provide essential nutrients, both enter the body through the mouth, etc.). This is because hunger has an object—food—to which it possesses an essential relationship. In fact, so essential is hunger's relationship with its object that it will refuse other objects which could serve as suitable substitutes, such as, bugs, for instance. Indeed, hunger will even discriminate amongst food itself, refusing to be satisfied except only by certain kinds of food. Thus, one person requires meat to sate their hunger while another requires vegetables while still another requires sweets to supplement either their meat or their vegetables. In this way, hunger possesses an object, not in the sense that it can force an object to appear but, rather, in the sense that it shares an essential link with an object, a link that can only be loosened "in the most extreme instances."[9]

While the instinct of nutrition exhibits an "energetic retention of its objects," the same cannot be said of the drive.[10] In his discussion of so-called "Sexual Aberrations," in *Three Essays*, Freud observes the sheer range of things that can serve as objects of the drive. As Freud notes, even objects that are not normally considered sexual by social and cultural norms, like children and animals, can become objects of the drive, albeit as "sporadic aberrations." The reason Freud brings up pedophilia and bestiality, however, is not to condone or defend them. To be sure, he describes these behaviors in strictly negative terms, especially pedophilia, which he says, quite plainly, is "sexual abuse." Rather, he brings them up only to demonstrate the sheer variety of things that can become objects of the drive. That is to say, Freud brings up pedophilia and bestiality precisely because they are aberrant. They are edge cases that demonstrate the extreme limit of what can become an object for the drive. He writes of these phenomena this: "Nevertheless, a light is thrown on the nature of the sexual instinct by the fact that it permits of so much variation in its objects and such a cheapening of them."[11] The only reason we are not in the habit of acknowledging the compromises the drive is willing to make in terms of object-choice—compromises that are not seen in hunger—is because, Freud tells us, we mistakenly take heteronormative sexuality, "where the object appears to form part and parcel of the instinct," as the drive itself. "We are thus warned," Freud concludes, "to loosen the bond that exists in our thoughts between instinct and object," for "[i]t seems probable that the sexual instinct is in the first instance independent of its object."[12]

IV

However, it is also true that even in the case of heteronormative sexuality, variability in the objects of the drive can still be observed. Heteronormative sexuality, at its simplest and most reduced, "is regarded as being the union of the genitals in the act known as copulation."[13] For this reason, the genitals are thought to be the natural object of the drive. But even here, at its simplest and most stripped down, there is ambiguity in regard to what precisely the drive aims. Does the drive truly aim at the other's genitals? Surely, this cannot be the case, for if the other's genitals were presented to us separate and isolated from their body—on a platter, for example, as in Francisco de Zurbarán's painting, *Saint Agatha of Catania*—we would find them disturbing or disgusting, not satisfying.[14] Indeed, as Freud points out, "It is only in the rarest instances that the psychic valuation that is set on the sexual object, as being the goal of the sexual instinct, stops short at its genitals." In the main, "appreciation," he continues, "extends to the whole body of the sexual object."[15]

And yet, it is also too crass to say that the object in question is simply the other's body as a totality. There is always some particular aspect of the other's body, some piece of it, that makes it stand out from all the rest. Perhaps, it is their penetrating eyes or their luscious hair. Perhaps, it is a mole, like with Cindy Crawford, or a scar, like with Padma Lakshmi. Whatever the case might be, whether it is an eye or a scar, this particular body part, like a signature or a fingerprint, defines them as a person. In that case, is it this particular body part, and not the genitals, that captures the drive? Indeed, it might not even be a particular body part at all, but simply, a feature of it like its color or shape. As the title of the Marylin Monroe film has it, *Gentlemen Prefer Blondes*, and so, it may not matter if the other's hair is long, short, curly or straight, so long as it is blonde, in which case, the drive seems to aim at the blondness of the hair, and not the hair itself, much less the body as a whole. And, of course, it might not even be the body itself but, rather, some extraneous artifact, like the pearl earring in Johannes Vermeer's famous painting, which lacks particular significance on its own but makes the wearer, whoever they might be, an object of fascination.

We find this vacillation of the drive on full display in Alfred Hitchcock's celebrated film, *Vertigo* (1958). When John "Scottie" Ferguson (James Stewart) begins obsessively remaking Judy Barton (Kim Novak) into the image of Madeleine Elster (also Kim Novak) by getting her the same hairstyle, the same floral brooch, the same gray suit and brown shoes, it becomes unclear whether Scottie truly loves Judy or if he suspects that she is Madeleine. Is he giving these gifts to Judy because he loves her? Or is he simply remolding her in Madeleine's image? That is to say, is the drive aimed at the object of Judy or the object of Madeleine? To these possibilities, we must add a third: neither. Scottie is in love with neither Judy nor Madeleine. Rather, he is in love with the mementos of Madeleine themselves: the blonde hair, the sweptback hairdo, the floral brooch, gray suit and brown shoes, etc. That is to say, Scottie will love anyone who possesses these partial objects, no matter who they are.

In that case, the drive aims at neither Judy nor Madeleine but, rather, at those part-objects of Madeleine themselves.

If we are unable to construe moles, blondness, pearl earrings, or floral brooches as proper sexual objects, it is not because those things cannot be objects of the drive but, rather, Freud argues, because we are in the habit of conflating the sexual and the genital.[16] The point here, of course, is not that the drive always aims at something other than the genitals but, rather, that it aims at *all* of these body parts and *none* of them all at the same time. For the body is, as Lacan says, like a Mannerist painting, an image that is "the coalescence, combination, or accumulation of a pile of objects," which can, at any time, be separated and partitioned by the drive in what Lacan describes as "the ungrouping of the objects."[17]

V

Although all of these ways of construing the object are, as Freud admits, present in perversions like fetishism, Freud does not raise them here to argue that normative sexuality is secretly a perversion, however true that might be.[18] He raises them, rather, to argue that even in the narrowest definition of sexuality, variability in the object can still be observed. Indeed, as a result, Freud will go on to describe the object as "what is most variable about an instinct."[19] What this irreducible variability suggests to Freud is that there is no such thing as an object of the drive as such like there is in hunger. Whereas hunger exhibits an *energetic retention of its objects*—namely, food—the drive exhibits "the lack of object."[20] The object of the drive is, in other words, "a lost object."[21] This then is the source of our trouble with objects. Because the drive lacks an essential object, like hunger and food, we pursue all sorts of objects, hoping to one day find what is missing from the drive. But because there is no such thing as an essential object of the drive, we experience nothing but disappointment, as every object that we find falls short of our expectations.

There are of course objects, such as a bike, that will come to serve as the object of the drive "in the course of the vicissitudes which the instinct undergoes."[22] But these objects are "not originally connected with" the drive and become "assigned to it only in consequence of being peculiarly fitted to make satisfaction possible" at a particular moment in time.[23] They are not linked to the drive in an essential way like food is to hunger. The sense of an essential link with an object is completely missing in the drive. The drive does not have an object in that sense—the essential object is lost.

Indeed, it is precisely this loss of an essential object that constitutes the drive as such. That is to say, whereas with hunger, the link to the specific object of food characterizes and defines it as a phenomenon—distinguishing it from, say, thirst, which is linked to water—with the drive, it is precisely the absence of any such link that is decisive. "Under a great number of conditions and in surprisingly numerous individuals," Freud writes in summary, "the nature and importance of the sexual object recedes into the background." "What is essential and constant in the sexual instinct," he concludes, "is something else."[24]

In this way, the drive can be said to be lacking, and lacking in a way that it cannot be said in regard to its aim. There is to be sure variability in the kinds of aims the drive takes up. Thus, for one it is collecting stamps while for another it is complaining incessantly while for a third it is both at the same time. But importantly all these aims share something essential in common. They are all "different paths leading to the same ultimate aim" of "removing the state of stimulation at the source of the instinct" or, in a word, satisfaction.[25] So, while the drive may have various aims, like it does with its objects, it nevertheless cannot be said to be lacking an essential aim in the same way that it lacks an essential object, for it in fact has one: satisfaction. Indeed, it is not inaccurate to say that the drive is nothing but this aim of satisfaction. What it lacks, what it does not contain within itself, is the very thing through which it obtains its essential aim of satisfaction: namely, the object.

As such, the drive is a structure that is wanting, a structure that exerts enormous pressure on its host but is utterly incapable of removing that pressure, a structure that is incomplete or not all—an aim without an object. This idea of the drive's incompleteness—what Freud elsewhere calls the "bedrock" of castration—conveys an important, indeed, the most important, psychoanalytic insight regarding human ontology: namely, that we, as humans, are fundamentally discontented creatures because we lack, in an original and irreducible way, the very thing that would bring us satisfaction, and not simply as a function of our inability to manipulate the world, as Freud originally thought, but, rather, as a fundamental fact of our being.[26]

It is indeed because of this lack in the drive that we have such trouble with objects. We believe that the next object we find will be the one that is essentially linked with the drive, thereby bringing permanent satisfaction. But, of course, it is not, since the drive lacks just such an object. Thus, when we find the next object, we experience disappointment, and not satisfaction like we had hoped.

And yet, rather than confront the "bedrock" of our castration, we prefer to believe that the source of our disappointment has to do with the object. We think that the object has some sort of flaw or deficiency; perhaps, it is not perfectly symmetrical or its corners are bent. Thus, a parent squashes their child's desire, believing that this desire prevents them from fulfilling the parent's hopes and dreams. Or a lover changes all the quirks and eccentricities of their beloved, believing that these oddities prevent them from finding satisfaction with the beloved. In these ways, and many more besides, we inflict considerable damage on the objects in our lives, running roughshod over what is unique and incomparable in them—what Mari Ruti describes as "the singularity of their being." In the interest of avoiding the uncomfortable truth that discontent is inherent to who we are as people, we "violate the integrity of our loved ones," writes Ruti, "by placing upon them hopes and expectations that have little to do with the singularity of their being" and everything to do with "our own sense of exceptionality or existential belonging."[27]

But this is not the genius. When the genius creates an object, they do not create the essential object which is missing from the drive—what we ordinarily call the masterpiece. This is because the genius accepts that there is always something not or null in the drive, a lost object that "will never be found again."[28] Rather, what the genius creates is an object that signifies the nonexistence of the essential object, an object that brings this nonexistence itself into discourse, thereby allowing us to face it and come to terms with it. Unlike me, the genius doesn't find in the flaws and shortcomings of their bike, the sign that they need a new bike, as if any bike could serve as the drive's essential object. Rather, what the genius finds in those flaws and shortcomings are the traces left behind by the nonexistence of the perfect bike. And while owning a flawed and imperfect bike might be disappointing for me, the genius finds in that disappointment a strange pleasure all its own.

In this way, the genius presents an alternative to the kind of violation of the other's singularity, which Ruti describes. When the genius considers the object, they do not see a lump of clay or a bundle of potential waiting to be molded and smoothed into the perfect object. Rather, they see a dignified object whose singularity must exist in the world, a thing whose "inimitable uniqueness" must be signified.[29]

7

Acute Nostalgia or, The Strange Case of Coca-Cola

I

There is no denying our obsession with objects. We have built an entire culture—indeed, an entire civilization—around their production, circulation, and consumption. We clamor for the newest products. We want the latest gadget to replace the one we already have, even though the one we already have is still perfectly serviceable. And so, to paraphrase the hymn, we endure many dangers, toils, and snares in order to acquire it. But no matter how many objects we acquire—whether bikes, shoes, books, or partners— we always want "just a little bit more," to quote Rockefeller. We tell ourselves that this is it, the next object will be the last one. We convince ourselves, and our loved ones, to let us acquire it, promising that once we have it, we will need nothing else. But no sooner have we acquired this coveted object than we are already eyeing the next one, and so, the relentless pursuit continues.

This obsession with objects—which encompasses everything from the way objects preoccupy our imagination, through our relentless pursuit of them and the pleasure, often intense, that we experience when we acquire them, to the magical belief that the right object will fulfill us once and for all—is a direct consequence of what I have described as psychoanalysis's greatest insight into our ontology: that the drive lacks an essential object. Indeed, it is precisely because the drive lacks a single essential object that any object can become an object of the drive. But this same lack in the drive is also responsible for a very different and, in some ways, contradictory, phenomenon; namely, the acute feeling of *nostalgia* that accompanies the acquisition of an object.

By *acute nostalgia*, I am referring to that feeling of familiarity, of homeliness or fit, that turns the acquisition of an ordinary object into the acquisition of the so-called right object or perfect object—the object that seems to uncannily fill out a hole, as if it had belonged there in the past, like the missing piece of a puzzle. One feels acute nostalgia, for example, when sitting in the cockpit of a car for the first time and somehow sensing that it was designed specifically for us, as if it was made, not in a factory by human hands but in heaven by the angels themselves. Or when we try on a cute sweater and feel that it was tailor-made especially for us, despite the fact that it was mass produced in a factory somewhere. Or when, in *The Shawshank Redemption* (1994), Andy Dufresne (Tim Robbins) and his fellow prisoners drink beer on the rooftop of the prison at 10 o'clock in the morning. At that moment, those ice-cold Bohemia-style beers don't feel like any ordinary beer. They feel like the only objects on earth that could produce satisfaction, the only objects that could make Andy and his friends feel like free men again, like they were "the Lords of all Creation."

But where this feeling of acute nostalgia is most evident is in the phenomenon of falling in love. When we fall truly and madly in love with someone, there is a feeling of destiny that attends our experience, a feeling that the beloved is precisely the one we had been searching for our entire lives—even if we didn't know we had been searching. Not some ordinary other, however true this might be objectively speaking, but a unique other, a perfect match—a soulmate, as we like to say.

It is this feeling of uncanny familiarity or acute nostalgia that Aristophanes, in *The Symposium*, attempts to account for in his panegyric to love. According to Aristophanes, all human beings were originally conjoined creatures, complete with "four arms and four legs, and two faces, both the same, on a cylindrical neck, and one head."[1] The original humans were ornery and unruly creatures, having to do with their completeness. So, to deal with their contemptuousness, Aristophanes says, Zeus split these creatures in two, thereby creating the humans of today. Each one of us, therefore, Aristophanes tells us, is one half of a whole, "forever seeking the half that will tally with himself"—or, as the philosopher Jerry Maguire (Tom Cruise) so pithily put it: "You complete me."[2]

II

Given that an object which is essential and original to the drive does not exist, one would expect that every encounter with an object would feel fresh and new. And yet, this is not the case at all. What we find instead is that every encounter with an object, even completely new ones, feels oddly familiar. Freud captures this strange phenomenon thus: "The finding of an object is in fact a refinding of it."[3]

Take, for example, the case of Coca-Cola. On May 8, 1886, the first Coca-Cola was sold at Jacobs' Pharmacy in Atlanta, Georgia. Whoever drank the first Coke that day must have felt a kind of pleasure that seemed to fill a deep and profound lack—what Lacan calls "the pleasure of the mouth" (as opposed to, say, the pleasure of the gastrointestinal system or the pleasure of the brain's dopamine receptors, as neither of those pleasures conveys the sense of pleasure that exceeds the satisfaction of bodily need which is at stake in the drive).[4] What makes this case so strange, however, is that on May 7, 1886, this "lack" of Coca-Cola didn't exist—indeed, couldn't exist—since no such thing as Coca-Cola yet existed. And yet, when that person drank the first Coke on May 8, 1886, it was like they found the very thing they had been looking for their entire life, like the Aristophanean other half itself. How could that be? How could that person feel nostalgic for Coke, if Coke did not exist prior to that moment? What "lack" then was filled that fateful day in May? Freud offers a possible answer.

According to Freud, this nostalgic feeling, which surrounds every finding of the object—the feeling of "refinding," as he describes it—is rooted in our earliest experience of loss. "At a time at which the first beginnings of sexual satisfaction are still linked with the taking of nourishment," writes Freud, "the sexual instinct has a sexual object outside the infant's own body in the shape of his mother's breast." He continues: "It is only later that the instinct loses that object, just at the time, perhaps, when the child is able to form a total idea of the person to whom the organ that is giving him satisfaction belongs."[5] So, as Freud has it, during infancy, the drive in fact has an object in the shape of the mother's breast, but it loses that object at the moment when we realize to whom the breast truly belongs. Based on this constellation of relationships, Freud proposes that every pursuit of an object is therefore an attempt to recover—or, to use Freud's locution, refind—the missing breast. On this account, if the first Coca-Cola felt uncannily familiar that fateful day in May, it is because it was a repetition—a "refinding"—of the mother's breast, and the lack that the Coke filled was none other than the lack left behind by the mother's missing breast.

Thus, on Freud's account, the feeling of acute nostalgia comes from "refinding" the lost breast in the shape of the new object. Yet, is there not something familiar about this account of Freud's? Indeed, does it not sound strikingly similar to Aristophanes' myth of love? The parallels are undeniable. In place of the conjoined creatures, we have the child–breast dyad; in place of a splitting by a god, we have the separation of the child from the breast by the mother; and in place of the longing to reunite with our missing half, we have the search for the missing breast in its various avatars. Indeed, it seems that Freud's account of the lost breast is nothing more than a psychoanalytic reimagining of the Aristophanean love myth, which alone should be enough to disqualify it. Still, if Freud's account is to be rejected, it should be done on more substantive grounds than its unfortunate similarities with Aristophanes' myth. Thankfully, a more substantive critique exists, which is, perhaps, not all too surprising, given the nature of Freud's account. What is surprising, however, is the source of that critique, for it comes from none other than Freud himself.

III

The ego, Freud asserts in *Civilization and Its Discontents*, "appears to us as something autonomous and unitary, marked off distinctly from everything else."[6] Consequently, "there is nothing of which we are more certain than the feeling of our self, of our own ego."[7] The reason for this feeling of certainty is not too difficult to ascertain, as having a strong sense of the ego confers a distinct adaptive advantage. For once the self is clearly defined and distinguished from the rest of the world in the shape of the ego, it is easily defensible against "a strange and threatening 'outside.'"[8]

However, there is a problem with the ego. Namely, this: "Some of the things that one is unwilling to give up, because they give pleasure, are nevertheless not ego but object; and some sufferings that one seeks to expel turn out to be inseparable from the ego in virtue of their internal origin."[9] That is, when we distinguish the ego from the external world, we make a critical misrecognition. We associate the pleasure-giving parts of the world with the ego and the unpleasure-producing parts of the ego with "a strange and threatening 'outside.'" And this, despite the fact that we made this distinction between ego and world originally as a way to protect ourselves from external danger. On second thought, isn't it precisely this motive of self-protection that causes this misrecognition in the first place? Indeed, in wanting to protect the self from all unpleasure, the ego deals with "unpleasurable excitations arising from within" in the only way it knows how. It treats them as "unpleasure coming from without."[10] So, as it turns out, this feeling of certainty in one's own sense of self—that is, in one's own ego—is erroneous from the start, a fiction predicated on the misrecognition of the actual source of our trouble. "Thus," Freud concludes, "even the feeling of our own ego," of which we are so certain and in which we place so much stock, "is subject to disturbances" because "the boundaries of the ego are not constant."[11] So much for the ego!

The paradigmatic case of the ego's misrecognition of self and world is none other than the breast-feeding infant—and not simply for us but incredibly for Freud himself. This is what he writes: "An infant at the breast does not as yet distinguish his ego from the external world as the source of the sensations flowing in upon him."[12] From this position of false discernment, the infant divides the world into two parts, "a part that is pleasurable, which it has incorporated into itself, and a remainder that is extraneous to it."[13] To one part, the infant says, "I should like to eat this," and to the other part, "I should like to spit it out." Caught up in this mistaken division is none other than the mother's breast itself. Insofar as it is a source of pleasure (indeed, it is the first pleasure), the infant "eats" the breast—that is, the infant associates the breast with itself—saying to it, "It shall be inside me."[14]

At the same time, the infant also "has separated off a part of its own self," a part that is, to be sure, a source of unpleasure, "which it projects into the external world and feels as hostile," like, for example, its own hunger.[15] As a source of irritation and unpleasure, the infant breaks off the association between itself and its hunger, saying to the latter, "I should like to spit it out," and thus, the infant no longer experiences hunger as something of its own making, as something caused by its own body, but, rather, as something done to it, something with an external cause. For example, the infant will blame the mother as the true cause of its hunger insofar as she withholds the breast (after all, isn't the breast the child's?) or otherwise cannot provide it. Or the infant will lament its hunger as a curse of nature, a fate that it must endure as part of the never-ending struggle for survival. The point, of course, is not that an unfed infant will not go hungry or that there is something unnatural in hunger. Rather, the point is that the infant refuses to accept responsibility for its hunger, delegating that responsibility to the other, whether it is the mother or nature.

To return then to Freud's account of the lost breast in *Three Essays*, the problem with this account, to put it simply, is that it construes the breast from the perspective of the ego. When Freud writes "the sexual instinct *has* a sexual object outside the infant's own body in the shape of his mother's breast," he repeats the misrecognition of the ego, for in actuality, the breast never belonged to the infant, and therefore, the breast was never the infant's to lose in the first place. For Freud to characterize the loss of the breast as a subsequent event—*It is only later that the instinct loses that object*—he must first accept the ego's premise that the breast was once a part of the infant. But as Freud himself recognizes, not only in *Civilization and Its Discontents* but elsewhere throughout his work, this association of the breast with the infant, as well as the feeling of possession that comes with it, is a fiction, an effect of the misrecognition that occurs with the formation of the ego itself.

Here is the point. The infant cannot lose the breast because it was never theirs to lose in the first place. That the infant eventually forms "a total idea of the person to whom the organ that is giving him satisfaction belongs" is therefore irrelevant. While it may be true that the infant eventually comes to the realization that the breast in fact belongs to the mother, it is a mistake to consider the breast the infant's possession until that point. To attribute the loss of the object to this realization or to make the two events coincide, as Freud does in *Three Essays*, is to fall into the same trap as the ego. The point is that the breast was always lost to the infant, and not simply when the infant realizes it. The breast is, in this sense, a lure, producing the feeling of having an object when in fact it was never there in the first place. As Lacan rightly recognizes, "It is in its nature that the object as such is lost. It will never be found again."[16] Or to put it paradoxically, albeit in terms that I imagine Freud himself would have appreciated, the breast is itself already a refinding of the lost breast.

IV

The great temptation is to fall for our acute nostalgia—that is, to misrecognize in the object the image of our missing half—as if we really were those bisected creatures from Aristophanes' myth. Or, to put it another way, the temptation is to misconstrue the object as the repetition of the mother's breast. Avoiding this temptation, I want to claim, is what distinguishes the genius from the nongenius. Recall that in Chapter 2, I argued that sublimation loosens the significance of the object to the drive—sublimation is *an aim without an object*, I put it—and that this loosening of the significance of the object enables the genius to engage in inquiry without any expectation of finding the solution. With this in mind, we may then say that the genius avoids the temptation of acute nostalgia by deemphasizing the significance of the object. The genius does not find the image of the missing breast in the object because the genius is not searching for the missing breast in the first place. Rather, they are enjoying the forepleasure of inquiry itself.

So, what are we reexperiencing in the object, if not the mother's breast? To answer this question, we must focus on Lacan's contention that the object, even a completely brand new one, is always "a refound object." "The object," he contends, "is by nature a refound object." "That it was lost," he adds, "is a consequence of that—but after the fact."[17] The key phrase here is *after the fact*. Lacan's keen insight here is that the object's quality of being lost—its lostness, if you will—is an *effect* of its finding. That is, we lose the object, but that loss, paradoxically, takes place only *after* we have found it. This is frankly an astonishing insight by Lacan, and we would do well to dwell on it a bit longer.

As we discussed above, Freud believes that the loss of the object took place sometime in the past. He specifically identifies the infant's loss of the mother's breast as that moment, but it's not important what the decisive moment is. What matters is that, for Freud, it occurred in the past. For example, one could read Freud's account of the infant losing the breast in nonliteral terms—as a reconstruction of a primal past, say—but that would not change the fact that, for Freud, the object is lost to the drive *prior* to the finding of a new object, such that this finding is always a refinding of the lost object. The situation is however very different with Lacan. In fact, it is the exact opposite. For Lacan, the loss of the object is paradoxically a *consequence* of the object itself: not something that happens before the object has been found but, rather, something that happens *after the fact*, as a result of it, which is why, for Lacan, the object is always "a refound object."

Thus, for Lacan, the loss which is responsible for that acute feeling of familiarity, that feeling of having found the missing piece of a puzzle, is an effect of the found object itself, which changes what is at stake in that loss. With Freud the identity of this loss is straightforward, if incorrect. Because the found object reminds us of a loss which took place in the past, what is at stake in the loss is whatever that lost object was—Freud claims it was the mother's breast. With Lacan, however, the issue is more complicated. Because that feeling of loss is an effect of the found object itself, it can't refer to a lost object in the past. Indeed, no such object ever existed. So, then, what object does it refer to? Why, none other than the found object itself! That is to say, the lost object that the found object makes us feel acutely nostalgic for is none other than the found object itself. This is why, for Lacan, the found object is always *a refound object.* There is always a redoubling—a "double affirmation," to use Alenka Zupančič's term—in the object that makes it feel familiar, like the missing piece of a puzzle, even when we have found it for the first time.[18] Acute nostalgia is therefore always a nostalgia for the present.

Though Lacan directly contradicts Freud on this point, it is Lacan, and not Freud, who shows himself to be more faithful to the Freudian cause, for it is Lacan who effectively deploys Freud's own temporal logic of belatedness or retroactivity—*Nachträglichkeit* in Freud's German—to grasp the paradoxical relationship between the drive and the object. Thus, it is Lacan, and not Freud, who avoids falling into the Aristophanean trap—that is, the trap of positing a mythical time in the past when we once in fact possessed the object—for it is Lacan, and not Freud, who recognizes this nostalgia for what it is: the retroactive effect of the object itself.

While we experience the loss of the object as occurring before the finding of the object—and logic tells us that it really must be this way—Lacan's argument is that we only experience this loss through the finding of the object, as a retroactive effect of it: "It is thus refound without our knowing, except through the refinding, that it was ever lost."[19] *Except through the refinding*: that is the key phrase. It is not that we become aware of our loss, and then go searching for its replacement. Rather, it is that we find an object and then experience this loss through it, as a retroactive effect of it.[20] This is why someone can flip through a catalog without any thought of purchasing an item, and then, upon seeing the merchandise on sale, suddenly feel the need to make a purchase. This is acute nostalgia: the feeling of loss that is retroactively cast back onto the past. And so, if we ever felt that a car filled a specifically car-shaped hole in our lives or that the beloved, a beloved-shaped hole, it is not because those specifically shaped holes already preexisted in us and that we, in a stroke of luck, happened to find their matching objects, as Aristophanes or Jerry Maguire believes. Rather, it is because those shaped holes are themselves the effect—the consequence—of those objects. In other words, every object carries within itself the precise loss that it itself fills.

V

We are now in a position to solve the strange case of Coca-Cola. The lack which was filled that fateful day on May 8, 1886, by the first Coca-Cola was none other than the lack created by the presence of the first Coca-Cola itself. Or, to put it another way, Coke filled the loss of Coke. Steve Jobs was therefore right: "People don't know what they want until you show it to them."[21] Despite what the market ideologues believe, an object, like the iPhone, does not come into existence to meet some preexisting need. No one in the history of the world ever needed an iPhone—and no one ever will. Rather, it comes into existence entirely to fill a lack. The trick, however, is that we only experience this lack through the finding of the object—that is, *after the fact*. I don't first desire an iPhone and then go to Apple and demand that they invent one, as the Economics textbooks tell us happens. Instead, I see its image in an advertisement or someone using one on the subway, and then suddenly, almost naturally, I feel its absence in my own life, thereby causing me to desire one of my own.

Once, I was putting gas into my car when I was suddenly struck by an irresistible urge for a Red Bull energy drink. I thought it was odd, since I only had Red Bull once in my life, and it was decades ago, when I was an undergraduate in university. But still, I had this deep longing for Red Bull, like Zeus had separated me from Red Bull a long time ago. It was not until I put the pump back into its holster that I noticed an advertisement for Red Bull on the handle. What had happened is that I had seen the Red Bull advertisement without knowing that I had seen it, and, as a result of having seen it, I felt its loss. In this way, the object always comes first, and only through that object, the experience of its loss and the subsequent desire for it, even if that loss and desire feel as natural as thirst itself. So, in a very literal way, the iPhone arrives on the scene, in the nick of time, to fill the lack that it itself creates. Or, to put it another way, Apple didn't produce the iPhone because people lacked it; people lacked the iPhone because Apple produced it. *People don't know what they want until you show it to them*, indeed!

And yet, having this insight did not make Jobs a genius. The problem for Jobs is that the very gesture of inventing the iPhone—that is, the gesture of showing people what they don't know they lack—falls into the Aristophanean trap. That is, by showing us what we want, Jobs mistakes the iPhone as our missing other half. And this makes Jobs, not a genius but simply another capitalist, someone who uses the object simply to turn a buck. Steve Jobs, not as a genius but, rather, as someone who was always busy, industriously inventing to order and becoming rich.[22]

What would have made Jobs a genius is if he offered the object, not as the compensation for our lost object—not as the Aristophanean other half—but, rather, as the dignified signifier of the null of that loss. Or, in other words, if he offered the object as the placeholder for the loss which we feel comes from the past but, in actuality, comes from the present. Compare Jobs's iPhone with Leonardo's *Coition of a Hemisected Man and Woman*, which we discussed in Chapter 3. The iPhone purports to be a useful object—perhaps, the most useful object in human history—and insofar as it is useful, it offers itself to me as something that compensates me for my loss, like, say, my poor sense of direction. Without the iPhone, I cannot find my way around the city, but with the iPhone, I am never lost. (Of course, I never knew I couldn't find my way around the city until the iPhone.) In this way, the iPhone presents itself to me as my missing other half, the sense of direction that I was separated from by Zeus.

By contrast, there is absolutely nothing useful in Leonardo's *Hemisected Man and Woman*, as it is riddled with "remarkable errors."[23] As such, when I view the sketch, I learn absolutely nothing about human sexuality. I am no more knowledgeable about human sexuality after viewing it than I was before viewing it. In fact, if anything, I am more likely to walk away from the sketch misinformed about human sexuality. To put it another way, *Coition of a Hemisected Man and Woman* doesn't provide the knowledge of sexuality that I feel I lack when I view it. What it does, rather, is hold the place of that lack in my knowledge, the place where the signifiers that would make human sexuality meaningful cannot be found, the place of the null. In this way, Leonardo's *Hemisected Man and Woman* is not an object but, rather, "the Thing beyond the object," the thing that is in the sketch which outlives its usefulness as a piece of knowledge.[24]

Unlike Jobs, the genius does not offer to give us the object that we lack. The genius recognizes that acute nostalgia always refers to the loss in the object itself, not to a mythical lost object in the past. Thus, the genius does not claim to reunite us with the mother's breast. What the genius offers instead is to make us more keenly aware of the fact that we never possessed the breast in the first place, that the object was always lost. They do this by offering us objects that signify the nonexistence of the lost object, objects that represent this nonexistence as the null within the drive. These are objects that bore a hole in our knowledge or, to paraphrase Jerry Maguire, objects that *decomplete* us. As such, the genius is in a very different kind of business than the one Jobs was in. Not the business of inventing objects that might supply what we feel we lack, but, rather, the business of creating objects that bear witness to that lack, objects that signify it. Objects that make us realize that what we are truly nostalgic for is the experience of loss itself. A money-losing endeavor, if there ever was one!

8

A Problem of Narcissism

I

Psychoanalysis has a name for our obsession with objects. That name is *narcissism*. But that can't be right, can it? Isn't narcissism—at least, in the popular sense of that word—the love of oneself? Therefore, isn't narcissistic the vain person or the self-interested person, and not the person who loves an object, like the doting parent or the infatuated lover? In fact, don't we say of the person who loves an object, who devotes themselves entirely to it and sacrifices everything for it, like the parent or the lover, that they are selfless, altruistic—the precise opposite of narcissistic? So, then, how can the love of objects be narcissistic?

There would even seem to be support for this popular version of narcissism in none other than Freud himself. In his pivotal paper, "On Narcissism," Freud develops the notion of "'anaclitic' or 'attachment' type" object-choice, a kind of object-choice that takes as its model, not the ego or the self but, rather, the other.[1] The earliest of these, call them, anaclitic objects are, Freud claims, the mother and the father, who are themselves the first other. Once we have formed an attachment to our primary caretakers, we seek objects that follow in their model. With this emphasis on the other, anaclitic object-choice appears to be a direct contradiction of narcissism. In this way, Freud appears to endorse, not reject, the popular notion of narcissism. So, how could I call object love narcissistic? However, to come away from the Narcissism paper with this lesson would be to completely misunderstand it.

II

To begin, while it is true that, in "Narcissism," Freud develops the concepts of anaclitic and narcissistic object-choice, they are not, for him, opposites. They are rather interrelated, always simultaneously operative within us. He writes, "We have, however, not concluded that human beings are divided into two sharply differentiated groups, according as their object-choice conforms to the anaclitic or to the narcissistic type." He continues: "we assume rather that both kinds of object-choice are open to each individual."[2] This simultaneity of anaclitic and narcissistic object-choice alone should be enough to dissuade us from thinking of anaclitic object-choice as the counter or antidote to narcissism, but Freud goes even further.

The whole reason Freud takes up the question of narcissism in the first place is the proximity he finds between narcissism and psychosis. In psychosis, the individual completely withdraws "from people and things in the external world."[3] But "the libido that has been withdrawn from the external world," Freud goes onto say, does not disappear from the world but, rather, is "directed to the ego and thus gives rise to an attitude which may be called narcissism."[4] That the libido, under psychosis, can turn from objects back onto the ego—in other words, that psychosis is even possible at all— leads Freud to make one of his most important theoretical advances: the idea that the libido itself is split between the ego and objects or, between, what he calls, *ego-libido* and *object-libido*.

Before "Narcissism," Freud understood things very differently. At that time, for him, sexuality manifested strictly through the formation of attachments to objects or, as it is called in psychoanalysis, object-cathexis. Thus, the libido functioned either by taking as its object a part of the subject's own body (i.e., auto-erotically), as in the case of thumb-sucking, or an external object, like the mother's breast, but never the subject's own ego— that is, never narcissistically. It is not until Freud deals with the psychoses that he reckons with the possibility of the libido taking the ego as its object. If the libido can turn back on the ego, then it must be because part of it is oriented around the ego (ego-libido) while another part is oriented around objects in the external world (object-libido).

But there is more. The psychoses confront Freud with a further puzzle, which has to do with timing. Narcissism, as it is clearly demonstrated by the fact that psychosis can occur in adults, is not simply prior to object-cathexis but also after it, which suggests that narcissism and object-cathexis are not a matter of development. To be sure, Freud argues that the drive is "at the outset attached to the satisfaction of the ego-instincts," but he doesn't argue, for all that, that we then mature onto object-cathexis, never to deal with narcissism ever again.[5] As the phenomenon of psychosis clearly demonstrates, narcissism never fully disappears. And so, even if the objectification of the ego can be explained by theorizing a split within the libido, the question still remains: what becomes of ego-libido while the psychotic exhibits object-cathexis? "Are we to suppose," Freud asks, rhetorically, "that the whole amount of it has passed into object-cathexes?" "Such a possibility," he replies, "is plainly contrary to the whole trend of our argument."[6] Freud's answer—and it is quite a remarkable answer indeed—is rather that "they exist together," one hidden inside the other, such "that our analysis is too coarse to distinguish them."[7]

Object-libido, Freud thus concludes, does not overcome or outgrow ego-libido but, rather, contains the latter within itself, such that narcissism always functions, albeit from the background, in object-choice, whether that choice is of the narcissistic type or the anaclitic type. Anaclitic object-choice therefore should not be construed as the antithesis of narcissism but, rather, as another mode or form of it: narcissistic object-choice forming the direct or *active* form of narcissism while anaclitic object-choice forming its indirect or *passive* form.

III

What makes our obsession with objects narcissistic therefore is not the amount of ego at stake in it. It is rather the purpose we have for the object. When the ego first develops, it exists, Freud claims, in a state of *primary* or *original narcissism*, a state of perfect contentment in which the drive enjoys an essential relationship with the object. The paradigmatic image of original narcissism is the breast-feeding infant. Of this image, Freud writes, "There are thus good reasons why a child sucking at his mother's breast has become the prototype of love."[8] In this image, the infant has its two original love objects: the mother's breast and itself. From our discussion of this image from the previous chapter, we know that this image represents a time that never existed. There was never a time in which the drive had an essential relationship with the object. Or, more to the point, there is no such thing as original narcissism. Nevertheless, the ego emerges from a feeling that it has lost this original narcissism, a feeling that leads to "a vigorous attempt to recover that state." Thus, recovering that lost original narcissism, as impossible as it is, becomes our highest aim in life. As Freud puts it, "To be their own ideal once more, in regard to sexual no less than other trends, as they were in childhood—this is what people strive to attain as their happiness."[9]

The object is instrumental to the project of reclaiming original narcissism since it is the loss of the essential object that led to the loss of original narcissism in the first place. This is why we are so obsessed with objects. We wishfully believe that we will one day find the object which will bring about the return of our lost narcissism. This is also why our obsession with objects is at bottom narcissistic. Not so much because our ego is at stake in it but, rather, because we want to use the object "to restore the happiness that has been lost."[10] And finally this is the source of the object's value for us. Insofar as we believe that the object has the ability to bring us our lost happiness, we regard it as possessing great value. And insofar as we believe the object lacks that ability, we disregard it as worthless.

There are two ways in which people will use objects to recover original narcissism. The first way is what Freud calls narcissistic object-choice or, as I am calling it, *active narcissism*. Active narcissism is when a person believes original narcissism was lost to them when something went missing in themselves—that is, in their own ego. Thus, the active narcissist believes the key to recovering original narcissism lies in recovering that lost something in the form of the object. "In that case a person will love in conformity with the narcissistic type of object-choice," writes Freud, and "will love what he once was and no longer is, or else what possesses the excellences which he never had at all."[11]

The prototype of the active narcissist is the doting parent. "If we look at the attitude of affectionate parents towards their children," Freud comments, "we have to recognize that it is a revival and reproduction of their own narcissism, which they have long since abandoned."[12] Though all the affections lavished on the child by the doting parent appear altruistic and selfless, even excessively so, Freud contends, they are all done in an effort to reclaim, through the child, the narcissism which was lost to the parent. Thus, when the doting parent looks upon the child, they don't see the child as they are but only as a reflection of themselves. Or, as Freud puts it, in the child, "a part of their own body confronts them like an extraneous object."[13] After all, don't parents even say of their children that they are the spitting image of themselves?

This kind of parental love can be said to be imaginary, not in the sense that it is a cover for some ulterior emotion but in the sense that the child functions as an image of the parent.[14] And so, when the parent sees to it that the child's every need and want is met and then some, that "illness, death, renunciation of enjoyment, restrictions on his own will, shall not touch him," they do it, not for the child's sake but for their own sake, insofar as the child is the bearer of their image, in the ultimate hope that in doing so, they will ensure that "the child shall fulfill those wishful dreams of the parents which they never carried out."[15] The imaginary quality of the parents' so-called unconditional love is then revealed when the child, say, drops out of university, abandons the family religion, marries someone of a specific race or nationality, reveals that they are gay—that is to say, when the child ceases to function as the parent's image, for it is then that the parents' love for the child magically evaporates.

Though the resemblance at stake in parental love is quite literal, this need not always be the case in active narcissism. In many cases, the object simply possesses a quality that the narcissist possesses. An American traveling abroad, for example, might strike up a spontaneous friendship with another American for no other reason than they are both American. Or a person will hire a graduate from their alma mater. But the object need not even possess a quality that the narcissist possesses. It is enough that they possess a quality that the narcissist used to possess or never possessed but wishes they possessed. A person therefore will buy a red sports car, believing that it conveys the same coolness which they once possessed when they were young. Or they will become obsessed with guns, as they see in the gun the same potency that they do not possess but wish they possessed. In all these ways, and many more besides, narcissism can be seen working through object-choice, not against it, as we use objects to recover the keys to our lost narcissism, thereby demonstrating Freud's keen insight that "where the libido is concerned, man has here again showed himself incapable of giving up a satisfaction he once enjoyed."[16]

IV

The second way that people will attempt to recover original narcissism is what Freud calls anaclitic object-choice, and what I am calling *passive narcissism*. Passive narcissism is when a person believes original narcissism is lost to them but can still be found in the perfect object, such as, the mother or the father. Thus, the passive narcissist believes the way to recover original narcissism is to become proximate to that perfect object. Ideals, for example, work in this passive manner. "What he projects before him as his ideal," writes Freud, "is the substitute for the lost narcissism of his childhood in which he was his own ideal."[17] I do not possess original narcissism, but the ideal does; so, if I associate myself with the ideal, I can partake in the ideal's original narcissism as the compensation for my lost narcissism. It is the passivity of this narcissism by proximity that I mean to convey with the term "passive narcissism".

For Freud, the model of the passive narcissist is the infatuated lover. The beloved object, Freud claims, "displays the marked sexual overvaluation which is doubtless derived from the child's original narcissism and thus corresponds to a transference of that narcissism to the sexual object."[18] When Romeo extols the beauty of Juliette or when Gatsby obsesses over Daisy Buchanan, while we may think of their devotion as a sign of the depth of their love, on Freud's view, it is nothing more than a transferral of the lover's lost narcissism onto the beloved. Like the doting parent, the infatuated lover doesn't love the beloved for who they are but, rather, for the image they bear—

in this case, the image of original narcissism itself. "The subject's narcissism," Freud therefore keenly observes, "makes its appearance displaced on to this new ideal ego, which, like the infantile ego, finds itself possessed of every perfection that is of value."[19]

In this way, the lover's infatuation with the beloved is also imaginary. The lover lavishes the beloved with all sorts of expressions of love, from words to deeds, but the lover makes these gestures only insofar as the beloved approximates their ideal beloved. If and when the beloved reveals itself to be different from this ideal—that is, when the beloved, like Lisa Fremont, bares their thing—the lover's infatuation breaks like a magic spell.

So, when I overlook the Grand Canyon and I admire its beauty and grandeur, my admiration is still caught up in narcissism. It is not the same narcissism as the active narcissist's, although this is not impossible either. For example, I may see in the Canyon a sublimity, which I can conquer by hiking through it, thereby proving my superiority over the Canyon itself, or alternatively, I may see in the Canyon a self-similar beauty, which I may capture with a selfie. Rather, it is a narcissism that I experience through the perfection that I confer upon the Canyon. The Grand Canyon, I think to myself, is a masterpiece of Nature, a veritable object of perfection. It is an object that lives up to its reputation, an object that takes my breath away. And so, while I myself may not have original narcissism, I still believe it exists in the shape of the Grand Canyon. For this reason, I am able to experience a small sample of original narcissism through the Canyon, which is of course why I love it. This is why I think to myself that I am better than all those visitors who are disappointed that the Grand Canyon is simply a large hole in the ground or all those unfortunate souls who have never been to the Canyon at all. I am privy to a secret narcissism by virtue of my love for the grandest of canyons.

V

Is there an answer to narcissism? Is there a way to relate to the object that is not narcissistic? For the genius, the only way to relate to the object that is beyond narcissism, whether one is talking about active or passive narcissism, is to give up original narcissism itself. Only by giving up original narcissism will we be able to relate to objects, not for what they can be for us but, rather, for what they are in themselves. But how does one give up something that never existed in the first place? An answer—or at least the beginnings of one—can be found in Freud's short but very powerful essay, "On Transience."

Written shortly after the outbreak of the First World War, "Transience" recounts an incident Freud had while walking with a friend and an unnamed poet through the Dolomites one summer.[20] Observing the beauty surrounding them, the poet, Freud recollects, refused to take any joy in it knowing that it was all destined to disappear with winter. "All that he would otherwise have loved and admired," Freud recalls, "seemed to him to be shorn of its worth by the transience which was its doom." Freud, however, rejects the poet's assessment. For Freud, the transience of the summer countryside does not detract from its beauty but, rather, enhances it. "Transience value," he argues, "is scarcity value in time," and "[l]imitation in the possibility of an enjoyment raises the value of the enjoyment."[21]

What accounts for the difference between the psychoanalyst and the poet's respective outlooks? Freud suggests that it has to do with mourning. "What spoilt their enjoyment of beauty," that is, the enjoyment of both the poet and Freud's friend, "must have been a revolt in their minds against mourning."[22] Without the capacity to mourn, Freud argues, we cannot love new objects. Only by slowly, and indeed painfully, releasing the psyche from all its attachments to the lost object can we then form new attachments to new objects. In this way, the ability to mourn is integral to our capacity to love. What, we may then ask, was the poet refusing to mourn? Here, Freud is somewhat equivocal. On one hand, he seems to suggest that the object at stake in the poet's refusal of mourning was nature itself, that by refusing to mourn the inevitable loss of nature, he did not have the capacity to enjoy all the beauty it possesses. In this case, transience is a future-oriented stance. It is a mourning for a loss to come, a preemptive form of mourning. But on the other hand, Freud also seems to suggest that it has to do with the ideal of beauty itself, that this ideal forms its own kind of object in the poet's mind, which then prevents him from appreciating the transient beauty of nature.

Freud interprets the poet's "aching despondency" at the inevitable loss of nature's beauty as a kind of protest against its transience. "Somehow or other," it seems to say, "this loveliness must be able to persist and to escape all the powers of destruction." Far from commendable, this requirement that beauty be eternal has to do, Freud claims, with an unreasonable "demand for immortality."[23] The poet's unhappiness seems to say that only the immortal object deserves his enjoyment, anything less is unworthy. This attitude is thoroughly narcissistic. It devalues nature's beauty for its failure to adequately bear the image of immortality, an image that derives from none other than the poet himself. To quote Freud again, "What he projects before him as his ideal is the substitute for the lost narcissism of his childhood in which he was his own ideal." To put it another way, the ideal of immortality is a substitute for the immortality that was lost to the poet.

The problem, of course, is that the ideal of immortality does not exist. It is a piece with original narcissism itself, a form of perfection that exists only insofar as it is lost. And yet, because the poet had not yet mourned the loss of his original narcissism, he believed it was reasonable to hold nature to its standard. "The idea that all this beauty was transient," Freud writes, "was giving these two sensitive minds a foretaste of mourning over its decease." He continues: "[A]nd, since the mind instinctively recoils from anything that is painful, they felt their enjoyment of beauty interfered with by thoughts of its transience."[24] Transience therefore must be, not only a mourning aimed at the future but also a mourning aimed at the imaginary objects that capture our minds, the objects that don't exist but prevent us from loving what is real all the same. Genius is a transience of this kind.

I find an example of this ethic of transience in Denis Villeneuve's 2016 film *Arrival*. Villeneuve's film tells the story of the "heptapods," a group of mysterious aliens who have landed on earth for some unknown reason, and Louise Banks (Amy Adams), the brilliant linguist who is recruited by the military to decode their indecipherable language. The film opens to a sequence of scenes that give us glimpses into Louise's relationship with her daughter, Hannah, at various points of their life together, beginning with Hannah's birth and ending with her untimely death. Based on its position within the film, the presence of Louise's voiceover—"I used to think that this was the beginning of your story," she begins the film—and importantly the music of Max Richter's elegiac "On the Nature of Daylight," this sequence leads us to believe that Hannah had died prior to the arrival of the heptapods. It is not until well into the film, when Louise is deep into her work with the heptapods, translating their obscure language, that she learns—and we along with her—she *will have* a daughter. At this moment, like an act of secondary revision itself, we realize that the opening sequence of the film was a glimpse into Louise's future, not her past—indeed, we also used to think this was the beginning of Hannah's story![25] Hannah will one day die; she has not died yet. In an extraordinary way, *Arrival* daringly uses the entire science fiction plot of the alien arrival as a mere device to stage an ethical question. Should Louise give birth to Hannah, knowing full well that she will die an untimely death? As Louise asks Ian Donnelly (Jerry Renner), her colleague and future husband, and Hannah's father, "If you could see your whole life from start to finish, would you change things?"

Louise, as we know from the opening sequence of the film, indeed decides to have Hannah, but the morality of her decision is ambiguous. Slavoj Žižek, for example, criticizes Louise's decision, calling it "an extremely selfish act of neglecting others' suffering." The film's great irony, he adds as a kicker, is that "while Louise literally saves the world … with her final choice she ruins her world."[26] The film itself does not necessarily disagree with Žižek on this point. While the film is told from Louise's point of view, it gives voice to this criticism of Žižek's through Ian, whose relationship with both Louise and Hannah is destroyed when he learns of Louise's foreknowledge—as Hannah says to Louise in one scene, "He doesn't look at me in the same way anymore."

While there is certainly substance to Žižek's—and Ian's—excoriation of Louise's decision, could we also not say of it that, like the poet's "aching despondency," it evinces a revolt against mourning? Could we not ask of it: why should the knowledge of Hannah's transience make her life any less beautiful? "On the contrary, an increase!"[27] After all, every parent—not just Louise—brings a child into the world knowing that life itself is impermanent and therefore their child will one day die. To chide Louise for her decision is to somehow forget this fact; it is to make immortality the ideal against which we measure Louise's love as a parent.

To my mind, while there is certainly pain and suffering at stake in her choice, Louise chooses to have Hannah, not because she is callous to other people's suffering but, rather, because she has a changed relationship to the future. Because of her work with the heptapod language, Louise is able to experience the future, and as such, she is able to mourn the loss of Hannah *before* she is born. That is to say, Louise is able to mourn the loss of a *nonexistent* Hannah, which frees her to enjoy an existent Hannah when she is born. As a result, Hannah's transience no longer interferes with Louise's ability to cherish her, like it does with Ian (and Žižek). Indeed, it is this transience, and not her ability to fulfill the ideal of immortality, that is the source of Hannah's value. This is why Louise is able to say with quiet defiance, "Despite knowing the journey, and where it leads, I embrace it. And I welcome every moment of it." It is not that Louise is selfish but, rather, that she has already mourned the loss of immortality. As such, Louise is able to relate to Hannah, not as the "revival and reproduction" of Louise's narcissism but, rather, for who she is in herself.

Thus, the genius's relationship to the object must be like Louise's relationship to Hannah: a relationship of transience. The genius may not have worked with an alien language, but the genius still must mourn the loss of a nonexistent original narcissism from their position in the present in the same way that Louise mourns the loss of the not yet existent Hannah from her position in the present. Let me illustrate what this might mean by revisiting the Grand Canyon example from above and rewriting it from the standpoint of transience. By experiencing the transience of the Grand Canyon, I no longer feel that its beauty comes from its perfection, from its status as a masterpiece of Nature. Whatever perfection I once saw in the Grand Canyon, I now sense was a projection on my part, and I mourn it as lost. Thus, when I visit the Grand Canyon, I no longer receive a sense of smug self-satisfaction. Yet, this doesn't mean that I no longer think the Grand Canyon beautiful, like a despondent poet. On the contrary, more so. But where does its beauty come from? It comes from the fact that nearby uranium mines threaten to pollute its waters with arsenic and uranium, that corporations constantly seek to commercialize its land with designs of erecting hotels and shopping malls along the Canyon floor, that coal-fired power plants and urban pollution frequently darken its sky, that years of drought caused by climate change endanger life as we know it throughout the Canyon, that visitors launch golf balls or throw padlocks into the Canyon to uplift their own egos. That is to say, the beauty of the Grand Canyon comes, not from its perfection, not from its status as a masterpiece, but, rather, from its impermanence, its transience, from the fact that at any moment it can be taken away from us and destroyed. The Grand Canyon, not as the signifier of original narcissism but, rather, the signifier of transience. Is there any satisfaction in loving such a signifier? There certainly is. But it takes a genius to see it.

Part Three

Group Psychology and the Analysis of Genius

In this book, I have examined genius from two angles: first, from the angle of the aim, and second, from the angle of the object. Now, I want to switch my focus to a topic that is somewhat tangential to the genius: the theory of groups or, group psychology. Whereas the first two parts of this discussion were focused on breaking down the genius to its most basic components, this discussion will focus on applying the genius to group psychology. My motivation is twofold. First, there is a certain stereotype about the genius which imagines the genius as a single, solitary individual. This is the genius as the savant. It is a stereotype that goes hand in hand with the notions of natural talent and innate intelligence insofar as it envisages the genius growing up in isolation and acquiring their gifts directly from Heaven. I want to attack this idea by thinking about the genius in a group context. What might the group based on genius be?

Second, there is a certain idea about psychoanalysis itself. Psychoanalysis, in many ways, is a theory of groups. This is something that Sartre understood and appreciated about psychoanalysis.[1] All the theorizing about family drama—the so-called Oedipus complex, and so on—can be seen as one grand attempt to situate the psyche within a group context. However, many believe that what psychoanalysis has to say about the group is purely negative. Indeed, nowhere is this negativity more evident than in Freud's *Group Psychology and the Analysis of the Ego*, which dismisses the idea that human beings are herd creatures as a saccharine illusion.[2] This has led some to advance the idea that psychoanalysis is incapable of offering a positive vision for the group, only a deconstructive one. I want to push back on this idea by thinking through, not only what psychoanalysis claims is problematic about the group but also what it thinks is possible.

In the "Postscript" to *Group Psychology*, Freud discusses the distinction between a drive that is inhibited in its aim and a drive that is uninhibited in its aim, a distinction that plays a significant role in his theory of the group.

Of the shift from uninhibited aims to inhibited aims, Freud writes this: "If we choose, we may recognize in this diversion of aim a beginning of the *sublimation* of the sexual instincts."[3] Freud's evocation of sublimation here is significant, as it does two things. First and foremost, it offers the basis for a positive vision of the group, a group based on the sublimation of the drive or, in other words, a group based on the inhibition of the sexual aim. Second, it implicates the genius in that vision insofar as the genius is a figure of sublimation.

Freud continues. "Those sexual instincts which are inhibited in their aims," he writes, "have a great functional advantage over those which are uninhibited." And what advantage is that? He answers, "Since they are not capable of really complete satisfaction, they are especially adapted to create permanent ties."[4] The drive that is inhibited in its aim—that is, the sublimated drive—is capable of creating *permanent ties*. If psychoanalysis offers a positive vision for the group, then it is a vision predicated on the inhibition of the drive insofar as the inhibited drive creates enduring ties. What that means, and what that group might look like, will be the topic of this, the third and final part of *Genius After Psychoanalysis*. But to begin, we will examine Freud's critical account of the group, what in *Group Psychology* is called *the artificial group*.

9

The Secret Life of Groups

I

Toward the end of *Leonardo da Vinci and a Memory of His Childhood*, Freud quotes Leonardo thus: "He who appeals to authority when there is a difference of opinion works with his memory rather than with his reason." As with Leonardo's formulation on love, which we discussed in Chapter 1, Freud finds this saying of Leonardo's noteworthy, not because it gets our relationship to authority right but, rather, because it gets it so wrong. "In most other human beings," Freud contends, "the need for support from an authority of some sort is so compelling that their world begins to totter if that authority is threatened."[1] It is this exact sentiment of Freud's that Lacan conveys in his most well-known formulation of desire: "[D]esire is the desire of the Other."[2]

At least part of what Lacan means with this formulation is that we receive the coordinates of our desire from an authority figure, the Other with a capital "O." To illustrate this point, Lacan looks to the history of psychoanalysis itself. Against the tendency to interpret Josef Breuer's patient, Anna O.'s false pregnancy as the fulfillment of *her* desire for a child, Lacan reads in it the Other's desire, which in this case is the desire of Breuer himself. "Why do you not go as far as to think that it was Breuer who had a desire for a child?" he asks.[3] Lacan's proposal is that Anna O.'s false pregnancy was not the fulfillment of *her* desire for a child but *Breuer's*. Or, more accurately, Anna O.'s false pregnancy was the fulfillment of her desire for a child insofar as her desire is Breuer's desire—desire is the desire of the Other.

However, Freud's claim is that this was not the case with Leonardo. Leonardo, as Freud understands him, did not need "support from an authority of some sort" to orient his desire. To put it in Lacanian terms: for Leonardo, the Other did not exist. If Leonardo had desired what others desired of him, then he would no doubt have been busy "industriously painting to order and becoming rich," and he wouldn't have picked up the scientist's notebook or dared leave an artwork unfinished, acts which were both integral to his sublimation.[4] Only by throwing off the authority of the Other could Leonardo achieve "the highest sublimation attainable by man."[5] In this chapter, I want to consider what it is that the genius rejects when they throw off the Other's authority. Is the genius simply an independent spirit or an egoist? Or is there something more at stake in this rejection? To do this, I will examine Freud's theory of the group from *Group Psychology and the Analysis of the Ego*, as I will place the genius's rejection in its context.[6] Or, in other words, I will frame the genius's rejection of the Other's authority as a rejection of the group's authority.

II

Groups, as far as Freud theorizes them in *Group Psychology*, come to exist under two specific psychic conditions. The first psychic condition is *identification*. "Identification," Freud writes, "is known to psycho-analysis as the earliest expression of an emotional tie with another person," a tie that "endeavours to mould a person's own ego after the fashion of the one that has been taken as a model."[7] A child who identifies with a parent, for example, will take on their behaviors, ways of speaking, mannerisms, and even their thoughts and opinions. An infant who identifies with another infant will also cry if that infant cries. A student who identifies with the other students in class will catch the yawn if the others yawn, and so on. Identification is not always motivated by admiration or love. It may also come from a place of rivalry or even hatred. A person in love may take on the attributes of a rival in order to garner the attention of the sought-after beloved. Whatever the case might be, whether out of admiration or rivalry, what remains constant is that identification always manifests in *being like* the other. In short, in identification, "one would like to *be*," as opposed "to *have*," the other.[8]

The group then forms, in part, when a collection of individuals identify with each other. One could say that identification forms the *horizontal* axis along which a group is constituted, as it enables them to overcome those petty differences—what Freud calls "the narcissism of minor differences"—that normally separate them.[9] Every social formation, Freud observes, "contains a sediment of feelings of aversion and hostility." Whether one is talking about a married couple, neighboring towns, fanbases of sporting teams, or even entire groups of people, like nations or ethnic groups, the other's difference, no matter how small, is always a source of aversion or "an almost insuperable repugnance," as Freud describes it.[10] But all this intolerance and hatred—this "insuperable repugnance"—disappears in the group. Freud writes,

"So long as a group formation persists or so far as it extends, individuals in the group behave as though they were uniform, tolerate the peculiarities of its other members, equate themselves with them, and have no feeling of aversion towards them."[11] By what power are the members of a group able to overcome the "insuperable repugnance" that normally divides them? Is it magic? Ideology, perhaps? No, the answer is identification.

Freud is therefore committing a slight inaccuracy when he writes that individuals in a group will "*tolerate* the peculiarities of its other members," for tolerance has nothing to do with it. Indeed, a group that is bound by tolerance is not a group at all but, rather, a collection of individuals who are held together by willpower. For these individuals to become a group, it is not enough that they simply tolerate one another; they must identify with each other. They must see their image in each other. Or, to put it another way, the members must not tolerate the "peculiarities" of the other members; they must identify with those peculiarities. And if for whatever reason the members of a group cannot identify with a given person—because they cannot overcome their "insuperable repugnance" of, say, a racial or sexual difference—that person will not belong to the group, even if they possess all of the same ideological beliefs as the rest of the group, for it is identification, and not common ideology, that determines membership. This is why in 2022 the Texas state Republican Party barred the so-called Log Cabin Republicans—a group of LGBT republicans—from participating in their convention. The homophobic members of the state Party could not overcome their "insuperable repugnance" of their fellow Republicans' sexuality.

But not only does identification give the group its strength of bond, it also makes it hostile toward outsiders. Anyone who stands outside of the group's tie, because they do not reflect the group's image, will be subject to the same hostility and aversion—that insuperable repugnance which Freud speaks of—that ordinarily divides all people, and this goes, Freud argues, even for the religion of universal love itself, Christianity: "Therefore a religion, even if it calls itself the religion of love, must be hard and unloving to those who do not belong to it." "Fundamentally," he goes on, "indeed every religion is in this same way a religion of love for all those who it embraces; while cruelty and intolerance towards those who do not belong to it are natural to every religion."[12] But why stop at religion? Why not extend this critique to all groups? After all, aren't all groups—like, say, the fanbase of a sports team—a "religion of love" to its members while cruel and intolerant toward the outsider? Indeed, hostility toward the outsider is not a feature that is endemic to religion; rather, it is a feature of the group as such insofar as it is a feature of identification itself.

III

There is a third characteristic that identification gives the group, which Freud overlooks. I will call it *internal cruelty*. Not only does identification give the group the ability to overcome the insuperable repugnance of its members (first characteristic), and not only does identification make the group hostile toward the outsider (second characteristic), but identification also makes the group cruel toward its own members—that is, it makes the group internally cruel.

In his other important text on identification, "Mourning and Melancholia," Freud notes that, in melancholia, identification splits the ego between a portion that is identified with the object, on one side, and a portion that is occupied by a critical, observing agency, on the other. As a result of this split, the critical agency in the ego is able to castigate the object by castigating the ego itself. In other words, the ego becomes an object of its own critical functions: "Thus the shadow of the object fell upon the ego, and the latter could henceforth be judged by a special agency, as though it were an object."[13] The two sides of the ego exist in a state of civil war, as each side fights for exclusive control over the ego.

From this standpoint, identification does not appear to be a cost-free way of establishing harmony between the members of the group. Rather, it appears as a kind of violence in which the members eliminate the differences that exist between them. The "insuperable repugnance" that separates the group from the outsider also exists within the group, separating the members from each other. For this reason, the group will act cruelly toward the outsider, yes, but it will also act cruelly toward its own members, as the members will fight to remove the minor differences that exist between them. This is why fans of a sports team will often verbally abuse fans of the *same* team. For example, if the fanbase hates the team's coach, they will verbally abuse any fan who supports that coach. It is not enough that they support the same team. They must also support that team in the exact same manner. For the same reason, believers of a religion will harshly criticize the look and appearance of believers of the same religion. It is not enough that the believers all hold the same doctrine. They must also look and dress the same as well. Fidelity to the group always means fidelity to the group's image.

To assuage this inner turmoil, the group will insist upon more identification, not only identification of thoughts and beliefs but identification of appearance and habits as well. But more identification will not help any, for as identification increases, so too will the criticisms, for nothing will suffice except the complete elimination of difference itself. So long as it is predicated on identification, the group will always be internally cruel—it is its destiny.

One way to understand the genius rejection of the Other's authority is then to understand it as a rejection of identification. Others have no authority over the genius's desire because the genius does not identify with them. At the same time, we should take care to avoid thinking of this rejection as a concern for the genius's individuality or ego. The genius is not a Howard Roark or a Howard the Duck. Rather, it has to do, at least in part, with the genius's peculiar relationship to love—what I called in Chapter 1 cool indifference. For what is identification if not a form of love? Indeed, it is its earliest and most primitive form, when love was still to be like the beloved object. And the genius, as we know, refrains from love until they've thoroughly investigated what it is they are being asked to love. But there is a second way to grasp the genius's rejection of the Other's authority, which brings me to the second psychic condition under which groups form: *idealization*.

IV

As Freud explains, one of the sources of identification is the existence of "a common quality." That common quality might be a shared trait, like a common language or affiliation. Travelers in a foreign country who speak the same language, for example, may feel an instant bond, even if they would've never associated with each other in their home country. Teammates on the same sports club may share the same habits of speaking because of their shared affiliation with the club. Two people who have a common hobby may fall in love because of their shared interest. Members of a political party may unite behind their party's candidate, and so on. Of course, the common quality need not always be positive; it may be a shared hatred as well. To use the same examples: travelers may bond over their mutual hatred for their foreign context, teammates may unite against a common opponent, two people may bond over a shared dislike of a mutual acquaintance, members of a political party may coalesce in opposition to a rival party's candidate. Whatever the case might be, whether a shared trait or a shared hatred, "the more important this common quality is," writes Freud, "the more successful may this partial identification become."[14]

Toward the beginning of *Group Psychology*, Freud clarifies that he is not concerned with groups in general but, rather, with a highly specific kind of group: namely, the group with a leader or, as Freud also calls it, *the artificial group*. Of this group, Freud makes the rather obvious claim that the most important common quality is "the tie with the leader."[15] But then he makes a less obvious, more contentious claim. He claims that the nature of this "tie" with the leader is *idealization*. "Idealization," writes Freud, "is a process that concerns the *object*; by it that object, without any alteration in its nature is aggrandized and exalted in the subject's mind."[16] A son who idealizes his father, for example, will believe that he is the biggest and strongest father in the whole world, even though he is the exact same man that he was before the son was born. A lover who idealizes the beloved will believe they are the most beautiful person who has ever lived. Fans who idealize a celebrity will think them incapable of committing a crime, despite all evidence to the contrary. In other words, idealization always exalts and uplifts, transforming even the most ordinary object into a paragon.

Idealization is the second psychic condition under which the group forms. If identification is the horizontal axis along which the group is constituted, then idealization is the *vertical* axis. The group therefore is not simply a collection of individuals who identify with each other but, rather, a collection of individuals who idealize the same leader. Or, more accurately put, it is a collection of individuals who identify with each other *because* they idealize the same leader. That is, idealization works hand in hand with identification by lending it content, such that to be like the members of the group is always to be like the leader. Or, as the Apostle Paul once put it, "be imitators of me, as I am of Christ."[17]

Thus, putting identification and idealization together, Freud defines the artificial group this way: "A primary group of this kind is a number of individuals who have put one and the same object in the place of their ego ideal and have consequently identified themselves with one another in their ego."[18]

V

While identification and idealization are ultimately two different relations—or ties, to use Freud's locution—it is not inaccurate to say that there is some commonality between them. Where they are similar is that both are relationships of likeness. While it is true that the members exalt the leader to a station higher than themselves, it is equally true that the members strive to be like the leader, just as they strive to be like each other—indeed, in the group, to strive to be like each other is to strive to be like the leader. In this way, idealization is a kind of identification, a species of identification. Where they are different, however, is that idealization is also a relationship of difference. That is, idealization always elevates the object above the ego. A son who idealizes his father sees in the father the strength that he himself does not have but wishes to have (of course, the father doesn't have it either). Likewise, by idealizing the leader, the members of the group impute to the leader the very qualities that they themselves aspire to possess. Whether the leader actually possesses those qualities is beside the point. It is enough that the members believe the leader has them. Idealization, in other words, turns the leader into the model of perfection, a paragon, which is why it is difficult to find a member who will criticize the leader. It is not that they are brainwashed, as people often think. It is simply that they have idealized the leader.

Thus, idealization exists in a state of tension between likeness and dissimilarity. On one hand, idealization invites the members to emulate the leader. On the other hand, it insists on the exemplarity of the leader. If it goes too far in one direction, the leader becomes exactly like the members, thereby losing their status as exemplar. But if it goes too far in the other direction, the leader loses touch with the members, becoming a leader in name only. Idealization must therefore maintain the tension between these two poles, which it does by introducing an exception to identification, an exception that limits the members' identification with the leader. Whereas with identification proper, there is no part of the object that the ego cannot emulate, with idealization it is the obverse. There is always one aspect of the leader that the members cannot emulate, one aggrandized aspect that is excluded from identification. It is the introduction of this exception that enables idealization to maintain the tenuous balance between likeness and dissimilarity. For examples of this exception, let us look at the two artificial groups that Freud discusses in *Group Psychology*: the army and the Church.

The common object in the army is the commanding officer, and as such, the soldiers of the army form a unit by idealizing the same commanding officer. It is erroneous to assume that this means the soldiers love or admire the officer, for as Freud notes, idealization may take the form of a shared "hatred against a particular person."[19] For an example of idealization as hate, we need only think of the platoon's mutual hatred of the drill sergeant. It is through their mutual hatred of the harsh drill sergeant that the soldiers coalesce into a cohesive unit. What is essential in idealization is only that the soldiers take the commanding officer as their model, not that they love them. Thus, whether they love or hate them, the soldiers strive to be good soldiers by striving to be like the commanding officer.

At the same time, however, the soldiers must be careful not to place themselves on the same level as the commanding officer. That is, they must be careful not to fully identify with the commanding officer. If a soldier were to ever completely emulate the commanding officer, they would be accused of insubordination. The commanding officer's rank places a limit or restriction on the soldiers' identification with them. It is the one aspect of the commanding officer which the soldiers cannot emulate, the exception that is excluded from identification.

In the Church, the leader is Jesus Christ. As such, what it means to be a christian is to be like Jesus—*What would Jesus do?* as the slogan goes. At the same time, christians don't simply consider Jesus to be a role model or a good teacher. They also believe that he is the Son of God—a title which means that he is God himself. This title of the Son of God is the difference between idealization and identification proper. Idealization means that the christian can be like Jesus in every way—including even the performance of miracles—except in this one aspect: they cannot be the Son of God. This title is precisely that aspect of Jesus which falls out of identification, an exclusion that constitutes idealization as such. If a christian were to ever proclaim that they are, like Jesus, the Son of God—like the former soccer player turned conspiracy theorist, David Icke did, for example—they would be accused of blasphemy or, perhaps, simply of being insane. Jesus's deity is the exception that limits the christian's identification with him, the aspect that is subtracted from identification.[20]

Though it may appear to be an impediment to the group, given that it limits the members' identification with the leader, this point of exception, which constitutes and differentiates idealization, is actually the very source of the group's cohesion. It functions this way because it ensures the equality of the members by introducing a structural gap between the members and the leader. Despite whatever differences they might have, there is at least one way in which the members are equal: none of them have this exceptional quality of the leader.

As such, it makes no difference from the standpoint of the group's structure itself if the commanding officer favors some soldiers over others. What matters is that none of the soldiers share the commanding officer's rank. It is the exclusion of their rank that guarantees the commanding officer's leadership over all the soldiers, including even the favored ones, which in turn lends the army its structure. Likewise with the Church. Though Jesus had 12 disciples, his deity ensures one way in which even the most common christian is like the Apostle Peter. Neither one of them are the Son of God. As such, Jesus is the Lord over all christians, including even the 12 disciples.

There is a style of leadership that has been growing in prominence in the United States, since at least the 1980s. It is a style of leadership that seeks to mobilize the passions of its followers by deconstructing the point of exception that separates the leader from the followers—that is, by collapsing idealization into mere identification. This is why Reagan contrived to eat jelly beans, instead of peanuts, on national television, why Clinton played his saxophone on *The Arsenio Hall Show*, why the second Bush went to great lengths to distance himself from his Yale education, and why Obama filled out a March Madness bracket every year. They were attempting to appear accessible to their followers—as mere Americans—thereby closing the gap that separates them. As Paul Eisenstein reminds me, that a potential voter could ask Clinton whether he prefers boxers or briefs—and that he would answer!—indicates the extent to which this style of leadership has been successful.[21] Other signs of its success are voters, in 2000, overwhelmingly telling pollsters that they'd prefer to have a beer with ole W than with Gore and an obscure Republican congressman, in 2009, disrupting President Obama's address to Congress by shouting "You lie!"

In this way, Trump—who has gone the farthest in this direction by eschewing the semblance of presidentiality itself—is simply the fruition of a political style that has been decades in the making. Isn't it therefore hypocritical for the surviving former presidents to ostracize Trump? After all, he is simply the truth of their political style. Or, perhaps, this is precisely why they ostracize him?

And yet, this "buddy" style of leadership plays a dangerous game, toying with the very gap that structures the group itself. It believes naively, even arrogantly, that it can maintain the structure of the group by simply reasserting the gap between leader and follower whenever it wishes. And never does it occur to it that once the gap has been removed, the group itself disintegrates, turning, not into a collection of individuals without a leader but, rather, a collection of individuals in which everyone is the leader, leaving it with no group to restructure.

VI

The second way in which to understand the genius's rejection of the Other's authority is then to understand it as the rejection of idealization. The Other has no authority over the genius's desire because the genius does not idealize the Other. This rejection of idealization is thus the ultimate reason why the genius falls out with the group. It has nothing to do with a concern over individuality or ego. In a certain way, it doesn't even have to do with identification with the members. Or, I should say, it does have to do with identification with the members only insofar as identification with the members depends on the idealization of the leader. But there is something else at stake in the genius's rejection of idealization. Not only is it a rejection of the leader's authority, it is also a rejection of the fulfillment of original narcissism, which the leader offers the group. To get at this other dimension of the genius's rejection, we should take a closer look at Freud's account of the formation of ideals.

Recall that for Freud the infant exists in a state of original narcissism, a kind of prelinguistic harmony that is best captured by the image of the breastfed infant. Original narcissism, Freud argues, does not last very long. Soon after the infant is born, others impose social and cultural ideals—part of what Lacan refers to as the symbolic order—on the infant, thereby forcing it to give up a piece of its narcissism as the price to be paid for entering into symbolic relations with them. So, for example, the infant is weaned off the breast or is told to stop touching its genitals, as these satisfactions are not permitted in society (and if it were not these particular satisfactions, then it would be some other ones).

But there is an ambiguity here. It is unclear in Freud whether original narcissism ever truly existed at all, as it is unclear when the infant was ever free of social and cultural ideals. For when was the infant ever outside symbolic relations? Even before the infant is ever born, parents give them a name, choose the colors of the nursery walls, determine the signifiers with which they will identify, plan their future, etc. Indeed, the infant may even be the fulfillment of a wish that was made by the parents when they were still themselves children. The symbolic is not imposed upon the infant after it has been born; rather, the infant comes into the world already immersed in the symbolic. To paraphrase Marx, the infant comes into the world, dripping from head to toe, from every pore, with the symbolic. Although Freud does not spell it out like this, given the absolute immersion—or *aphanisis*, in Lacan's locution—of the child in the Other's ideals, we should think of original narcissism as a retroactive fantasy that we construct to help make sense of our current state of discontentment.[22] To wit, there was a time when things were great, but that time is lost, and now I am unhappy. In this way, original narcissism is the originary lost object—the object that exists only insofar as it is lost—whose loss explains the discontent which is part and parcel of life itself.

That it is lost, and lost in an originary way, however, does not mean that we simply forget about it. On the contrary, the specter of original narcissism continues to haunt the psyche, thereby giving the ego an acute nostalgia for a bygone time. But how can the ego get original narcissism back? Without a readymade answer to this question, the ego looks to the ideal for guidance. Precisely because the ideal appears to have taken away original narcissism, it appears to hold the secret to recovering it. When I give up my desire to become an artist to adopt my parents' ideal of becoming an optometrist, I imagine that becoming an optometrist holds the key to recovering my lost narcissism. In other words, I impute to the ideal the original narcissism that

I seek to recover, and in this way, I idealize the ideal itself. So, while it is true that I don't have the original narcissism that I desire, I have the ideal, which I imagine possesses the lost narcissism that I seek, and I am therefore compensated for my loss.

But there is more to the ideal's compensation than simply substituting for original narcissism. Not only is the ideal "the heir" to original narcissism, but "satisfaction is brought about from fulfilling this ideal."[23] So, while original narcissism is originarily lost, the ego receives something of that lost narcissism back by approximating the ideal. The ego is like an investor who receives a dividend—a dividend paid in libidinal satisfaction—from its investment in the ideal. Thus, I receive a small piece of satisfaction when I receive an A in biology class, and another piece, this time larger, when I am admitted to a good university, and another piece, this time the largest yet, when I am admitted to optometry school, and so on. To be sure, if I ever attain the ideal by actually becoming an optometrist, I don't finally receive the original narcissism that I seek, since it doesn't exist as such. Rather, it becomes displaced onto some other ideal—now, owning a yacht or traveling into space—as it continues to elude my grasp, over and over again.

In their function as the group's ideal, the leader offers the members this same kind of compensation—a point that Freud himself, at times, seems to not fully appreciate.[24] To be sure, a considerable portion of the leader's appeal indeed comes from their appearance as the living embodiment of original narcissism as such. But it is also true that the leader's connection with original narcissism is imaginary—a product of the members' collective projection—and so, the leader cannot really deliver on the promise that they embody. And yet, to hold onto their position as the ideal, it is not enough that they offer empty promises. There must be a real libidinal satisfaction at stake in their relations with the members. It is here then that the compensatory satisfaction of idealization comes into play.

While the leader cannot deliver the members' original narcissism, since it doesn't exist as such, they are able to offer a compensatory satisfaction that issues directly from the idealization of their imago—a kind of return on the members' investment, if you will. *You may not have original narcissism,* the leader seems to say, *but you have me; so, idealize me, and I will compensate you for your loss.* What draws the members of the far right to a leader like Trump? Is it the promise to "make America great again"? No, it is Trump himself. This is what the media doesn't seem to understand. When they quiz Trump's followers about whether their leader has made good on his promise, they think they are scoring points by revealing how hollow Trump is. But the joke is on them because the satisfaction Trump's followers receive doesn't come from the return of this mythical Great America; rather, it comes from

Trump himself. That is, they enjoy how he mocks the disabled, engages in so-called locker-room talk, has extramarital affairs, belittles a rape victim for her looks, dodges paying taxes, and so on. He embodies every excellence that the members wish for themselves, and in this way, they enjoy him directly, not his ability to return some lost America. To use Lacan's words, Trump offers himself as "an idol offered to the desire of the other."[25] A perverse offer, if there ever was one![26]

How long can the members of the group hold out before they demand the leader make good on their promises? How long can the compensatory dividends that issue directly from the leader satisfy the members? This may be surprising, but the answer is indefinitely. The members can live indefinitely on the compensatory dividends of idealization because they know on some level that they cannot get their lost narcissism back. While the members may *consciously* demand original narcissism, they are *unconsciously* invested in the perverse dividends that they reap from the leader. This is the real satisfaction that they want. In that case, the ultimate source of Trump's appeal is not his ability to "make America great again," but, rather, his *inability* to make America great, since it is this inability that keeps the perverse dividends coming. The promise to make America great is the lie that Trump's followers have unconsciously known all along but consciously believed all the same. So, Mark Edmundson is wrong: we don't fall in love with power.[27] We don't fall in love with the leaders who have the goods. As strange as it may sound, the truth is we love the leaders who *don't* have the goods—what Joan Copjec calls, "the *unvermögender* Other" or, the Other without means—for it is they who are best able to compensate us for our lost narcissism with the perverse dividends of idealization.[28] And it is our love for them that gives them their power, that gives them the appearance of having the goods in the first place, not the other way around.

The rejection of this perverse dividend is then the third and final way in which we should understand the genius's rejection of the Other's authority. The ideal has no power over the genius because the genius rejects the authority of this perverse dividend. But the genius doesn't reject it because they are wiser than the members of the group. It is not that the genius knows better or that they are able to spot a lie. After all, the members also know it is a lie, unconsciously at least. No, the genius rejects the lure of the leader's perverse dividend because they recognize that original narcissism is lost— not empirically lost but ontologically lost—and they have already mourned it, experienced its transience. As such, the dividend offered by the leader simply has no appeal for them.

As long as the group is organized around the recovery of the lost object of original narcissism, the genius has no truck with it. But is there another way of organizing the group which could involve the genius? A group that is organized, not around the recovery of original narcissism but, rather, around the avowal of its loss? A group made up of members who don't seek compensation for their loss but, rather, who identify themselves with that loss? If such a group is possible, then it would represent a form of collective life that the genius finds worth living, a form of collective life that is worthy of the name *sublimation*. But is such a group possible? The genius wonders.

10

The Logic of Debasement

I

In his seminar *Lacan*, the philosopher Alain Badiou takes psychoanalysis—and, in particular, Lacan—to task for its stance on the group. The group, as I discussed in the previous chapter, is an imaginary collective, not in the sense that it is unreal but in the Lacanian sense that it depends on the members seeing their image in the other members (identification) as well as in the leader (idealization). To Badiou's point, this is not a very flattering portrayal of the group. The group, as far as Freud theorizes it, appears in strictly negative tones, as a kind of negative ideal, a fate to be avoided at all costs, which has the effect of casting suspicion on every form of collectivity. This suspicion of the collective has a consequence. It casts suspicion on the possibility of social and political change as such, as this kind of change requires, not individual but collective action. Thus, it is not enough that psychoanalysis critiques the artificial group. Unless psychoanalysis is able to think a new form of the collective, beyond the imaginary relation, its suspicion of the group is destined to appear as a suspicion of change as such.

The natural place to begin thinking about an alternative to the artificial group is the imaginary relations of identification and idealization. The new form of the collective should move beyond these imaginary relations. But here Badiou puts the question to psychoanalysis. "In what conditions is [the group] not under the sway of imaginary coalescence?" he asks.[1] Badiou's critique of Lacan—and by extension of psychoanalysis at large—is that he cannot say. To drive home this point, Badiou turns to Lacan's own group, the Cause freudienne. Lacan can say all he wants that "the imaginary effect must be avoided" and that the Cause freudienne "must avoid the group effect," but Badiou asks, "how can the group effect be avoided?"[2] On this question of how, Lacan founders. He simply doesn't have any ideas or proposals on how to avoid the so-called group effect. In the absence of anything concrete from Lacan, Badiou speculates as to what this principle might be through which the psychoanalytic group is able to avoid the group effect. That principle, Badiou argues, is "dissolution." Simply put, "the Cause freudienne group will only last temporarily."³ The only way for the psychoanalytic group to avoid fetishizing a figure like Lacan and requiring its members to mirror each other as they all mirror Lacan is simply to disband before it happens with the assumption that it is inevitable. "Thus," Badiou exclaims, "the analysts were disbanded and disbanded they remain!" "Because," he concludes, "that is indeed the imperative that was bequeathed to them: 'Disband!'"⁴

If Badiou is correct—if the only way psychoanalysis can think past the problems of identification and idealization is to make dissolution the central principle of the group—then the prognosis for psychoanalysis is indeed grim. As Badiou tells us, this principle of dissolution constitutes "Lacan's true political vision," namely, "a tyrannical anarchism." As bad as this verdict may already sound—and Badiou assures us that he doesn't use the term "tyrannical" with "any value judgment" (what a relief!)—Badiou wants to argue that the true problem with dissolution is not that it prescribes bad politics but, rather, that it falls short of politics altogether.⁵ For politics, as far as Badiou argues here, is not a temporary formation. It is not people coming together to fix a problem and then disbanding. "*That*," Badiou says, "might be a movement ... a group, or a grouping, or an assembly, or a gathering," but it is not politics. Politics is not solving a series of isolated problems, one by one; it is rather the metonymic movement from problem to problem through a long chain of problems, what remains consistent across problems. Therefore, in politics, Badiou argues, "there's a need to switch from one thing to another;" or, in other words, politics needs organization, longevity, or that watchword of Badiou's: fidelity. The political collective therefore cannot be the one that dissolves. Rather, it must be the one that endures, not a finite group but an infinite one, which is why Badiou believes Lacan's "final thesis is that ... there is no politics."⁶

II

No doubt there will be some in psychoanalysis who find it a relief to hear Badiou say "psychoanalysis ... remains silent about politics," and some who would even agree.⁷ And perhaps Badiou is correct. Perhaps, psychoanalysis cannot think the collective outside the imaginary relation. Perhaps, the best it can offer is some vague model of a group that is always in the process of self-dissolution. And therefore perhaps psychoanalysis does indeed fall short of politics, like Badiou suggests. But then one finds this enigmatic comment from *Group Psychology and the Analysis of the Ego*: "It is interesting to see that it is precisely those sexual impulses that are inhibited in their aims which achieve such lasting ties between people." *Lasting ties*! Could it be that psychoanalysis is not so silent on the question of the political tie after all? Freud continues, "It is the fate of sensual love to become extinguished when it is satisfied; for it to be able to last, it must from the beginning be mixed with purely affectionate components—with such, that is, as are inhibited in their aims—or it must itself undergo a transformation of this kind."[8] Leaving aside for the moment the question of whether the love at stake in group psychology is inhibited or uninhibited—that is, whether it is, in Freud's words, affectionate or sensual love—what should strike us here is how Freud seems to indicate that psychoanalysis does indeed have a concept of the enduring group tie. It is the tie predicated on components that are *inhibited in their aims*. Is it possible that Badiou passed judgment too quickly?

Later, in the postscript to *Group Psychology*, Freud returns to this question of inhibited versus uninhibited sexual aims. He writes, "If we choose, we may recognize in this diversion of aim a beginning of the *sublimation* of the sexual instincts."[9] That Freud would evoke sublimation in this context is not too surprising, given that he defines sublimation as the drive's *power to replace its immediate aim by other aims which are not sexual*—or, otherwise put, the drive's power to have its aim inhibited. He continues: "Those sexual instincts which are inhibited in their aims," in other words, the sublimated drives, "have a great functional advantage over those which are uninhibited." Namely, this: "Since they," meaning the inhibited or sublimated drives, "are not capable of really complete satisfaction, they are especially adapted to create permanent ties."[10] There it is again! *Permanent ties.*

So, Freud does have a notion of the permanent group tie after all. It is the tie that is predicated on the inhibition of the sexual aim or, in other words, sublimation. What we might call, the *inhibited* or the *sublimated tie*. Thus, as it turns out, the artificial group, along with its imaginary relations of identification and idealization, is not psychoanalysis's last word on group psychology after all. There is something else it can say about it. Namely, the possibility of the group forming around the inhibition of the drive, a relation that possesses the permanence needed to "switch from one thing to another," which Badiou claims is necessary for politics. The only question is: what does this group look like?

III

At times, in *Group Psychology*, Freud seems to suggest that the group which forms around the inhibition of the drive is none other than the artificial group itself. For example, he describes hypnosis as a relation with the factor of "sexual satisfaction excluded" and then goes onto to call it "a group of two."[11] And when comparing the artificial group to neurosis, he says neurosis involves "love instincts which still pursue directly sexual aims," while the artificial group involves "love instincts which have been diverted from their original aims."[12] But this cannot be right. The group that is constituted through the sublimated tie cannot be the group that is constituted through the imaginary relations of identification and idealization for two very important reasons.

The first reason is Freud's own claim that sublimation creates permanent ties. Earlier in *Group Psychology*, Freud argues that the artificial group depends on the "illusion" of a leader "who loves all the individuals in the group with an equal love." "Everything," he writes, "depends upon this illusion," and if this illusion were to ever be broken, then, he argues, the group itself "would dissolve."[13] It would indeed be odd to describe illusion as a permanent tie. Based as it is on an illusion, the artificial group is always susceptible to dissolution, as Freud himself admits. This susceptibility to dissolution is most evident in the phenomenon of panic. "Fear in an individual is provoked either by the greatness of a danger or by the cessation of emotional ties," writes Freud. "In just the same way," he continues, "panic arises either owing to an increase of the common danger or owing to the disappearance of the emotional ties which hold the group together."[14] It seems then that either the imaginary relations of the artificial group do not arise to the level of permanent or Freud is working with a highly specific, and counterintuitive, definition of that word.

The second reason the sublimated group cannot be the artificial group comes, once again, from Freud, only this time it comes from his definition of sublimation as the introduction of nonsexual aims or, as he puts it, aims that are "not capable of really complete satisfaction." This reason is more problematic than the first given that Freud implicates the artificial group in the satisfaction of narcissism everywhere throughout the book. Here is just one example: "We love it," meaning, the ideal, "on account of the perfections which we have striven to reach for our own ego, and which we should now like to procure in this roundabout way as a means of satisfying our narcissism."[15] To this single example, we could add Freud's various claims from the Narcissism paper that the fulfillment of the ideal produces satisfaction, claims that he reiterates here in *Group Psychology*.[16] We could also add my own argument that the members use idealization to elicit a perverse dividend from the leader. Indeed, the artificial group is saturated in sexual satisfaction and couldn't exist without it.

Clearly, Freud was mistaken when he suggested that the ties which bind the artificial group are inhibited as far as sexual aims are concerned. But what should we make of this contradiction? There are two possibilities. The first is that Freud is quite simply wrong about the group. Psychoanalysis is misplaced when it is outside the clinic, and so by applying psychoanalytic categories to a social phenomenon like groups, Freud simply takes psychoanalysis too far afield. Group psychology as an instance of wild psychoanalysis.[17] The second possibility is that he is wrong about the inhibition of sexual aims. While the inhibition of sexual aims may exist at the level of the individual—for example, the genius—it doesn't exist at the level of the group, and so, in applying this category to the group, Freud simply takes his theorization in the wrong direction. Though coming from different directions, both possibilities, if true, would have the same effect. They would nullify Freud's work on group psychology. Maybe this is a necessary move, if not an inevitable one, as one must take seriously the very real possibility that psychoanalysis is quite simply not equipped to speak on group psychology, and therefore it finds itself too far afield on its terrain.

But before jumping to this conclusion, there is one more possibility we must consider. It is the possibility that with the idea of the sublimated tie, Freud found the basis for a new kind of group but could not recognize it himself, much less theorize it, as he was focused on the immediate task of critiquing the artificial group. On this view, the problem is no longer that Freud goes too far or that he takes psychoanalysis too far afield but, rather, that he doesn't go far enough, that he stops short, that psychoanalysis still has more to teach us about group psychology. That Freud could not think past his own impasses doesn't invalidate the entire inquiry; it only means that it is left for us to take up.

Thus, based on Freud's claim that "sexual instincts which are inhibited in their aims" are "especially adapted to create permanent ties," I want to claim that *inhibition* is the sublimated tie, the tie that is capable of creating permanent group relations. This claim, however, will be met with immediate suspicion due to certain other comments made by Freud in his 1912 paper, "On the Universal Tendency to Debasement in the Sphere of Love." In that paper, Freud draws the exact same distinction that he draws in *Group Psychology* between *affectionate* or *sexually inhibited* aims, on one side, and *sensual* or sexually uninhibited aims, on the other. Only this time, he draws this distinction to implicate it in that degradation of the object known as *debasement*. I will elaborate more fully on the ways in which inhibition creates group ties in the next chapter, but for the remainder of this chapter, I want to respond to the objection that debasement potentially raises against my claim.

IV

"If the practising psycho-analyst asks himself on account of what disorder people most often come to him for help," Freud opens the Debasement paper, "he is bound to reply ... that it is psychical impotence." This condition, which Freud claims affects "men of strongly libidinous natures," presents, not in a physical inability to perform the sex act, as these men profess to have no issues with performance in the main, nor in a waning of sexual interest as such, as they still possess "a strong psychical inclination to carry it out," but, rather, in a psychic inability to perform the sex act with a particular kind of woman: namely, the woman whom these men love.[18] The problem is that the man loves this woman—typically, his wife—but he does not desire her sexually. It is as if the man's sexual desire has become splintered off from his love, such that they are now at cross purposes with each other, or, as Freud pithily puts it: "Where they love they do not desire and where they desire they cannot love."[19]

Turning his attention away from the obsessional on the couch and toward the man on the street, Freud observes that this splintering of love between its sensual current (sexual desire) and its affectionate current (love as such) is not at all uncommon. Rather, it is observable in the everyday man, making it a particularly *male* form of love. "There are," he goes onto say, "only a few very educated people in whom the two currents of affection and sensuality have become properly fused"—a far cry from only a few pages ago when he described the union of these two currents as the "normal attitude in love"![20] (Or is Freud's point that only a very few men are normal?)

Whereas this impasse in the capacity to love and desire the same object throws the obsessional into crisis, even driving them to analysis for help, the man on the street seeks to work around his difficulties using a vulgar, yet effective, strategy. He simply splits his love and desire between two separate women. The first woman is the woman in which the man finds the aim of sexual satisfaction inhibited. As such, he feels free to pour out all his affections onto this woman, the sublime object. There is no limit to the amount of esteem he feels toward this woman, no limit to the respect he has for her, as she has become for him the ideal object. This woman, we might say, is *the object of love*. In the visual language of Hitchcock's classic *Vertigo* (1958), this object of love is John "Scottie" Ferguson's (Jimmy Stewart) platonic friend, Marjorie "Midge" Wood (Barbara Bel Geddes). Scottie has the utmost respect for Midge, but crucially, he does not desire her sexually. Instead, Scottie regards Midge strictly in a familial way. Indeed, when Midge visits Scottie in the hospital, where he is recovering from shock, after having witnessed the horrific death of Madeleine Elster (Kim Novak), she even refers to herself as "mother"—the quintessential object of love.

The second woman is the opposite of the first. She is the woman in which the man's aim of sexual satisfaction is completely uninhibited. As such, the man feels no compunction exploiting her for his own sexual satisfaction. He has no qualms exposing her to the full force of the sensual currents within him, which includes many "perverse sexual aims" that he harbors yet keeps secret.[21] He feels neither esteem nor respect for this woman but in fact actively debases and demeans her, the debased object. This woman, we might say, is *the object of desire*. Once again, in the language of *Vertigo*, Judy Barton (Kim Novak) acts as the object of desire to Midge's object of love. Unlike Midge, Judy fascinates Scottie, awakening the sexual desire within him. I say sexual desire *within him* rather than *for her* because Scottie's desire has nothing to do with Judy herself. Whatever desire Scottie appears to have for Judy is revealed to be a lie by his mistreatment of her. His complete lack of regard for Judy makes it clear that his sexual desire is concerned, not with Judy but with Madeleine (or, as I suggested in Chapter 6, the little part-objects of Madeleine).

As opposed as these two women may appear—indeed, they are the exact opposite of one another—it is important to recognize that they do not exist independently of each other but, rather, as an interrelated pair within the man's psyche. This is why Midge is so important to the structure of *Vertigo* and why the film would not work without her. Far from extraneous, it is Midge's presence as the object of love that enables Scottie to desire Judy/Madeleine, thereby setting the gears of the narrative in motion. In other words, it is precisely because the man esteems the object of love that he can then debase the object of desire. Freud puts it this way:

> He is assured of complete sexual pleasure only when he can devote himself unreservedly to obtaining satisfaction, which with his well-brought up wife, for instance, he does not dare to do. This is the source of his need for a debased sexual object …. It is to such a woman that he prefers to devote his sexual potency, even when the whole of his affection belongs to a woman of a higher kind.[22]

Note the logical precision with which Freud describes the man's way of love. It is because the man devotes his love to one woman, whom he exempts from the debasement of his sexual impulses, that he feels free to unleash the full force of his "sexual potency" on every other woman. One could formalize the man's logic this way: all women can be debased because there is at least one woman who cannot be debased. A masculine form of logic, if there ever was one![23] As such, there is no point in convincing this man to respect women, for his respect for women is baked directly into his debasement of them. For him, respect and debasement do not negate one another but, rather, form a logical pair. Misogyny as respect.

If the man is to truly love the object of love, it is not enough that he respect her, Freud argues. To truly love the woman, the man must allow the stain of desire to appear within her. This would be like Scottie desiring Midge, which is a thought that Scottie finds absolutely revolting, tantamount to incest. We learn this when Midge presents Scottie with a portrait she has made of Carlotta Valdes (the imago of Madeleine), except with her face in place of Carlotta's. Midge's intention with the painting is to make Scottie pay attention to her, but Scottie finds it deeply disturbing, "not funny." Why? Because it puts Midge in the position of the object of desire, which is a thought that Scottie finds disgusting. Thus, Freud writes, as if he were commenting on *Vertigo* itself, "anyone who is to be really free and happy in love must have surmounted his respect for women and have come to terms with the idea of incest with his mother or sister."[24]

V

The interrelation between these two women—the object of love, on one hand, and the object of desire, on the other—becomes even clearer when viewed through a Lacanian lens. From a Lacanian standpoint, these two women are not two distinct objects at all but, rather, two parts of the same debased object. Specifically, the object of desire is the element of desire that has been separated from the object of love and given its own form. To put it, once again, in terms of *Vertigo*: Midge can appear to Scottie as a pure object of love because the stain of desire has been removed from her and given external form in the person of Judy.

Insofar as desire may fall off the woman, like an object in itself, the woman—as with all objects—proves to be a "complex grouping" of partial objects, which can fall apart at any moment.[25] A prime example of such a "deciduous object" is that most familiar of psychoanalytic objects: the breast.[26] "On what side does the breast stand? On the side of what sucks or on the side of what is sucked?" asks Lacan.[27] To get at Lacan's meaning here, we may think of the dissociation that a mother may feel with her breast while nursing a child. When the child relentlessly demands the breast, the mother may come to feel as though the breast is not hers anymore but the child's. She might, for example, complain that she "feels like a cow." That is to say, she may feel that her breast is an object that exists strictly for the child's nourishment—not a member of her own body but an extension of the child's insatiable appetite—and, as such, she may feel her breast as something that has fallen away from her, something that was once a part of her body but now no longer belongs to her. The "complex grouping" of mother and breast becomes ungrouped, as it were. It is indeed moments like these, when a part of our own body falls away, that give the lie to the imaginary feeling that we were ever whole in the first place.[28]

The reason the man needs to separate the object of desire from the object of love is not so that he can desire her, the object of desire, but, rather, so that he can desire the other woman, *the object of love*. To put it bluntly, it is not that the man wants to lovingly cuddle with his wife and have dirty sex with his mistress, as Freud sometimes thinks it is. It is that he wants to have dirty sex with his wife too! But in order to desire the object of love in this way, the man feels he must encounter the *cause* of his desire outside of her, a task that he accomplishes by removing the stain of desire from the object of love and externalizing it in the form of the debased object of desire. This is the dynamic that we find in Denis Villeneuve's *Bladerunner 2049* (2017). Like a man who must look at pornography to jump start his desire for his wife, K (Ryan Gosling) must have Joi (Ana de Armas), a holographic woman, superimpose herself on the replicant, Mariette (Mackenzie Davis), in order to have sex with the latter. As a replicant, Mariette lacks the object of desire, and so, if K is to be sexually aroused by her, he must supplement her with Joi, who functions in this triadic relationship as the externalization of the stain of desire. Thus, in *Bladerunner 2049*, there are not two categories of people, as there are in the original *Bladerunner* (1982), but, rather, three: humans, replicants, and Joi. That is, respectively, a person with the object of desire, a person without the object of desire, and the object of desire itself as the externalization of the difference between the first and second categories.

At the same time, we should resist any inclination, as tempting as it might be, to construe the debased woman's presence in the man's, call it, debasement fantasy as a sign of his enjoyment of her, as if their relationship— or, more accurately put, nonrelationship—is some cute Hollywood romance, like *Pretty Woman* (1990). While it may appear as though the man enjoys the debased woman—and may appear so even to the man himself—the man relates to this woman only as the *cause* of his desire, and so, "the more the man approaches, encircles and caresses what he believes to be the object of his desire, the more he is in fact diverted and distracted from it." The debased woman is emphatically not the object that the man desires—despite how it may appear—but the object that "lies *behind* desire."[29]

But if the man doesn't enjoy the debased woman, then what exactly is he enjoying? The object of love, of course! The debased woman, in her function as the object of desire, lights up the man's desire for the object of love. For the man, the object of desire is not a full and rich woman, complete with wants and desires of her own—to put it in the language of Part Two, she is not a thing. Rather, she is a debased object that has been reduced to a single trait: namely, the cause of the man's desire. She is that small residue of the object of love that makes the man desire her—not an object in her own right but a part of an object, which has fallen away from the object proper. Or, to put it yet another way, the object of desire is not a woman with a lovely breast; she is rather the lovely breast itself.

Debasement thus performs a kind of reversal of the logic of disavowal found in fetishism. If the fetish is a substitute for the mother's missing penis, then it is, Freud argues, a highly peculiar one. Peculiar because, while it allows the fetishist to go on believing that the mother has a penis in the form of the fetish, it also accedes to the falsity of this belief in the very act of standing in for the missing penis. That is, if the mother has a penis, then why does it need a substitute? Thus, the fetishist "has retained that belief" in the mother's penis, "but he has also given it up."[30]

Fetishistic disavowal is thus, as Octave Mannoni classically formulates it, an "I know well, but all the same ..." sort of logic: I know well the shoe is not the mother's penis, but all the same ....[31] Debasement follows this same logic but with terms reversed. Whereas fetishism disavows the knowledge of the other's *lack*, debasement disavows the knowledge of the other's *presence*. With debasement, the man has the breast (in the form of the debased woman) without the woman to whom it is attached. He knows very well that the breast belongs to the woman, but he can nevertheless act as if it does not, as if the breast is an object without the other. As opposed to the fetish, which is the part that is missing from the other, the debased object is the part-object that is missing the other itself. Not an "I know very well that the mother does not have a penis, but all the same ...," but an "I know very well that this breast belongs to the other, but all the same ...."

Thus, the jouissance that the man receives from the debased woman is not a jouissance that he experiences *with* this woman, nor is it even a jouissance *of* this woman; it is, rather, the jouissance he wants to receive from the *other* woman, the object of love, a jouissance that he can only access *through* the debased woman, for as Lacan puts it, "jouissance shall know nothing of the Other except by this remainder"[32] Not only has the man divided up the woman into the object of love and the object of desire, but he has also divided up his desire and jouissance, locating his desire with the debased object of desire, insofar as it is the cause of his desire, and his jouissance with the sublime object of love. As such, the sex he has with the debased woman is not aimed at enjoying her at all but at enjoying the object of love, which he can only access *through* her. Not sex *with* the debased woman, but sex *through* the debased woman. Isn't this why Joi is a hologram? So that K can enjoy Mariette literally through her?

VI

What the man achieves in the debasement fantasy is therefore none other than his ideal woman. A woman who is much like the Francisco de Zurbarán painting, *Saint Agatha of Catania*. In this painting, Saint Agatha is depicted carrying a platter with a pair of breasts on it. Anyone who is acquainted with Saint Agatha's story will immediately recognize that these are her breasts on the platter.[33] Some may find this image of Saint Agatha carrying her breasts on a platter distressing, even anxiety provoking, if not outright disgusting, and when pressed as to why they feel this way, they will point to the breasts that have been separated from Saint Agatha's body. Lacan, however, disagrees with this assessment or at least finds it imprecise.

Though Lacan will eventually agree that Zurbarán's painting can be unsettling, he nevertheless begins by praising *Saint Agatha* for its "beguiling" quality—a quality that he claims stems from its excellent portrayal of "the objects of our desire."[34] Lacan's claim is bound to appear puzzling at first, even distasteful. How exactly does *Saint Agatha* depict the objects of desire? Is Lacan simply saying, in a roundabout way, that we desire breasts? What could he possibly mean? Lacan's claim, I believe, becomes less mysterious when it is put into the context of the logic of debasement that we have been discussing.

For the man, the ideal woman is a woman from whom the stain of desire has been excised—or, "enucleated," as Lacan puts it—a woman like Saint Agatha: a woman without the breast, so to speak.[35] And it is this idealization by enucleation that Zurbarán captures in his painting. That is, Saint Agatha appears saintly precisely because she is juxtaposed with the vulgar breasts on the platter. Far from a detraction, the very vulgarity of the breasts accentuates Saint Agatha's saintliness—that is to say, it accentuates her lack of breasts. And yet, it is also true that the man cannot do without the object of desire. As much as the man desires a woman without the breast, he needs the breast without a woman to fuel his desire. As such, the ideal woman will not be the woman without the breast by herself but the woman as she appears with or next to the object of desire: that is, a woman, like Saint Agatha, who carries her breast on a platter (or a replicant, like Mariette, who superimposes the breast on herself, in the form of Joi).

So, when Lacan lauds Zurbarán for presenting us with "the objects of our desire," he is not simply referring to the breasts on the platter but, rather, to the entire composition as such. *Saint Agatha of Catania* does not capture the object of desire simply because it has a pair of breasts in it. It captures the object of desire because it depicts the *form* in which the object must appear in order to appear desirable within the debasement fantasy: that is, as a "complex grouping" of woman and breast, of object of love and object of desire. In this way, Midge's portrait of herself as Carlotta Valdes serves as the exact obverse of *Saint Agatha of Catania*, as it obliterates the gap between the object of love and the object of desire—that is, between the woman and the breast—which is of course why Scottie finds it so offensive. For the same reason, in *Bladerunner 2049*, K is unaffected by the sexual advances of his superior, Lt. Joshi (Robin Wright). For K, Joshi is a woman with the object of desire, not on a platter but incorporated within her image.

The ideal woman for the man is therefore someone like *Saint Agatha of Catania*, someone who is always "a complex grouping" of the woman who is *without* the breast and the woman who *is* the breast. And if Zurbarán's painting is distressing, it is not because he presents the woman and the breast as two separate objects, Lacan argues. Indeed, there are a plethora of pornographic images that present the breast, as well as every other body part imaginable, in isolation from the rest of the body, and none of these images are meant to cause anxiety. Zurbarán's painting is distressing, not because it presents the woman and the breast as *separate* objects but as "*separable* objects," that is, objects with a certain "stuck on" quality to them, like they are always on the verge of "falling-away," a falling away that would mean the falling apart of desire.[36]

VII

It is indeed tempting to read Freud and Lacan's respective accounts of debasement as a criticism of the inhibition of the drive. On this view, it would be the fact that the man encounters an obstacle in the object of love, which "gives rise to the inhibition of his male potency," that is to be blamed for all his infidelities and debasements.[37] Perhaps, then, sublimation is what removes this obstacle—the tie that stitches the object of love and the object of desire back together again—thereby reuniting desire and love. But this would be the exact wrong lesson to learn. The problem is not that the man encounters the obstacle to his sexual satisfaction in the object of love. Rather, the problem is that he ever believed in a woman that could perfectly satisfy him in the first place, a woman without an obstacle. For it is this belief that causes him to misrecognize in the encounter with the obstacle the sign that another woman exists who is capable of perfectly satisfying him—a misrecognition that sends him on a search for that perfect woman. Indeed, what the man doesn't realize is that the object of love is exactly like every other woman he will ever meet insofar as *all* women, like all objects, possess some irreducible otherness—some unassimilable component or thing—that obstructs or inhibits his ability to find satisfaction through them. While it may be true that the man is indeed able to find a woman through whom he can satisfy his sexual impulses, he is only able to do so by blotting out or excising this otherness—the thing—through the logic of debasement. For this reason, sublimation will definitively not be the tie that binds the object of love to the object of desire nor will it be the uninhibiting of sexual satisfaction in the former. Rather, sublimation will be the signification of the thing in the beloved—the thing that inhibits the path to satisfaction—and a deflection or reorientation of the drive *toward* it (insofar as sublimation aims at something other than and remote from satisfaction), such that this thing is experienced now as the very impetus for love.

Love, Lacan claims in the seminar *Transference*, is like a hand reaching out of an object just as one is reaching toward it:

> If, in the movement of reaching, drawing, or stirring, the hand goes far enough toward the object that another hand comes out of the fruit, flower, or log and extends toward your hand—and at that moment your hand freezes in the closed plentitude of the fruit, in the open plentitude of the flower, or in the explosion of a log which bursts into flames—then what is produced is love.

This "other hand that reaches towards us," Lacan clarifies, is the object's "desire."[38] What Lacan is getting at in this rather enigmatic image of love is that love is only possible when the beloved object is allowed to have a desire of its own—that is, when the beloved object ceases to be an object simply given for the lover's satisfaction and becomes an object with a desire of its own. Only then are we able to experience true love for it. Or, to put it in the language of debasement, only when the man ceases his attempts to uninhibit his sexual impulses will he be able to truly love the woman, for as long as he seeks sexual satisfaction in either the object of love or the object of desire, he debases both women as mere objects given for his sexual pleasure.

Thus, far from a point of frustration, the unassimilable thing of the beloved, which obstructs every attempt at sexual satisfaction, is the most precious and dignified of objects insofar as it opens up the possibility of love. For by thwarting our attempts at securing satisfaction, this thing forces us to experience the beloved's desire, insofar as desire is the desire of the Other. And it is only by remaining true to that desire, by not giving ground on it, that we become receptive to what the beloved is in itself. As such, it is not a coincidence when, in Yosujiro Ozu's wonderful *The Flavor of Green Tea over Rice* (1952), Taeko Satake (Michiyo Kogure) falls in love with her husband Mokichi Satake (Shin Saburi) at the precise moment when she eats Mokichi's favorite meal: green tea over rice. This meal, which is Mokichi's thing, was the source of an almost insuperable repugnance for Taeko earlier in the film. Thus, she could not stand to be in the same room with him when he ate it. Yet, when Taeko eats the soupy rice herself, rather than blot out Mokichi's thing she encounters it, which reaches out to her like a hand emerging from an exploding ember. It is at this moment that Taeko and Mokichi, after years of marriage, finally become a married couple. The lesson that Ozu imparts to us in *Green Tea over Rice* is that we become a group—even if only a group of two—when we finally construe the other's thing, not as an obstacle to our satisfaction but, rather, as the source of our bond.

The genius's group then is like Taeko and Mokichi's marriage. It grows from an encounter with the other's thing, an encounter that occurs only when we inhibit the aim of satisfaction. When we inhibit this aim, the oddities and idiosyncrasies in the other are allowed to emerge like the Lacanian hand reaching out from a flower. And rather than reading this emergent hand as the sign that the ideal must save us, this group reads it as the signifier of the nonexistence of original narcissism, the nonexistence of the perfect object, the masterpiece, a signifier that the other gives us as a sign of their love insofar as "love is giving what you don't have."[39]

11

Toward an Ethics of Subjective Cession

I

In *Group Psychology and the Analysis of the Ego*, Freud makes use of his infamous construction of the primal horde, first developed in *Totem and Taboo*, in order to give a structural account of how relations in the artificial group take hold.[1] As this construction has it, the primal horde is led by a ruthless and narcissistic father who "loved no one but himself," loved others "only in so far as they served his needs," and "gave away no more than was barely necessary."[2] To protect his monopoly on the uninhibited pursuit of his happiness, this father "prevented his sons from satisfying their directly sexual impulsions" and pressed them into "emotional ties with him and with one another which could arise out of those of their impulsions that were inhibited in their sexual aim."[3] There is that phrase again: *inhibited in their sexual aim.*

Continuing this argument, Freud then suggests that the equality of renunciation that the primal father imposes upon his sons is the structural homologue for "the illusion that the leader" of the artificial group "loves all of the individuals equally and justly."[4] So, while the leader binds the artificial group together through identification and idealization, and not domination and subordination, the equal love that the leader has for all their followers is nevertheless an implicit injunction that they renounce their claims to sexual satisfaction—in other words, that they *inhibit* their sexual aims. Of course, the same does not apply to the leader themselves. Like the primal father, the leader is an exception to the rule of equality, and so, while all the members must inhibit their sexual aims—after all, "social justice means that we deny ourselves many things so that others may have to do without them as well"—the leader can still be "of a masterful nature, absolutely narcissistic, self-confident and independent."[5]

If I were to hazard a guess as to what inhibition in the primal horde is, I would *not* say that it is to occupy the position of the sons, despite the fact that they are the ones in Freud's construction who must inhibit their sexual aims. The problem with this interpretation is that it ignores the position of the primal father itself, which introduces the possibility of uninhibited sexual satisfaction into the structure of the group. That is to say, construing the sons as representing the position of inhibition does not take into account Freud's construction as a whole. The inclusion of the primal father's position within the horde makes it impossible for the horde as a whole to create the kind of permanent tie that Freud believes is possible through inhibition. The temptation of uninhibited sexual satisfaction is simply too great. There will always be a son who breaks the bonds of brotherhood in a bid to take the position of the father for himself. Indeed, in *Totem and Taboo*, this temptation is so great that it leads the sons to band together and murder the father. Interestingly, in *Group Psychology*, Freud envisions the father's death as a natural death.[6] But even here, the mere vacancy in the father's position is enough to break the bonds of the sons, as one of them inevitably succeeds their dead father, as if to say that even natural death, as benign as it is, is enough to break the bonds of brotherhood.

Thus, if the complete inhibition of the sexual aims does indeed exist within Freud's account of the group, it must look something like the collective renunciation of the father's position as such. On this view, the genius's group would be the set of all the individuals who have renounced the father's inheritance of uninhibited satisfaction. And yet, this could not be all, for what is problematic is not simply the inheritance of uninhibited satisfaction but the father's position itself. For to renounce the goal of uninhibited satisfaction without affecting the father's position would be tantamount to conceding the irreducibility of uninhibited satisfaction in the structure of the group. Thus, the genius's group must go further. It must not simply be the group of individuals who have renounced the father's inheritance. It must also be what remains of the group after the father's position—that is, the position of uninhibited satisfaction—has been completely removed.

II

However, there is reason to doubt that eliminating uninhibited satisfaction from the structure of the group will be enough to secure the lasting group tie. This is because, as Lacan's analysis of debasement demonstrates, the sons' relationship with the father is more ambivalent than meets the eye. Whereas Freud envisions the father as possessing the means of complete satisfaction, and therefore diametrically opposed to the destitution of the sons, Lacan detects the possibility of a split. For the members of the horde, there is a difference between the person of the father, on one side, and the stain that makes him desirable, on the other. Or, to put it another way, the artificial group possesses the logic of debasement.

In Lacan's terminology, this stain of desire, which in the debasement fantasy is excised from the object of love and given external form as the object of desire, is *the object a*. The object *a* is the debased object. It is Saint Agatha's breasts, Kim Novak's Judy Barton, and Ana de Armas's Joi. It is "a kind of residue" that makes the object of love desirable. Though the man believes it is the object *a* that he truly desires, the object *a* is only the "cause" of his desire, the object that brings him back to the object of love.[7] And just as the man who is caught up in the logic of debasement comes to desire the object of love by encountering the cause of his desire in another woman, the members of the artificial group come to desire the leader by encountering the cause of their desire in some other object *a*. Freud comes very close to this idea when he theorizes the leader as possessing some sort of quality, like the hypnotist's "mysterious power" or the primal father's "mana," which allows the leader to elicit the desire of the members and "hold it riveted."[8] But he falls short of it when he fails to recognize the possibility of this so-called mana becoming separated from the person of the leader and given objective form.[9]

What the logic of debasement suggests is that the true source of the leader's appeal has nothing to do with person of the leader, as Freud assumes it does. It has to do with this object *a*—the mana—that has been split off from their person. We find this sort of dynamic in far right groups. The leaders of these groups are, as a rule, completely incompetent and buffoonish—*unvermögender*, as Joan Copjec might put it. Indeed, for those who do not belong to these groups, it is difficult to understand what their appeal is. What causes the members of these groups to desire such a moronic figure? This is where the figure of the minority comes in. This minority figure, whether it is the immigrant, the Jew, the woman, the racial other, etc., fills the position of the object *a* in the structure of the group. By becoming the object of the members' hatred, the minority causes their desire for the idiot leader. The minority figure is the mana that has fallen off the person of the leader. One cannot separate the two. They are like Zurbarán's *Saint Agatha of Catania*— one in the same object.

For this reason, the leader, as a person, need not be exceptional in any way. Indeed, they may be absolutely pathetic—completely bereft of mana, to put it in Freudian terms. The leader need not be a person of high moral character, a success in their private affairs, or aesthetically pleasing. The leader need not be seen as possessing the strong national identity that the members want for themselves. Indeed, the leader may even be someone who has lost this identity themselves, just like the members. The leader need not have the magic formula for keeping the minority in check but, instead, may be another one of their supposed victims. Indeed, the leader may be "an *unvermögender* Other," to use Copjec's term again—a leader without means.[10] And yet, the leader may also be the one who bucks the conventions of polite society in order to publicly air their grievances against the minority—imagined as they are—and in so doing, situates themselves alongside the object *a*. That is to say, the leader need not possess the object *a* or mana within themselves, as Freud believes they must. It is enough that they appear next to the object *a*—holding it on a platter, so to speak.

Could one imagine Freud theorizing this kind of primal father? Not a father who is "of a masterful nature," but a debased father who constantly whines and complains about how he is treated unfairly by the sons, how he doesn't receive a parade like the leaders of other hordes, how the father who preceded him ruined the horde and was in all likelihood from another horde anyway, how he was not in fact murdered by the sons at all but had the horde stolen from him by the deep-horde state. It is indeed unthinkable. But it is precisely Freud's inability to think this kind of father—not the absent father, but the debased father—that casts doubt on the efficacy of excising the position of uninhibited satisfaction from the group, for it is not clear anymore that the temptation of this satisfaction is what rivets the followers to the leader in the first place. While the fantasy of uninhibited satisfaction should certainly be given up, Lacan's version of debasement suggests that there is something else at stake in the group's unconscious love for the leader: namely, the presence of this externalized object *a*—this residue or stain—that causes the group's desire for the leader.

In terms of priority, it seems to me that the object *a* always comes first. The members have a vague sense that something has interfered with their satisfaction. In Chapter 9, I argued that this something is the symbolic order itself, as we all must give up original narcissism in order to enter into symbolic relations with each other. In other words, the object *a* is the name for our incommensurability with the symbolic order. But the members look for someone to blame for their state of discontent, someone who can serve as the face of the object *a*. Here enters the leader. The leader names the cause of the members' discontent; they attach a specific identity to it. It is the Jew or the immigrant or women or the liberal media—sometimes all of the above— who has stolen the members' plentitude. The specific identity of the leader is not important. They need not possess a unique charisma or mana. It can be anyone. Indeed, the more bereft of mana, the better, as it only makes it easier for the members to identify with them. A primal father with whom the sons can share a beer, we might call it. The only thing that matters is that the leader appears to the members holding the object *a* on a platter, like a political *Saint Agatha of Catania*.

What is crucial in this constellation, however, is that the members receive a perverse dividend directly from their idealization of the leader. As such, it is not the temptation of uninhibited satisfaction that keeps the members riveted to the leader but this perverse dividend. So, if the leader could in fact provide the means for eliminating the object a—which to be sure they cannot—would the members even go for it? Or would they find excuses to leave things as they are? For this reason, it is unclear if cutting the position of the primal father—that is, the position of uninhibited satisfaction—out of the structure of the group would be enough to create permanent ties. In fact, it is doubtful. What is necessary, in addition, is to transform the members' relationship to the object a itself. The members must relinquish the idea that the solution to their discontent lies in eliminating the object a, in its various avatars. Instead, they must accept their discontent as an inherent feature of life itself, an artifact of the drive's lack of an essential object. In other words, the members must identify with the object a, not avow it as the enemy. As Lacan puts it, "It is at this point of lack that the subject has to recognize himself."[11] That is, the members must place themselves on the same level as the object a. This then is how we should understand the genius's group. The genius's group is the collection of individuals who all recognize themselves as objects a. This new relationship with the object a is what Lacan calls *inhibition*. To get a better handle on how inhibition transforms us, we should turn to the account that Lacan gives of inhibition toward the end of his seminar *Anxiety*.

III

In the penultimate session of *Anxiety*, Lacan asks his audience: "What is inhibition for us in our experience?" His answer? The "introduction into a function ... of another desire besides the one that the function satisfies."[12] I admit that this formulation of Lacan's is practically incomprehensible. It bears some vague resemblance to Freud's already difficult definition of inhibition as "restrictions of the functions of the ego which have either been imposed as a measure of precaution or brought about as a result of an impoverishment of energy," but other than that it is absolutely opaque.[13] So, what could Lacan possibly mean by it, and what, if anything, does it have to offer group psychology?

A good place to start is indeed to compare it with Freud's own (relatively) clear definition. For while these two statements may appear to resemble one another, when placed side by side, an instructive difference appears. According to Freud's definition, an inhibition is a kind of ceasing or stopping of a function—*restrictions of the functions of the ego*, as he puts it. An activity, for example, like writing or walking, takes on a particular significance for a person (typically, sexual in nature), and therefore they stop engaging in it—that is, it becomes inhibited—as *a measure of precaution* against encountering that new significance. Lacan's formulation presents a slight deviation from this account. Inhibition, for Lacan, is no longer simply the ceasing of a function but now *the introduction into a function*—or, the unexpected appearing in a function—*of another desire*, which is errant or strange. A person doesn't simply stop writing or walking as "a measure of precaution" against encountering some particular significance, as in Freud. Rather, they find that their writing or walking has become infiltrated or invaded by "another desire," a desire that they find strange and disturbing. Though this difference with Freud is subtle, its implications are significant, for it takes inhibition from a precaution and changes it to a disruption or an intervention.

Thus, we have made a small piece of sense of Lacan's formulation. When he says inhibition is the "introduction" of desire into a function, he means that inhibition is an *intervention* into a function, an intervention made by desire—what he also calls "the incidence of desire."[14] And while there is still much more work to be done before we can say that we fully understand Lacan's formulation—if such a thing can ever be said—we can already appreciate what his formulation might contribute to our thinking on group psychology.

Whereas Freud finds inhibition already present in the group—specifically, in the type of relationships its members share with each other—Lacan begs to differ. In the first place, to construe the members' relationships with each other as inhibited misses the ways in which the group, like the debasement fantasy itself, functions to *uninhibit* satisfaction for its members, albeit in roundabout and circuitous ways (the perverse dividend that I discussed in Chapter 9 is one example). But, more importantly, the members' relationships to one another cannot be inhibited in the Lacanian sense because, for Lacan, inhibition is not something *in* a function at all. Rather, it is something that happens *to* a function. Inhibition is not a quality of a relationship already present *within* the group; it is, rather, an intervention that happens *to* the group. The appearing—or, to use Lacan's locution, "introduction"—of a desire that intervenes in the group and disrupts its function.

IV

Having established that for Lacan inhibition is the intervention of desire into the group, we may now ask: what kind of desire is this intervening desire? What is it a desire for? To answer this question, we must turn to the moment immediately preceding Lacan's comments on inhibition. There, we find Lacan discussing the case of Freud's famous patient, the Wolf Man.

The Wolf Man receives his pseudonym from a dream he had when he was young. In this dream, a window opens, revealing a tree with several wolves perched on its branches. The wolves "had their ears pricked like dogs when they pay attention to something."[15] Terrified by the sight of the alert wolves (Lacan suggests that it isn't simply the wolves themselves but their gaze, which the Wolf Man encounters only obliquely through their pricked ears), the young Wolf Man awakens from the dream. Lacan claims that this moment of confrontation with the wolves—and importantly, the Wolf Man's reaction to it—reveals something fundamental about the subject's relationship to the object *a*. He states, "If we are able to grasp it here, in some sense in a pure way, it is precisely in so far as, in his radical, traumatic confrontation, the subject yields to the situation."[16]

So, inhibition is the introduction of the errant desire to yield to the situation. But what is the desire to yield mean? Is it a lethargy or an apathy? Lacan clarifies that by *yields to the situation* he does not mean that "the subject wavers" or "flags." It is not an issue of exhaustion or "an impoverishment of energy," to use Freud's phrase. It cannot be an issue of wavering or flagging because, as Lacan points out, the Wolf Man *leaned into* the dream scene. Despite his rising anxiety alerting him to the danger awaiting him outside the window frame, the Wolf Man looked out the window and stared at the wolves instead of awakening immediately. For this reason, Lacan argues, we must think of the Wolf Man's yielding to the situation as "literally a cession."[17] That is, by yielding to the situation, the Wolf Man did not resign but, rather, ceded the object *a* to the Other. The desire to yield, not as a form of lethargy or apathy but, rather, as "the cession of the object *a*."[18]

To elaborate on what he means by "the cession of the object *a*," Lacan turns to that very familiar image in psychoanalysis of the breast-feeding child. Recall that for Lacan the mother is not a single unitary object but is, like all objects, a complex grouping of partial objects, a point that he reiterates here, reminding his audience that the breast is not simply a member of the mother's body but is an object that is a "part of the individual who is being fed," which is "merely *stuck onto* the mother."[19] What Lacan is emphasizing here is that as far as the child is concerned, the breast is a part of its own body, not the mother's. As such, whenever the mother takes the breast back, the child is faced with a decision: "[E]ither hold onto or leave go of this breast."[20] That is, either retain the belief that the breast is a part of its own body or recognize that it belongs to the mother. If the child retains its claim on the breast, when the mother takes it back, the child will experience the loss of the breast as a kind of theft perpetrated by the mother and will, as a result, resent the mother as the thief who has stolen, not simply a beloved object but a member of its own body. Very clearly, the group's own grievances over the loss of original narcissism are a repetition of this earlier theft of the breast, evincing that the group has only ever given up the breast physically, not psychically. Alternatively, if the child recognizes the breast as belonging to the mother—that is, if the child yields or cedes the breast to the mother—the child will not resent the mother, as the mother will have done nothing wrong from the child's perspective. It is in this sense that Lacan says the child always weans itself, for though it is the mother who takes the breast away, it is always the child who must ultimately *leave go* of the breast or, in other words, cede it to the mother.[21]

So, when Lacan says that the Wolf Man yielded to the situation, he is far from claiming that the Wolf Man simply resigned or withdrew. Rather, he is claiming that the Wolf Man made a decision—took a stand—to cede the object *a* to the situation. This is what Lacan means by "the cession of the object *a*." We *leave go* of the object *a* just as the child leaves go of the breast, the first "yieldable object."[22] It is impossible to overstate the gravity of the decision at stake here, for in ceding the object *a*, the Wolf Man, as much as the breast-feeding child itself, does not let go of something as simple as a cherished keepsake, like a favorite toy or blanket. Rather, he cedes a piece of himself. Just like the child who misrecognizes the mother's breast as a part of their own body, we misconstrue the object *a* as the little piece of ourselves which was lost when we entered the symbolic, the missing object of the drive which has been stolen from us. Thus, when the Wolf Man ceded the object *a* to the situation, as Lacan claims he did, he was, from the perspective of his ego, relinquishing a part of himself. Or, otherwise put, he was ceding his claim to original narcissism.

In light of its gravity, this decision to relinquish the object *a* deserves to be considered an ethics in its own right—call it, the ethics of "subjective cession."[23] It is the ethics of the object that supplements the ethics of desire, which I alluded to in Chapter 4. That is to say, refusing to give ground on our desire always requires the supplementary act of relinquishing the object *a*, for unless such a relinquishing takes place, our desire will always remain stuck within the gravitational pull of original narcissism. Viewed in this more elevated light, the decision to cede the object *a* no longer appears as simply another action, much less as a mere acting out, but now as an ethical *act* in its own right insofar as "the gap of desire," which Lacan says is written into all acts, "is written into it."[24] This desire which is written into the act of cession, Lacan says, is "the desire to hold back," and its general form is inhibition.[25]

V

We can now offer the following rendition of Lacan's formulation of inhibition: inhibition holds back the function so that the desire to cede the object *a* may appear. Yet, while we have made greater sense of Lacan's formulation, questions still remain, as the phrase *to hold back* is thoroughly ambiguous. Indeed, depending on the context, *to hold back* can have a variety of meanings. For example, it can mean to hold something in, as in the phrase "to hold back one's tears," or to put up a struggle, as in "to hold back the enemy," or even to let something go, as in "to hold back one's grip," to name just a few possibilities. Of course, there is a reason for this ambiguity. Lacan is deliberately playing on Freud's words, found in many places, regarding the child holding back their feces during potty training.[26] Lacan is playing on these words because he wants to break the link between the desire to hold back, on one hand, and the so-called anal stage, on the other. "A more general form is involved in the desire to hold back," insists Lacan, "and that is what we have to grasp."[27] Be that as it may, we must clarify Lacan's phrasing, for unless we do, we will not fully grasp the exact kind of intervention the desire to hold back is.

In the second half of Lacan's formulation, we find the suggestion that the function is already in the midst of satisfying a desire when it is interrupted by inhibition: *besides the one that the function satisfies*, he says. This gives us a clue as to what kind of desire the desire to hold back is. It is the desire to hold back—or inhibit—whatever desire this function is so busy satisfying. So, what desire is the function so busy satisfying? To begin answering this question, recall that the breast is not simply any object in a world full of objects but one that is unique among objects insofar as it is also a part of the subject itself, an object that the subject has "appended as a portion of himself," as Lacan puts it. As such, the act of subjective cession is not as simple as clipping off one's fingernails, for when the subject cedes the breast, they cede a part of itself. Thus, Lacan states, the cession of the object *a* is "the abandonment of this organ that is much more than an object, which is the subject itself."[28] That is, to cede the breast to the mother is to abandon *the subject itself*.

By implicating the subject, Lacan raises the stakes of subjective cession as it now reveals something about the very existence of the subject itself. Not only does relinquishing the breast mean that I must take up the cross of my castration, it also means that I must accept that I myself, as a subject, am also a "yieldable object" like the breast. For if the breast, which psychically has the same status as one of my own physical body parts, can be lost, then why not one of those physical body parts themselves, like my arm or my hair? Indeed, many people who have lost a part of their physical body—like, for example, their hair or their breasts—report feeling that they have lost something essential about themselves. Or think of men and their castration anxiety. For many men, losing the penis is worse than death itself, as it is tantamount to no longer being a man. But the chain of this reasoning goes even further. If one of my own physical body parts can be lost, then why not one that is less tangible, like the voice? As Lacan points out, while the voice is immaterial, it nonetheless appears "to be capable of belonging to the realm of yieldable objects."[29] And if something like the voice can be lost, then why not finally all of me? Indeed, to relinquish the breast, "we shall have to recognize ourselves as object *a*," Lacan claims.[30]

So, while it may appear that the child makes a decision on the breast alone when they cede the breast to the mother, they are always simultaneously making a decision on themselves. No wonder the weaning child cries! They are confronting the fact that they themselves are a lost object. In a way, then, the first "yieldable object" is not the breast at all but, rather, the subject itself, for only if the child has already ceded itself as a "yieldable object" can it then cede the breast. Or, to put it another way, when the child relinquishes the breast, it always retroactively relinquishes itself as the necessary precondition for this act. Or, if one wants a more Kantian formulation, the child must relinquish the breast *as if* it has already relinquished itself. Thus, only by identifying with the lost object and saying of oneself, "I am forever this yieldable object," can one ever hope to cede the object *a*.[31]

The decision to cede the object *a* is therefore an ethical decision of the highest order, and as such, it is one that we will go to great lengths to avoid. We will, for example, preoccupy ourselves with the acquisition of possessions, silently hoping that by recovering the drive's missing object, we will never have to face the decision to yield. Or we will fill up every waking moment with work and leisure, in order to bury the decision to yield underneath an avalanche of frenetic activity. Or we will develop intricate routines and rituals to prevent this decision from taking us by surprise. Of course, all these various strategies of avoidance can become oppressive and onerous in their own right. But we will engage in them anyways, even as we complain about them, because, as difficult as they might be, they all express the same exigent desire: namely, the desire to know nothing of the decision to cede the object *a*.

We are now in a position to identify the desire that the function is so busy satisfying. That desire is the desire to know nothing of the decision to cede the object *a*, the desire to remain passionately ignorant of it.[32] The phrase *to hold back* should therefore no longer be ambiguous. It is to hold back this ignorance that keeps us from confronting the desire to cede the object *a*. Thus, when inhibition intervenes in a function, it holds back this desire to remain ignorant of the decision to yield, which the function satisfies. With all this in mind, we may now return to Lacan's formulation of inhibition and offer the following rendition: inhibition holds back the passion for ignorance so that the desire to cede the object *a* may appear.

Now, there are many things that we do—many "functions" that we utilize—to remain passionately ignorant of the decision to yield, but the most potent one of all is none other than the artificial group. That is to say, the artificial group also satisfies the desire for ignorance. It does this by sustaining the fantasy that the members can recover original narcissism through the person of the leader. So, while the members may not have the object a, they do not have to face the decision to cede it because the group, as a form, allows them to continue believing that it will one day be restored to them by the leader. In this way, we may say that the ultimate authority, which rivets the members to the leader, is not the leader's mana or even the perverse dividend but, rather, this shared ignorance of the decision to yield, for by claiming to have the power to recover the group's lost narcissism, the leader allows the members, as well as themselves, to continue avoiding the decision to cede the object a. Indeed, one may even modify Freud's definition of the artificial group in this direction: a primary group of this kind is a number of individuals who all idealized the same leader, in order to remain passionately ignorant of the decision to cede the object a, and have consequently identified themselves with one another in their ego. In that case, we may think of the genius's rejection of the Other's authority as a rejection of this tyrannical ignorance that secretly binds the group together like a blood oath.

VI

It should now be clear that Lacan's conception of inhibition differs quite widely from Freud's. For Freud, inhibition is the inability to engage in an activity or task due to unsavory associations. For Lacan, however, inhibition is the appearing of the strange desire to cede the object a as well as a disruption of all the various means by which we remain passionately ignorant of that desire. Let us now take this idea of Lacan's and apply it to group psychology. What do we gain? As an answer to this question, I want to offer three claims or theses.

First thesis. Inhibition is an intervention into the artificial group. Inhibition disrupts the members' idealization of the leader by holding back their passionate ignorance of the desire to cede the object a. But if this were all that inhibition was, if inhibition were only an intervention, then Badiou would be right. Psychoanalysis can only offer a critique of the group relation. It cannot offer one itself. This then brings me to my second thesis.

Second thesis. Inhibition is the basis for a new group relation. By allowing the desire to cede the object a to appear, inhibition causes the members to give up their investment in original narcissism. They accept it as lost, and in so doing, they realize themselves as yieldable objects in "the same series as the a."[33] This series is the collective of geniuses.

Third thesis. The disruption of the artificial group and the creation of the collective of geniuses are not in fact two separate movements but, rather, two sides of the same movement. It is impossible to form a new group relation without disrupting the old group relation, and it is impossible to disrupt the old group relation without the help of others. Given that it means losing a part of oneself, there is always something disorienting about ceding the object *a*. For this reason, we need the help of another subject in our moment of disorientation, a subject that is able to help us find our place among that series of the *a* or, as Alenka Zupančič puts it, "someone who helps us get on the train at the right moment."[34] This is why there is no such thing as "self analysis." There is always the need of another desire that is able to capture the spirit of one's act. This, Lacan argues, is the function of the analyst's desire, "a desire which intervenes."[35] By fabricating the promoted signifier, the signifier of null, the genius offers exactly this kind of intervention. Thus, the genius is that extraneous subject who helps us find our way to the series of the *a*, the collective of geniuses.

12

Life after the Image or, *Cluny Brown*

I

What happens after the passion for ignorance is inhibited and we cede the object *a*? Does all become lost? Do we simply disappear into nothingness, never to be heard from again? I claimed at the end of the last chapter that there is a form of group life, based on inhibition, that emerges from the act of subjective cession. But what kind of life is it? Is it a life made up of the pulverized dust of those who have ceded themselves as objects *a*?[1] A life of nothingness? My answer is an emphatic No. The life that is possible in the sublimated group is rich and full. Indeed, insofar as it is removed from the impossible goal of recovering original narcissism, it is the only life that is real. To understand how this is possible, we must only remember that, for Lacan, who we are in the artificial group—the *I* that we present—is only ever an image, an image that is imposed upon us by that group, an image that we are forced to live up to.[2] What we lose then when we cede the object *a* is this image.

However, the image is not all that we are. As Paul Eisenstein so nicely puts it, there is always "something of substance internal to every identity that cannot be made to mean, and that we are forever cut off from … even as it is lodged within us."[3] A remainder that cannot be fully incorporated into the image, or overwritten by it, which, as a result, always threatens to disrupt our place within the artificial group. When we cede the object *a* and lose the image, it is this nonmeaningful "something" that remains—what Lacan calls, "the excremental *a*."[4] Lacan's claim is that we "cannot enter the world" as a subject "except as a remainder."[5] In other words, who we are as subjects is found, not in the image but in this remainder.

And yet, we ourselves do not possess an easy relationship to this remainder within us—as Eisenstein puts it, we are "cut off" from it. Freud observes in *Three Essays on the Theory of Sexuality* that we typically react to this "something" in us—for Freud, it is sexuality itself—with "shame, disgust, horror or pain."[6] This is why we accede to the group's image in the first place. Our hope is that the image will eliminate this remainder or at least normalize it. But if we are to realize ourselves as subjects, we must not disassociate ourselves from this remainder. On the contrary, we must recognize ourselves in it. And so, while life after the cession is possible, not only will it require us to cede the image, it will require us to identify with this excremental remainder as well.

II

To get a better handle on this dual act of abandoning the image and identifying with the remainder—and perhaps also to demonstrate that life in the sublimated group is full of laughter and love—I want to turn to Ernst Lubitsch's final film, the wonderful screwball comedy *Cluny Brown* (1946), for this film turns on this very dual act. The titular character, Cluny Brown (Jennifer Jones), is a woman out of place, as her Uncle Arn (Billy Bevan) constantly reminds her. "You don't know your place," he scolds Cluny after learning that she has fixed a clogged kitchen sink (and had a little too much to drink), and "You never will know your place." What makes Cluny out of place is her irresistible passion for plumbing. There is nothing strange about plumbing in itself. Indeed, in a man, the passion for plumbing would be proper, even laudable. What makes the passion for plumbing odd is that it is found in Cluny, a woman. There is no place in 1930s England for a woman with a passion for plumbing. For it, a woman who has a passion for plumbing is not zero; she is null. Thus, Cluny is a woman out of place in society because her passion for plumbing is out of place in her. To teach Cluny her proper place, Uncle Arn sends her to the countryside to become a housemaid at Friars Carmel manor, in an attempt at what might today be called "conversion therapy." At Friars Carmel, she reunites with the writer, Professor Adam Belinski (Charles Boyer), a Czech refugee whom she meets at the beginning of the film when she fixes the clogged kitchen sink, and from there, a love story unfolds.

This role of the housemaid is an excellent example of what Lacan calls the image. If Cluny wants to have a place in society, she must take on this image of the housemaid. It is not that society will consider her a bad woman if she is a plumber. Indeed, it is worse. It is that it will not consider her a woman at all, as it has no concept of a woman who is a plumber. Thus, to be legible as a woman at all—even as a bad woman—Cluny must fit within society's image of a woman, a woman like the honorable Betty Cream (Helen Walker), which means giving up her passion for plumbing and becoming a housemaid.

But as *Cluny Brown* clearly demonstrates, this image, which Lacan talks about, is not something of our own making. Cluny doesn't become a housemaid because she finds the role appealing or interesting. It is not a life she chooses for herself. Rather, she takes on the role because she is forced to by others, above all, Uncle Arn. The image of the housemaid is imprinted on her, we might say.[7] Thus, if Cluny wants to live a meaningful life, she has no choice; she must become a housemaid. To put it another way, Cluny's choice is forced. She must either choose to become a housemaid or live a nonmeaningful existence, which is of course no choice at all. Cluny is alienated. That is, she disappears underneath the image of the housemaid.[8]

And yet, *Cluny Brown* also clearly demonstrates another truth. Namely, this: the choice between the image and nonmeaning, though forced, is not strictly a product of subjugation or oppression. We don't choose the image because we are coerced or disciplined into it by some external power or apparatus. On some level, we desire it. Or, as Lacan puts it, desire is the desire of the Other.

Thus, after her first date with her new suitor, the local pharmacist, Jonathan Wilson (Richard Haydn), Cluny, still dressed in her maid's uniform, sinks down into her chair, and with a wide, self-satisfied smile on her face, tells Belinski, "You know Mr. Belinski, when I sat down in his parlor, and everything cozy and peaceful, and so homey, and Mr. Wilson playing the harmonium, I got all choked up. For the first time, I really felt what it must be like to have a place." By becoming a housemaid, Cluny seems to have finally found her place in society, a belonging that her relationship with Wilson epitomizes. But what is crucial in this scene is the genuineness of Cluny's satisfaction. After Cluny says this line, Lubitsch cuts to a reaction shot of Belinski. Importantly, he is completely serious. Belinski's reaction tells us that there is nothing funny or ironic in Cluny's happiness. It is absolutely genuine. Though the choice of becoming a housemaid was initially forced upon her, Cluny has come to desire it for herself. Why? For the same reason why any of us desire the images that are imprinted on us: because it gives Cluny a chance to feel "satisfactory and loved."[9] To paraphrase Lacan, Cluny's desire is the desire of Uncle Arn.

III

There is something else at stake in Cluny's investment in the image, something related to what Lacan calls "the function of oblativity."[10] Speaking of the obsessional, Lacan says this about our relationship to the image: "He gives this image to the other. He gives it so entirely that he imagines the other part would no longer know what to do should this image of him go missing."[11] What Lacan is getting at here is that we come to desire the image, not only for our own sake but also for the sake of the other. We give our image to the other in an act of oblation, a holy sacrifice. Why? Because, Lacan says, we imagine that "the other part" could not function without it. The issue here is not whether, in reality, the other can or cannot function without us playing our part. The issue is rather that, in our own psychic realities, we imagine the other not being able to function without us playing our part. The reason the other's well-being is a concern for us is not that we are altruistic creatures but, rather, that we need a fully functioning other to guarantee the meaning of our existence.[12] Or, to put it in a Freudian key, we play our part in order to keep our world from tottering.

So, while Cluny is forced to become a housemaid, she takes up the image jubilantly, in part, for herself but also, in part, for her Uncle Arn, for Lord and Lady Carmel, for Mrs. Maile and Mr. Syrette, for Jonathan Wilson, for the whole of Friars Carmel, and for the class system itself, for all these others need her to play her part so that the symbolic order they've created can function unproblematically, and Cluny needs the order to function unproblematically so that they may ensure that her life will have meaning.[13] And so, while Cluny may feel alienated by the image of the housemaid, she nevertheless identifies with it, for it is, for her, a kind of gift or holy sacrifice given to the Other in exchange for its meaning, which is why Lacan ascribes to the image "the function of oblativity."

IV

The trouble in *Cluny Brown* is that, try as she might, Cluny cannot extinguish her passion for plumbing. As she tells Belinski, "You know what plumbing does to me; just can't keep my hands off it." Plumbing is Cluny's thing, the unassimilable component in her that cannot be traced back to anything familiar in the symbolic order. As such, her passion constantly threatens to return and disrupt Cluny's tenuous grip on her place. In the climactic scene of the film, this threat finally comes to fruition. Cluny is attending the birthday party of Wilson's (hilariously) phlegmatic mother (Una O'Connor). Just as Wilson is about to announce his engagement to Cluny—thereby finally securing Cluny's place in society—the bathroom sink backs up. Hearing the sounds of the stopped-up sink, Cluny, once again, feels the urge to plumb. Unable to resist this urge, Cluny springs into action, fixing the sink. However, instead of impressing everyone at the party, Cluny horrifies them—including, above all, Wilson—which puts Cluny's status as an accepted member of society, which she had worked so hard throughout the film to obtain, in jeopardy.

This passion of Cluny's for plumbing is that "something of substance"—the thing—within her, which Eisenstein says, "cannot be made to mean." As far as her society is concerned, Cluny's passion is nonsensical, null. This is the whole point of the image of the housemaid. It is meant to eradicate or, at the very least, control Cluny's nonsensical passion—to make it mean, to put it in Eisenstein's terms. But as the birthday scene clearly demonstrates, the image is not up to the task. Somehow, something of Cluny's passion always leaks out, like a piece of excrement, marring the pristine image of the housemaid. Cluny's passion for plumbing is the point of anamorphosis within the image, where an errant sideways glance suddenly transforms the plentitude of the housemaid into "the figure of death's head."[14]

Though Cluny doesn't recognize it at first, her passion for plumbing is the source of her freedom. In his important book *Universality and Identity Politics*, Todd McGowan argues, "Freedom becomes apparent as a value when we experience our nonbelonging."[15] Cluny's passion for plumbing may leave her without a place in society, but precisely for this reason, it ensures that she is always free. "My belonging in a society always breaks down," McGowan explains, "which enables me to turn against this society when it takes a direction that I cannot accept."[16] Precisely because Cluny's passion drives a wedge between herself and her society—because her passion causes her belonging to "break down," as McGowan might put it—this passion ensures that she cannot be fully encaged by the image. A little piece of Cluny always escapes from the image—a remainder. As a result, Cluny is able to leave Friars Carmel. Unlike the passionless Wilson who was born in Friars Carmel and intends to die there, Cluny's passion for plumbing violently uproots her from the social order, and while this means that she'll never find a place in society, it also means that she'll always be free—free to leave Friars Carmel, for example—insofar as "[f]reedom emerges when one begins to depart from the givens of one's existence."[17]

Toward the end of the film, Belinski decides to leave Friars Carmel and return to London—as it turns out, there's no place for him there either. Cluny chases him down, and just as he is about to board the train, Cluny, still dressed in her housemaid's uniform, leaves with him. On the train, Belinski proclaims his love for Cluny with what are perhaps the most romantic words in all of Hollywood: "If I were rich, I would build you the most beautiful mansion with the most exquisite and complicated plumbing, and right in the middle of the most elegant housewarming party, I would hand you a hammer and say, 'Ladies and Gentleman, Madame Cluny-Belinski is about to put the pipes in their place.'" Then, Belinski asks Cluny to remove her maid's hat and apron—the small part-objects that she believed would make her whole—and he tosses them out the window. With this act of subjective cession, Cluny literally throws away the image of the housemaid, cedes it back to Friars Carmel. And while Cluny throws away the life that she tried so hard to make for herself throughout the film, all is not lost. Something remains. Something important and precious. In fact, we might say, it is the only thing that matters. It's her passion for plumbing. Having relinquished the image of the housemaid, Cluny is finally able to identify with her troublesome passion. She trades in one passion—the passion for ignorance— for another passion, the passion for plumbing. So, while it may have appeared to Cluny that life is only possible *through* the image—and others, including above all Uncle Arn, certainly want to believe this—what Cluny learns is that life is only possible *after* the image.

V

Crucially, Cluny is only able to realize herself as a plumber with Belinski's help—"You do make one see things," she tells him. While this detour through Belinski may appear to be evidence of Lubitsch's conservatism—that he is a product of his time—Alenka Zupančič finds in it "a sign of Lubitsch's revolutionary spirit."[18] The difference for Zupančič has to do with the objective status of comedy as such. This, what Zupančič dubs "Lubitschean chivalry," is not a statement on the inability of women to save themselves.[19] Rather, it is a statement on the objective nature of the thing at stake in Cluny's cession of the image. What Belinski saves, in other words, is not Cluny herself—which would indeed be a conservative form of chivalry—but, rather, the thing in Cluny, her odd passion. "It is not about saving or not saving Cluny Brown," Zupančič explains, "it is about not giving up on this surplus object, which not only drives the comedy, but is also the key to our objective, (un)human 'standing in the world.'" That is, Belinski saves Cluny because he believes the world needs her passion for plumbing, not her per se. Or, to put it another way, Belinski saves Cluny to preserve the signifier for a missing passion in the world, namely, the feminine passion for plumbing. "Cluny's survival," Zupančič thus concludes, is incidental to this objective salvation; it is the by-product or "collateral damage that comes with saving 'her' object."[20]

I find Zupančič's account of the objectivity of comedy to be an excellent way of grasping Belinski's role in Cluny's act of subjective cession. It clarifies that identification with the thing is always a group effort. This is because the appearance of the thing disrupts the image, and "precisely because of this interruption, this discontinuity of the subject," Zupančič argues, "it cannot be a solitary business, something that a subject can carry out all by herself." In our moment of disorientation, she continues, we need "someone who helps us get on the train at the right moment." For this reason, Zupančič insists, "to not give up on your desire takes (at least) two"—that is, a group.[21] Yet, as much as I support Zupančič account, I find that it overlooks one small detail, which I'd like to add. Namely, this: the objectivity of Lubitsch's idea of chivalry applies as much to Belinski as it does to Cluny. For what is important about Belinski is not so much him as a person—Belinski, the fellow human being—but the *position* he occupies, the position from which he enunciates the most famous line in the film, *squirrels to the nuts*.[22]

In the opening scene, when Belinski learns of the tension that exists between Cluny and her Uncle over her passion for plumbing, he tells her: "In Hyde Park, for instance, some people like to feed nuts to the squirrels. But if it makes you happy to feed squirrels to the nuts, who am I to say 'nuts to the squirrels'?" *Squirrels to the nuts*: Belinski gives this line to Cluny as a piece of advice (Zupančič likens it to a Lacanian matheme) to help her appreciate her unique passion. It is quite literally a genius formulation insofar as it signifies the nonexistent logic that would make sense of Cluny's strange passion. That is, if we all understood the legitimacy of feeding squirrels to nuts, then we'd understand Cluny. As Zupančič notes, it is this formula, rather than a common interest or emotion, that links Cluny and Belinski together. *Squirrels to the nuts* "becomes a kind of codeword between them." "It is the very form and substance of their bond," writes Zupančič, "the thing that binds them in the Real so to speak."[23] What I want to emphasize here, however, is that Belinski is able to formulate this genius statement, not because he himself is brilliant but, rather, because he sees Cluny from a certain position, the position of someone who doesn't belong.

Like Cluny, Belinski is a man out of place. He is in England, not because he is a citizen but because the Nazis have invaded his homeland. While at Friars Carmel, Belinski never quite fits in. He doesn't have the proper attire for the local morays, he refers to his borrowed dinner jacket as his "uniform," and it takes the entire duration of his stay there for Lord Carmel (Reginald Owen) to learn how to pronounce his name. Even in London, where he feels more comfortable, Belinski still doesn't have a place. With no abode of his own, he stays as a guest (or squatter?) in the homes of the people he meets— people like the Carmels' son, Andrew (Peter Lawford)—and he has his mail delivered "general delivery," since he has no address of his own. As Belinski tells Cluny, he is a man without a tent, "Not in the desert or anywhere."

What Cluny finds in Belinski then is someone who is like her passion for plumbing—that is, someone who occupies the place of what McGowan calls *nonbelonging*. Indeed, this is why Cluny is only able to recognize herself in her strange passion—to fall in love with it, as it were—when she falls in love with Belinski. McGowan argues that embracing the freedom of nonbelonging requires a shift in one's perspective. He writes, "rather than looking at nonbelonging from the perspective of belonging, we must look at belonging from the perspective of nonbelonging."[24] In *Cluny Brown*, McGowan's shift occurs when Cluny falls in love with Belinski. When Cluny falls in love with Belinski, she sees herself from his standpoint, which is the standpoint of someone who doesn't belong in pre-War England—the standpoint of "general delivery," we might call it—and seeing herself from this position, something about herself is revealed to her, something that she perhaps didn't pay enough attention to (indeed, we might say that Cluny becomes a genius): namely, that her passion for plumbing is not to be scorned but loved. In this way, the central love story of this screwball comedy is neither the love story that takes place between Cluny and Wilson nor the one that takes place between Cluny and Belinski; rather, it is the love story that takes place in the background of the two "human" love stories, that is, the love story that takes place between Cluny and her passion for plumbing.

Thus, we shouldn't think of chivalry in *Cluny Brown* as a personality trait. That is, we shouldn't think of it in subjective terms. Belinski is not chivalrous because it is part of his personality or character. Through an odd sequence of events involving Andrew Carmel and Betty Cream, we even learn that he is something of a womanizer. Indeed, this sequence of events, which otherwise feels out of place in the film, appears to exist for the sole purpose of demonstrating that Belinski, the man is not chivalrous. Instead, we should think of chivalry objectively, that is, as a structural position. What is chivalrous in Belinski, in other words, is not him but, rather, his position— that is, the position of nonbelonging itself. Just as Belinski saves Cluny's thing, and not so much Cluny herself, it is Belinski's position, and not so much Belinski himself, that saves Cluny. This is why Lubitschean chivalry is unlike conservative chivalry. What saves the other in a Lubitsch film is not the fellow human being. The flesh and blood individual is merely contingent. What saves the other is rather a structural position or, more precisely, a shift in a structural position.

Therefore, falling in love in *Cluny Brown* is unlike falling in love in most other romantic comedies. In other romantic comedies, like *She's All That* (1999) or *Pretty Woman* (1990), love is used as a way to normalize one of the partners, to find a place for what doesn't belong (typically, through an elevation of status). In *Cluny Brown*, however, love doesn't bring Cluny and Belinski together in order to normalize one, or even both, of the partners. Indeed, the exact opposite is the case. Love in this film pours fuel on Cluny's passion for plumbing, allowing it to burst forth like an exploding ember. Rather than normalize one of the partners, love in *Cluny Brown* brings the couple together so that they may not belong together. That is to say, Cluny falls in love with Belinski, not so that she can finally find her place in society (as a wife, for example). Instead, she falls in love with Belinski to signal that she too doesn't have a place in society, that she too is without a tent. This is why when Cluny asks Belinski where the train is going, he doesn't answer *London*, even though the train is indeed heading to London, but, rather, "general delivery." Where this group of two is heading is not to London or America, or any other *place* for that matter; rather, they are heading to the non-place itself, the place of "general delivery."

VI

McGowan claims that what doesn't have a place in the social order is the universal as such. Like the society that cannot incorporate Cluny's anamorphic passion for plumbing, no structure is complete. All structures, McGowan points out, contain a barrier, and "this barrier marks their failure." The structure's barrier is what doesn't have a place within it, and "the point that doesn't fit in within a structure," writes McGowan, "… is the point of universality."[25] Cluny's passion for plumbing is just such a figure of universality. Yet, it isn't universal because she shares this passion with Belinski, for universality, McGowan argues, doesn't form out of "a quality that multiple particulars possess in common." "The universal," he continues, "is what particulars share not having."[26] Otherwise put, the universal is a common absence between us, "a shared nonbelonging."[27] So, if Cluny's passion for plumbing is universal, it is not because she and Belinski share it in common; rather, it is because this passion doesn't have a place in society just like Belinski, and as such, it allows Cluny and Belinski to share the same status, the status of nonbelonging or general delivery.

What takes place on the train platform then is none other than the formation of a collective. When Cluny inhibits her search for a place, she forms a bond with Belinski insofar as he too has inhibited his search for a place. What makes Cluny and Belinski a collective therefore is not that they put their various eccentricities together—Cluny, the plumber and Belinski, the writer—as collectives do not form, McGowan writes, "by adding up individual elements together." "Instead," he continues, "collectivity exists from the beginning through the connection that forms in the shared limit that the particulars have, through their shared way of relating to the universal."[28] What makes Cluny and Belinski a collective, in other words, is their common link to the universal, a link that they make in their own way: Cluny through her passion for plumbing and Belinski through his status as a refugee. For this reason, for Cluny to form a couple with Belinski, she doesn't need to align her passion with Belinski's future aspirations, like a good supportive wife; that is, they don't have to find common ground. All that she must do is inhibit her desire to remain ignorant of what she already knows is true: that she too has her mail delivered general delivery.

This then is how I suggest we must read the final scene of *Cluny Brown*. In this scene, Cluny and Belinski are now married and living in New York. They pass by a bookstore window, which has on display Belinski's latest novel, a mystery entitled *The Nightingale Murder*. They kiss and are immediately confronted by a police officer. Cluny faints due to her pregnancy, and a new book appears in the window, *The Nightingale Strikes Again*, signaling that Belinski is hard at work supporting their growing family. This is an odd ending to be sure as it feels contrary to the rest of the film. There is no sign of Cluny's plumbing, and it appears that Cluny and Belinski have finally found their place in America. For that reason, it is easy to dismiss this scene or, worse, to read it as a betrayal of the film itself. However, I want to suggest an alternative reading. Instead of reading this scene as suggesting that Cluny and Belinski have betrayed the remainder within them for a new image, I want to read it as reiterating Cluny and Belinski's lack of place. In this way, I want to suggest that this final scene depicts, not a betrayal of the remainder but, rather, the life that is possible by ceding the image—the life of the universal collective.[29]

Crucial to my reading is this scene's composition. Instead of shooting the scene from outside the bookstore, so that Cluny and Belinski appear in the foreground and the bookstore in the background, which would have the effect of placing them on the same side as the audience, Lubitsch does the opposite. He shoots the scene from within the bookstore, such that the store window separates Cluny and Belinski from the camera and, through the camera, the audience. This is to be sure an odd way to compose the final— and arguably, most important—scene of the film, as we are unable to hear Cluny and Belinski speak. We can still make out what they are saying by reading their gestures and lip movements, but crucially, we cannot hear their voices. Because of this odd composition, the final scene feels somewhat anticlimactic, especially when compared to, say, the bombastic finale of *Bringing Up Baby* (1938) or the loquacious finale of *His Girl Friday* (1940). Nevertheless, it is not a mistake for Lubitsch to have composed the scene this way, for by placing the window between Cluny and Belinski and the audience, Lubitsch maintains the theme of nonbelonging by isolating them from us. That is to say, because the window literally separates us from Cluny and Belinski, they are prevented from finding a place with us, the audience; they are on the other side of us. This motif is then reiterated at the level of sound, as the window robs Cluny and Belinski of their voice. (And let's not forget that for Lacan the voice is "capable of belonging to the realm of yieldable objects."[30]) Because of their silence, it sounds as if the film's score, which plays over the image, belongs on our side of the window, not theirs. Or, to put it another way, the film's score makes it sound as if we're the ones in the film, not Cluny and Belinski. Somehow they have lost their place even in their own movie. So, Cluny and Belinski still don't have a place, which means that what is depicted in this finale is not the life that is possible if we betray our thing and find a place in the world but, rather, the life that is possible when we never find that place, the life of general delivery.

On this interpretation, this scene issues an implicit challenge to the audience. By placing the window between us and Cluny and Belinski, not only does Lubitsch underscore their lack of belonging; ingeniously, he also positions us in the place of belonging. In so doing, Lubitsch puts the question to us, the audience. Will we recognize in the Cluny-Belinski collective the signifier of our own lack of place and, therefore, reach through the glass and join them, just as the New Yorkers who've gathered around them seem to have done? Or, will we blot out "the something of substance" in their couple and remain on our side of the glass?

What the Cluny-Belinksi couple embody then is none other than the psychoanalytic group itself. Not the group of analysts that is forever dissolving itself and disbanding, as Badiou (and Lacan) thinks it is, but the group of all those who have abandoned the image by identifying their thing with the nonplace of the object *a*, not only the genius but "every single one of us" who "situate[s] the *a* as such in the field of the Other," which is simply another way of saying that the genius is *anyone* who inhibits their ignorance and cedes the image by situating themselves in "the same series as the *a*."[31] It is not a group that suffers from the so-called imaginary or group effect, as it is not predicated on the image, but one that is formed precisely in its inhibition—that is, not a collection of individuals who relate to each other as ego to ego, but a collective of geniuses who relate to each other as *a* to *a*. And it is not a group that idealizes a person and turns them into the leader, for it is not a group that is enamored with the prospect of recovering original narcissism, since it owes its very existence to the loss of that narcissism and the lack of place that comes with it. As such, it is not a group that stabilizes and hardens into a single Identity because it is a group that is permanently aware of the lack of this Identity, a lack that produces a forepleasure all its own. A group that can never dissolve because it is always under construction, as it is always adding those who don't belong to its number. Let this group be defined as such: *a psychoanalytic group of this kind is a number of geniuses who have ceded the image and have consequently taken up the place of the remainder, the place of the excrement.*

Conclusion: Drive within the Limits of Death Alone

I

As I bring *Genius After Psychoanalysis* to a close, I want to return to a topic that I left in abeyance in Chapter 3. The death drive. For a theory that defines the drive as a "continuously flowing source of stimulation," the idea of natural death is a problem.[1] If the drive is *continuously flowing*, then how can one ever die of natural or internal causes? Every death, it seems, would have an external cause. So, does natural death exist? In 1920, in one of his wildest and most speculative books, *Beyond the Pleasure Principle*, Freud set out to answer this exact question.

The ostensible occasion for *Beyond the Pleasure Principle* is the question of whether the pleasure principle—that is, the tendency "to free the mental apparatus entirely from excitation or to keep the amount of excitation in it constant or to keep it as low as possible"—serves as the ultimate horizon of human experience or if something else, some other motive or principle, exists somewhere beyond it.[2] By the time of its writing, Freud had accumulated decades of clinical experience, and nearly all of it pointed to the same conclusion. Pleasure is the ultimate principle governing all human behavior, and beyond it, there is nothing. And Freud would have indeed accepted this conclusion had it not been for one phenomenon which he encountered in the clinic: the compulsion to repeat.

II

In his clinical work, Freud saw a class of patients who, while various in their particularities, all exhibited one similarity. They all repeated their original trauma, as if they were "fixated" with it.[3] What is so puzzling about this phenomenon—Freud calls it *traumatic neurosis* but today we call it post-traumatic stress disorder—is that there is no pleasure at stake in it. And yet, these patients do it all the same, as if possessed. So, what is driving this compulsion to repeat, if not the pleasure principle?

Freud's initial hypothesis is that repetition comes out of an attempt to master the trauma. The inspiration for this hypothesis is Freud's grandson. One day, Freud observes his grandson playing a game. In this game, Freud's grandson tosses a wooden reel, which is tied to a string, out of his crib and then retrieves it with a yank of the string. On Freud's interpretation, this game of *fort/da* (gone/there), as it has come to be known, is an attempt to master the unpredictable movements of the mother. By tossing the reel out of his crib, Freud's grandson simulates the unpleasurable disappearances of the mother in order to feel that he is the one in control of the mother's otherwise inexplicable movements. "At the outset he was in a *passive* situation," Freud writes, "... but, by repeating it, unpleasurable though it was, as a game, he took on an *active* part."[4]

But there are two problems with this, call it, mastery hypothesis. The first problem is the mastery itself. Mastery cannot be "beyond the pleasure principle" because, while the process that leads to it might not be pleasurable, the end result certainly is. The child repeats the mother's disappearance, and while this repetition in itself is unpleasurable, as a result of it, the child now experiences the mother's disappearances as a fulfillment of its own wishes, and not as something done to it. "All right, then, go away! I don't need you. I'm sending you away myself," the child seems to say. Somewhere along the way, however, the repetition itself suddenly becomes pleasurable, revealing that mastery is not ultimately antithetical to the pleasure principle, despite how it begins. Freud thus concludes: "We are therefore left in doubt as to whether the impulse to work over in the mind some overpowering experience so as to make oneself master of it can find expression as a primary event, and independently of the pleasure principle."[5]

The second problem with the mastery hypothesis is the very experiences that are repeated. While it may be true that some experiences—such as, the mother's disappearances—can become pleasurable through their repetition, there are some experiences which, Freud admits, "include no possibility of pleasure, and which can never, even long ago, have brought satisfaction even to instinctual impulses which have since been repressed."[6] Very clearly, Freud here recognizes the existence of experiences that bring absolutely *no possibility of pleasure*. One such experience, he claims, is the trauma that his patients repeat in the consulting room. That is to say, Freud's point is not that all traumas—no matter how horrific—can eventually become a source of pleasure but, rather, the exact opposite. Certain traumas, no matter how many times they are repeated, never produce pleasure.

Freud enumerates a long list of such traumas—indeed, his list spans three pages.[7] Of these I only want to mention one, as it is relevant to the discussion of genius that has been taking place in these pages. That trauma is the failure of the infantile sexual researches.[8] Thus, some fifteen years after writing *Three Essays on the Theory of Sexuality*, Freud still insists on the failure of this, our earliest intellectual experiences. Indeed, if anything, his insistence has only grown stronger, as he names the infantile sexual researches to underline their unmasterability.

So, then, why do Freud's patients repeat their trauma, if not for pleasure? It can only be that pleasure is not the principle behind all human activity, that there is something else—something "more primitive, more elementary, more instinctual"—beyond it, which motivates the repetition.[9] That something else, Freud claims, is the death drive.

III

Freud defines death as the "return to the quiescence of the inorganic world."[10] Death, in other words, is the complete expenditure of all the psyche's excitations, and the return to the calm silence of inanimation—or, in a word, "complete satisfaction."[11] Life then, on this view, is not a mysterious phenomenon that requires complicated explanations, nor the by-product of some inherent striving for progress and development. Rather, it is quite simply the path that the organism takes toward this goal of quiescence.[12]

The picture that Freud leaves us with then is this. An organism wants to die in its own fashion—that is, it wants to return to its original inorganic state. But it is prevented from doing so by obstacles in the environment and is therefore forced to prolong its life in order to achieve its own unique death. This resolute determination to return to its original state— not simply to die but to die in its own particular manner—is what Freud calls *the death drive*. This is how he describes it: the death drive is "an urge inherent in organic life to restore an earlier state of things which the living entity has been obliged to abandon under the pressure of external disturbing forces."[13]

The death drive is what thwarts all those endeavors, both good and bad, that cause us to deviate from the path to our unique death. It is also what stands behind the phenomenon of repetition compulsion. Thus, if a person sabotages their relationships, even when these relationships are good and pleasurable, it is because these relationships take that person farther afield from its unique death. And if the patient repeats their trauma in the consulting room, it is because death has priority over all of life's pleasures. And if the genius repeats the failures of their infantile sexual researches, it is because this failure is the truth of our being—that "earlier state of things" to which we all strive, albeit unconsciously.

IV

That was Freud's conclusion in 1920. Something does indeed exist beyond the pleasure principle, and that something is the death drive. A truly radical conclusion! And though Freud would never again engage in the kind of wild speculation on animalcules and germ cells that is found throughout *Beyond the Pleasure Principle*, the conclusion to which this speculation led—namely, that the death drive exists and it is prior to the pleasure principle—would remain, informing the last two decades of his thought. And yet, for all its radicality, if we pay close enough attention to Freud's account, we can still detect the slightest hint of hesitancy on his part, as if he could not bring himself to finally remove the pleasure principle from its post as "the watchman over our mental life."[14]

This last claim of mine requires further elaboration, as it is not immediately obvious. Though it may appear that Freud's account of the death drive completely unseats the pleasure principle from its position of dominance, my claim is that it in fact preserves it, this time within the death drive itself. Death, we must remember, in Freud's definition, is the absolute expenditure of all stimulus and the return to quiescence—"complete satisfaction," to use Freud's own words. By making the death drive aim at this target of complete satisfaction, Freud introduces, if not the pleasure principle itself, then its underlying economic logic insofar as pleasure too is defined as "a *diminution*" in the quantity of stimulus.[15] Thus, the death drive—at least, as far as it is presented in *Beyond the Pleasure Principle*—is not so much beyond the pleasure principle as it is the pleasure principle in new form. Or, as Freud himself puts it, "The pleasure principle seems actually to serve the death instincts."[16]

The problem with smuggling pleasure into the death drive in this manner is that it puts the latter at odds with the idea of the drive as a "continuously flowing source of stimulation." If the drive is a source of continuous stimulation, as Freud claims, and if the death drive is the urge to return to the state of quiescence, as Freud also claims, then the death drive begins to resemble the pleasure principle insofar as it too aims at expending all the excitations that emanate from the drive. And if this is the case, then what accounts for the drive's constancy? Where does the "continuously flowing source of stimulation" come from? It is out of this confusion that Freud develops the idea of the so-called life drive or Eros.

The life drive, Freud claims, is a drive that is "constantly producing tensions whose release is felt as pleasure."[17] If this definition feels familiar, it is because it is the very definition of the drive as such, as the drive too is a constant source of tension. Doesn't this mean that the so-called life drive is none other than the drive as such? It seems then that what Freud has done is introduce a new drive—the life drive or Eros—in order to account for what is in reality the normal functioning of the drive as such. Yet, if this is indeed correct—if the drive's constancy derives from a life drive—then Freud would have to abandon any notion of natural death, since the originary force at work within the psyche would be life- and not death-giving. To be sure, it is still possible that this original life-giving drive can become sabotaged from within by the death drive, but the mere fact of its existence would throw the entire premise of natural death into question, as it would no longer be clear why the life drive would lose out to the death drive in the first place. And without the premise of natural death ready to hand, Freud would lose all ability to explain the phenomenon of repetition compulsion. To wit, if the drive is life-giving, even if only in part, then why do we repeat death, and not life? Perhaps, this is why Freud simply glosses over the issue of "internal excitations" in *Beyond the Pleasure Principle*, saying only that it is where the psychic mechanism of projection originates and that the pleasure principle is "especially on guard against increases of stimulation from within"—hardly a sufficient discussion![18]

It is of course possible to reconcile the death drive with the conception of the drive as a source of constant stimulation, but to do so, one must be willing to do what Freud could not. Namely, eliminate every last vestige of the pleasure principle from the death drive and finally unseat the pleasure principle, once and for all, from its position as that "watchman over our mental life." Only then can one be said to have gone truly beyond the pleasure principle.

V

The issue with Freud's account is not that it grasps death as the return to quiescence; it is, rather, that it conflates this notion of death with the death drive itself. Because of this conflation, the death drive appears to Freud as something at odds with the drive inasmuch as the one always impels toward the increase of tension while the other always toward its decrease. To resolve this seeming contradiction, Freud erects a dualism so that a separate and distinct drive can account for each of these movements: the so-called life drive or Eros for increase and the death drive or Thanatos for decrease.

Now, the problem with this dualism, as I have argued, is that it doesn't in fact surpass the pleasure principle, as Freud believes it does, but simply recreates it on a higher plane in the form of life and death itself. Thus, to reconcile Freud's account, what is needed is to decouple the death drive from death, and to grasp the former, instead, as integral to the drive itself. That is to say, we must grasp the death drive, not as a separate and distinct drive unto itself, which can then be turned around and opposed to some other separate and distinct drive, as if this opposition were an external opposition, but, rather, as an aspect or feature of the drive itself. Once reconciled in this way, there is no need for a dualist conception of the drive, for the opposition between life and death now appears dialectical—that is, not as an external opposition between life and death, as Freud mistakes it to be, but as an internal opposition within death itself.

What does it mean to grasp the death drive as integral to the drive itself? It means to grasp the death drive, not as a separate entity unto itself but as a function of the drive as such, a function that causes the pleasure principle to malfunction and fail. The drive is, as we know, constantly producing stimulus, which the pleasure principle wants to expend, thereby keeping "the amount of excitation in it constant" or "as low as possible."[19] And if nothing went awry in this relationship, the drive and the pleasure principle would form a perfectly complementary pair, resulting in the predictable ebbs and flows of psychic life. After consecutive days of rigorous exercise, one would, as a rule, take a day off. We would always complete our projects on time, and Freud's grandson would always make his lost spindle reappear. And, of course, we would have no memory of a past trauma. But, as we know from Freud's clinical experience, and perhaps from our own personal experiences as well, the rhythms of psychic life are never predictable. The pleasure principle may decree that it is good to avoid the increase of tension by expending the stimulus that flows from the drive, but inexplicably, the drive doesn't comply. After consecutive days of rigorous exercise, it does not always follow that we take that well-earned rest day. We sometimes choose another day of exercise instead, even if such a choice comes at the detriment of our own health. Delays preserve a state of tension, and yet, we choose to procrastinate, putting off our projects until the very last conceivable moment. Freud observed that his grandson often did not play his game to completion. Instead, "the first act, that of departure, was staged as a game in itself and far more frequently than the episode in its entirety, with its pleasurable ending."[20] And, of course, as we know from Freud's clinical findings, the human mind does indeed keep the memories of trauma stored up, such that they are repeatedly recalled and relived, as if the human mind doesn't so much possess traumatic memories as it is possessed by them.

Thus, the drive and the pleasure principle do not form a complementary pair at all. There is something about the drive, like it has some kind of design flaw, that puts it at odds with the pleasure principle, that makes it antagonistic toward the dual goals of "an avoidance of unpleasure" and "a production of pleasure," which skews the relationship always toward the accumulation of stimulus—that is, toward unpleasure.[21] That is to say, we should not think of the drive as passively supplying the stimulus that the pleasure principle expends. There is a force or initiative behind its production that gives it an element of intention, such that we must always think of the drive as actively producing stimulus in order to thwart or undermine the pleasure principle.

It may be tempting to construe the issue as a lack of incentive, but to do so would be a mistake, for the path of expenditure is absolutely laden with incentives—the pleasure principle guarantees it. The issue is not that the drive demands proper compensation from the pleasure principle and withholds its cooperation until it receives it. The issue is rather that the drive doesn't share the pleasure principle's imperatives: "an avoidance of unpleasure" and "the production of pleasure" are simply not what concerns the drive. Motivating the drive is something far different, an imperative that does not fit well within the language of the pleasure principle. Indeed, it is an imperative that is beyond this language—the imperative of the death drive.

VI

As you may have already noticed, we have already done away with Freud's dualist conception of the drives. In the account that I have just given, there are not two distinct drives—the life drive and the death drive—but only one: the drive as such, that is, the drive as a "continuously flowing source of stimulation." However, and this is the crucial point, it is not a drive that is fully reconciled within itself—and thus without contradiction—but, rather, one that bears a split. On one hand, it is a drive that must expend its surpluses in order to avoid tension and pain (i.e., the pleasure principle). But on the other hand, it is also a drive that constantly obstructs and sabotages the attainment of this aim by producing those very surpluses (i.e., the death drive). There may only be one drive, but it is a drive that is incommensurate with itself—a drive that is not whole.

Now, Freud knew very well that the idea of the death drive was—and still is—a difficult one to accept. But he also recognized that without it, one would turn the drive into a monism, much in the way that Jung did with the libido.[22] Indeed, it is for this very reason that Freud developed his dualist model of the drives in the first place. And so, it may appear that in rejecting Freud's dualism, and insisting on a single drive, that I myself have realized Freud's worst fears and turned the drive into a monism. But this is not in fact the case. Indeed, it is the exact opposite.

To avoid turning the drive into a monism, it is not enough to posit a second drive to stand against it—that is to say, it is not enough to create a dualism. The problem with this line of thinking is that it concedes to monism the assumption that the drive is indeed internally consistent. Though it contests monism by positing two drives instead of one, dualist thinking, like monism itself, accepts the premise that the two members of the dualism are internally coherent. Otherwise put, for the dualist, the life drive is understood to be a drive that in fact achieves life, and the death drive, death. As such, any conflict that these drives might experience can only be the result of an encounter with an externally opposed force, that is, with the other member of the dualism. If somehow these drives could be isolated from one another, such that they never interacted with each other, then they would in fact each achieve their respective aims and achieve them, presumably, in perpetuity. Thus, if the life drive fails to achieve life, it is not because there is something within it that prevents it from doing so. It is only because it encounters and conflicts with another fully developed drive external to itself called the death drive. So, while it may appear as if the monist conception of the drive has been repudiated, all that has actually happened is that a single monistic drive has been replaced by two monistic drives: the life drive and the death drive. Or, to put it yet another way, Freud's dualism is not opposed to Jung's monism, as Freud mistakenly believes it is, but is itself a kind of monism insofar as it shares with monism a common presupposition. Namely, the existence of a noncontradictory drive.

Thus, to properly oppose a monistic conception of the drive, one shouldn't posit a multiplicity of (monistic) drives but, instead, shed this presupposition of noncontradiction that underwrites it, which means grasping what appears to be an external conflict between two opposing drives as an internal conflict within a single drive. The death drive, on this account, is not simply another drive in a long series of drives, which can, in its independence, come into conflict with all the other members of the series. It is rather an aspect of every drive in this series. Or, as Lacan puts it, "every drive is virtually a death drive."[23]

The drive therefore cannot act as a monism because it does not have the requisite internal consistency to be one in the first place. Part of the drive aims at its own annihilation through the complete expenditure of all its stimulus—this is the part that is determined by the pleasure principle. But it is opposed or, rather, undermined by another part of *itself*, which aims at the constant production of stimulus—and this is the part that is determined by the death drive. And yet, despite the fact that the death drive opposes the return to quiescence, we should not construe it as the expression of life itself, for to do so would be to make the same mistake as Freud, albeit in the opposite direction: that is to say, we would once again be grasping the death drive as a monistic entity, although this time as a life-giving one. Rather, we must retain in Freud the death drive's association with death, even as we must reject its conflation with the return to quiescence, which is simply another way of saying that the death drive is death by the accumulation of stimulus. This then is that form of death which comes as the product of one's "*own metabolism*," which Freud finds so striking in biology: not only does the absolute expenditure of all stimulus kill the organism, so too does the ordinary activity of the drive itself, that is, the constant production of stimulus.[24]

Death therefore comes at the organism from two directions, both of them internal. On one hand, death comes from the direction of absolute expenditure (i.e., the return to quiescence), and on the other hand, it comes from the direction of the constancy of the drive itself (i.e., the death drive)—internal death indeed! Crucial, then, is the nonexistence of the life drive or Eros. There is no original or bare life. All there is in the organism is death—bare death, if you will. But, and this is absolutely crucial, it is a death that is at odds with itself, a death that seeks to accomplish its work, on one hand, by expending every last quantity of stimulus and, on the other hand, by contradictorily producing endless supplies of stimulus. Two halves that don't add up to a whole. That phenomenon called life emerges out of this contradiction within death, which is to say, if organisms don't die immediately, it isn't because there is some sort of life drive keeping it alive, as Freud mistakenly believes, but only because death fails to fully realize itself. We live, not because we possess some kind of originary bare life but simply because we fail to die: such is the ultimate implication of the death drive.

VII

In *Leonardo da Vinci and a Memory of His Childhood*, Freud gave an account that laid the groundwork for a psychoanalytic theory of genius predicated on the sublimation of the drive, that is, on the drive's "power to replace its immediate aim by other aims which may be valued more highly and which are not sexual."[25] The genius then is the one who has replaced the aim of the pleasurable expenditure of stimulus with the aim of its unpleasurable accumulation. Or, to put it within the language of *Beyond the Pleasure Principle*: the genius is the one who has replaced the aim of the pleasure principle with the aim of the death drive.

But despite all appearances, we must take care to avoid understanding this embrace of the death drive as a morbid or melancholic fixation on death. Indeed, the one who truly exhibits a morbid fixation on death is the hedonist who represses or otherwise denies the death drive by making the pursuit of pleasure the highest good. For in denying the death drive and pursuing the pleasure principle to its fullest, the hedonist eliminates the very source of life itself, namely, the contradiction within death. Far from embracing life, the hedonist's full-throated pursuit of pleasure is an attempt to find the shortest path to the complete expenditure of all stimulus—they are in other words the true being toward death.

The genius, on the other hand, embraces, not so much life itself as much as the other side of death. By sublimating the death drive, the genius prolongs life, not by directly aiming at it but by maintaining the contradiction that enables it: namely, the contradiction within death itself. Thus, if it can be said that the hedonist is a being toward death, insofar as it is they who abandon the contradiction that leads to life, then the genius is the being who fails at being a being toward death—a failure that puts them on that long detour called life.

Notes

Introduction

1. Søren Kierkegaard, "Of the Difference between a Genius and an Apostle," in *The Present Age: On the Death of Rebellion*, trans. Alexander Dru (New York: Harper Perennial, 1962), 68, original emphasis.
2. Francis Galton, *Hereditary Genius: An Inquiry into Its Laws and Consequences* (New York: Macmillan, 1892), v, 4.
3. Galton, *Hereditary Genius*, v.
4. Galton, *Hereditary Genius*, 1.
5. Catherine Malabou, *Morphing Intelligence: From IQ Measurement to Artificial Brains*, trans. Carolyn Shread (New York: Columbia University Press, 2019), 20.
6. Immanuel Kant, *Critique of the Power of Judgment*, trans. Paul Guyer and Eric Matthews (Cambridge: Cambridge University Press, 2000), 186, original emphasis. Catherine Malabou offers a new interpretation of nature in Kant as epigenesis, which has the potential of changing Kant's relationship to innatism. See, Catherine Malabou, *Before Tomorrow: Epigenesis and Rationality*, trans. Carolyn Shread (Cambridge: Polity, 2016).
7. Full disclosure: one of my children was identified as "gifted."
8. Malcolm Gladwell, *Outliers: The Story of Success* (New York: Back Bay, 2008), 19, original emphasis.
9. Gladwell, *Outliers*, 46.
10. Gladwell, *Outliers*, 42, 43.
11. Gladwell, *Outliers*, 55.
12. Hegel writes, "True thoughts and scientific insight can only be won by the labor of the concept." Georg Wilhelm Friedrich Hegel, *The Phenomenology of Spirit*, trans. Terry Pinkard (Cambridge: Cambridge University Press, 2018), 44.
13. Despite my criticism of Stratchey's translation of *Trieb*, I will make no attempt to correct the text when I quote from the Standard Edition in the interest of avoiding confusion. Instead, I will rely on the reader to understand that where Stratchey uses the word "instinct," Freud is using the word *Trieb* or drive.
14. Assuming Dion spent one hour per shoe shopping, does that make her a genius of shoes?
15. Slavoj Žižek, *The Parallax View* (Cambridge, MA: MIT Press, 2009), 4. For the notion of parallax, Žižek is heavily indebted to Kojin Karatani, who himself is indebted to Kant. See, Kojin Karatani, *Transcritique: On Kant and Marx*, trans. Sabu Kohso (Cambridge, MA: MIT Press, 2005).

16 Sigmund Freud, *Group Psychology and the Analysis of the Ego*, trans. James Strachey, in *The Standard Edition of the Complete Psychological Works of Sigmund Freud*, ed. James Strachey, vol. 18 (London: Hogarth, 1955), 113.
17 Freud, *Group Psychology*, 100.

Part One

1 Sigmund Freud, *Leonardo da Vinci and a Memory of His Childhood*, trans. Alan Tyson, in *The Standard Edition of the Complete Psychological Works of Sigmund Freud*, ed. James Strachey, vol. 11 (London: Hogarth, 1957), 63. I would be remiss if I did not address the issue of mistranslation in *Leonardo*. Freud devotes considerable space to a fantasy of Leonardo's, supposedly involving a vulture. The word that Freud takes to mean "vulture" is the Italian word *nibio*, which means *kite*, not *vulture*. For some, this mistake of Freud's invalidates the entire book. I, on the other hand, share Strachey's opinion: "It will, however, be a good plan to examine the situation more coolly and consider in detail the exact respects in which Freud's arguments and conclusions are invalidated." Freud, *Leonardo*, 61. If one disregards the vulture fantasy, what remains valid—and therefore valuable—in *Leonardo* are Freud's speculations on Leonardo's relationship to science, the incompletion of his artworks, and his relationship to love and hate, all of which is independent of the vulture fantasy. More than that, what remains valid—and vitally important—is the account of sublimation he gives in it, which is still the most comprehensive account we have of this enigmatic concept, and which also has nothing to do with the vulture fantasy. What will serve my purposes in this book therefore are those aspects of *Leonardo* only, and definitively not the vulture fantasy. Thus, the thorny issue of Freud's mistranslation has absolutely no bearing on what will follow in these pages.
2 Freud, *Leonardo*, 63, 64.
3 Freud, *Leonardo*, 63.
4 Freud, *Leonardo*, 76.
5 Freud, *Leonardo*, 65.
6 Freud does devote some critical attention to *Mona Lisa* (the rest of Leonardo's artwork receive barely more than a mention). He offers a reading of the painting as a reconstruction of Leonardo's childhood—"the synthesis of the history of his childhood," as he puts it—and of Mona Lisa herself as the condensation of the various important women in Leonardo's life. But, crucially, Freud does not use *Mona Lisa* as the material for his theory of genius. Freud, *Leonardo*, 112.
7 Freud, *Leonardo*, 92, emphasis added.
8 Freud, *Leonardo*, 78.

Chapter 1

1. Sigmund Freud, *Leonardo da Vinci and a Memory of His Childhood*, trans. Alan Tyson, in *The Standard Edition of the Complete Psychological Works of Sigmund Freud*, ed. James Strachey, vol. 11 (London: Hogarth, 1957), 66.
2. Freud, *Leonardo*, 65.
3. Freud, *Leonardo*, 64.
4. Freud, *Leonardo*, 77.
5. Giorgio Vasari, *The Lives of the Artists*, trans. Julia Conaway Bondanella and Peter Bondanella (Oxford: Oxford University Press, 1998), 294.
6. Freud, *Leonardo*, 66.
7. Freud, *Leonardo*, 66.
8. Freud, *Leonardo*, 68.
9. Freud, *Leonardo*, 69.
10. Freud, *Leonardo*, 69.
11. Freud, *Leonardo*, 73, 74.
12. The idea that love motivates learning is one that has a basis in philosophy. See Socrates's speech in *The Symposium*. Plato, *The Symposium*, trans. Michael Joyce, in *The Collected Dialogues of Plato: Including the Letters*, eds. Edith Hamilton and Huntington Cairns (Princeton: Princeton University Press, 2009), 526–74.
13. Freud, *Leonardo*, 74.
14. See Sigmund Freud, *Group Psychology and the Analysis of the Ego*, trans. James Strachey, in *The Standard Edition of the Complete Psychological Works of Sigmund Freud*, ed. James Strachey, vol. 18 (London: Hogarth, 1955). I return to the topic of groups in Part Three of this book.
15. Freud, *Leonardo*, 74, original emphasis.
16. Freud, *Leonardo*, 74.
17. Freud, *Leonardo*, 74.
18. See, for example, Søren Kierkegaard, *Fear and Trembling*, trans. Howard V. Hong and Edna H. Hong, in *Fear and Trembling/Repetition: Kierkegaard's Writings*, eds. Howard V. Hong and Edna H. Hong, vol. 6 (Princeton: Princeton University Press, 1983), 1–124.
19. Freud, *Leonardo*, 77.
20. Freud, *Leonardo*, 76.
21. Freud, *Leonardo*, 77.
22. Freud, *Leonardo*, 76.
23. Freud, *Leonardo*, 77.

Chapter 2

1. Sigmund Freud, *Three Essays on the Theory of Sexuality*, trans. James Strachey, in *The Standard Edition of the Complete Psychological Works of Sigmund Freud*, ed. James Strachey, vol. 7 (London: Hogarth, 1953), 168.

Because he defines the drive in quantitative terms, this aspect of Freud's metapsychology is known as the "economic" dimension. The other two dimensions are the "topological" and the "dynamic"—that is, the ego, the id, and the superego; and repression, respectively.

2 Freud's word for the opposite of pleasure is *Unlust*, which translates literally to "unpleasure." While there is a nuanced difference between "unpleasure" and "pain" (i.e., not everything that is an unpleasure is pain), I will use the two terms interchangeably for the sake of readability, preferring in most cases the more idiomatic "pain."

3 Sigmund Freud, "Formulations on the Two Principles of Mental Functioning," trans. M.N. Searl, in *The Standard Edition of the Complete Psychological Works of Sigmund Freud*, ed. James Strachey, vol. 12 (London: Hogarth, 1958), 219.

4 Sigmund Freud, *Beyond the Pleasure Principle*, trans. James Strachey, in *The Standard Edition of the Complete Psychological Works of Sigmund Freud*, ed. James Strachey, vol. 18 (London: Hogarth, 1955), 7.

5 Sigmund Freud, "Instincts and Their Vicissitudes," trans. C.M. Baines, in *The Standard Edition of the Complete Psychological Works of Sigmund Freud*, ed. James Strachey, vol. 14 (London: Hogarth, 1957), 137.

6 Freud, "Instincts and Their Vicissitudes," 139.

7 Freud, "Instincts and Their Vicissitudes," 118, original emphasis.

8 Freud, "Instincts and Their Vicissitudes," 118, original emphasis.

9 Freud, "Instincts and Their Vicissitudes," 118.

10 Freud, "Instincts and Their Vicissitudes," 118.

11 Freud, "Instincts and Their Vicissitudes," 119.

12 Sigmund Freud, "On Narcissism: An Introduction," trans. C.M. Baines, in *The Standard Edition of the Complete Psychological Works of Sigmund Freud*, ed. James Strachey, vol. 14 (London: Hogarth, 1957), 85–6.

13 Elsewhere, Freud presents the mind in more passive tones: "Thinking was endowed with characteristics which made it possible for the mental apparatus to tolerate an increased tension of stimulus while the process of discharge was postponed." Freud, "Formulations on the Two Principles of Mental Functioning," 221.

14 Sigmund Freud, *Leonardo da Vinci and a Memory of His Childhood*, trans. Alan Tyson, in *The Standard Edition of the Complete Psychological Works of Sigmund Freud*, ed. James Strachey, vol. 11 (London: Hogarth, 1957), 80; Freud, "Formulations on the Two Principles of Mental Functioning," 224; Freud, *Leonardo*, 80.

15 Freud, *Three Essays*, 136.

16 Freud, "Instincts and Their Vicissitudes," 122.

17 Freud, *Leonardo*, 78.

18 On sublimation representing a contradiction in Freud, Jacques Lacan comments: "[Freud], therefore, introduces the idea of an opposition, an antinomy, as fundamental in the construction of the sublimation of

an instinct. He thus introduces the problem of a contradiction in his own formulation." Jacques Lacan, *The Seminar of Jacques Lacan, Book VII: The Ethics of Psychoanalysis, 1959–1960*, ed. Jacques-Alain Miller and trans. Dennis Porter (New York: Norton, 1992), 95. Todd McGowan has demonstrated the crucial importance of contradiction in social and political life. See Todd McGowan, *Emancipation after Hegel: Achieving a Contradictory Revolution* (New York: Columbia University Press, 2001).
19 Freud, *Leonardo*, 78.
20 Freud, *Leonardo*, 79.
21 Freud, *Leonardo*, 79–80.
22 Freud, *Leonardo*, 80.
23 Freud, *Leonardo*, 80.
24 Freud, *Leonardo*, 80.
25 Strachey speculates that sublimation may have been the topic of a lost metapsychological paper.
26 Freud, *Leonardo*, 80.
27 Freud, *Three Essays*, 135.
28 Freud, *Three Essays*, 149.
29 Freud, *Three Essays*, 149.
30 Freud, *Three Essays*, 184.
31 So, Adam Phillips is wrong. Psychoanalysis is not "what two people can say to each other if they agree not to have sex." Adam Phillips, "Introduction," in *Wild Analysis*, ed. Adam Phillips (London: Penguin, 2002), xx. What this clever-sounding formulation overlooks is the sexual factor of talk itself. Simply because we're not in the habit of thinking of talk as sexual doesn't make it a nonsexual aim, at least not as far as psychoanalysis is concerned. Compare Phillips's comment with this one from Lacan: "[F]or the moment, I am not fucking, I am talking with you. Well! I can have exactly the same satisfaction as if I were fucking." Jacques Lacan, *The Seminar of Jacques Lacan, Book XI: The Four Fundamental Concepts of Psychoanalysis*, ed. Jacques-Alain Miller and trans. Alan Sheridan (New York: Norton, 1981), 165–6. Unlike Phillips, Lacan recognizes that talk itself can be a sexual aim. Perhaps, a better description of psychoanalysis might be: psychoanalysis is what two people can say to each other if they agree to have sex *only* by talking.
32 Freud, "Instincts and Their Vicissitudes," 122.
33 Freud, "Instincts and Their Vicissitudes," 122.
34 Sigmund Freud, "'Wild' Psycho-Analysis," trans. Joan Riviere, in *The Standard Edition of the Complete Psychological Works of Sigmund Freud*, ed. James Strachey, vol. 11 (London: Hogarth, 1957), 222.
35 Freud, "Narcissism," 94.
36 Sigmund Freud, "Types of Onset of Neurosis," trans. James Strachey, in *The Standard Edition of the Complete Psychological Works of Sigmund Freud*, ed. James Strachey, vol. 12 (London: Hogarth, 1958), 232.

37 This is of course Kant's formula for aesthetic judgments, and not his formula for the genius, which as we discussed in the introduction is predicated on natural talent.
38 Freud quotes Reitler thus: "The male genital on the other hand is depicted by Leonardo much more correctly." Freud, *Leonardo*, 71 n.
39 Freud, *Leonardo*, 72 n.
40 Freud, *Leonardo*, 70 n., 71.
41 Freud, *Leonardo*, 70 n. While Freud doesn't challenge Reitler directly, he cites the fact that Reitler's views have been criticized: "These remarks of Reitler's have been criticized, it is true, on the ground that such serious conclusions should not be drawn from a hasty sketch, and that it is not even certain whether the different parts of the drawing really belong together." Freud, *Leonardo*, 72 n.
42 Freud, *Leonardo*, 77.
43 Sigmund Freud, "On the Sexual Theories of Children," trans. D. Bryan, in *The Standard Edition of the Complete Psychological Works of Sigmund Freud*, ed. James Strachey, vol. 9 (London: Hogarth, 1959), 215.
44 Freud, *Leonardo*, 122.

Chapter 3

1 Sigmund Freud, "Two Encyclopedia Articles," trans. James Strachey, in *The Standard Edition of the Complete Psychological Works of Sigmund Freud*, ed. James Strachey, vol. 18 (London: Hogarth, 1955), 256.
2 Sigmund Freud, "The Economic Problem of Masochism," trans. Joan Riviere, in *The Standard Edition of the Complete Psychological Works of Sigmund Freud*, ed. James Strachey, vol. 19 (London: Hogarth, 1961), 160.
3 Jacques Lacan, *The Seminar of Jacques Lacan, Book XX: On Feminine Sexuality, The Limits of Love and Knowledge, 1972–1973 (Encore)*, ed. Jacques-Alain Miller and trans. Bruce Fink (New York: Norton, 1998), 4.
4 Sigmund Freud, *Three Essays on the Theory of Sexuality*, trans. James Strachey, in *The Standard Edition of the Complete Psychological Works of Sigmund Freud*, ed. James Strachey, vol. 7 (London: Hogarth, 1953), 211. He also calls them "preliminary sexual aims." *Three Essays*, 149.
5 Freud, *Three Essays*, 209.
6 Freud, *Three Essays*, 210.
7 Freud, *Three Essays*, 211.
8 Freud, *Three Essays*, 209.
9 Freud, *Three Essays*, 210.
10 Jacques Lacan, *The Seminar of Jacques Lacan, Book VII: The Ethics of Psychoanalysis, 1959–1960*, ed. Jacques-Alain Miller and trans. Dennis Porter (New York: Norton, 1992), 152. The full quote is as follows: "It is only insofar as the pleasure of desiring, or, more precisely, the pleasure

of experiencing unpleasure, is sustained that we can speak of the sexual valorization of the preliminary stages of the act of love." Interestingly, Lacan links the pleasure of unpleasure to desire, thereby suggesting a link between desire and sublimation. I will address the issue of desire in Chapter 4.

11 Freud, *Three Essays*, 210.
12 While "The Economic Problem of Masochism" makes no mention of *Three Essays on the Theory of Sexuality*, the latter does refer to the former in a footnote that Freud added in 1924: "I have made an attempt at solving this problem in the first part of my paper on 'The Economic Problem of Masochism.'" Freud, *Three Essays*, 209 n.1. So, clearly, Freud had access to the concept of forepleasure—if it was not directly on his mind—when he was writing the Masochism paper thus making its omission even more curious.
13 See Sigmund Freud, *Jokes and Their Relation to the Unconscious*, trans. James Strachey, in *The Standard Edition of the Complete Psychological Works of Sigmund Freud*, ed. James Strachey, vol. 8 (London: Hogarth, 1960) and "Creative Writers and Day-Dreaming," trans. I.F. Grant Duff, in *The Standard Edition of the Complete Psychological Works of Sigmund Freud*, ed. James Strachey, vol. 9 (London: Hogarth, 1959).
14 Freud, "Masochism," 161.
15 Freud, "Masochism," 159.

Chapter 4

1 Sigmund Freud, "Types of Onset of Neurosis," trans. James Strachey, in *The Standard Edition of the Complete Psychological Works of Sigmund Freud*, ed. James Strachey, vol. 12 (London: Hogarth, 1958), 232.
2 Sigmund Freud, *Civilization and Its Discontents*, trans. Joan Riviere, in *The Standard Edition of the Complete Psychological Works of Sigmund Freud*, ed. James Strachey, vol. 21 (London: Hogarth, 1964), 128.
3 Freud, *Civilization and Its Discontents*, 129.
4 Freud, *Civilization and Its Discontents*, 129.
5 Depending on what one considers Freud's first major work on guilt, the difference between his account of sublimation and his account of guilt is anywhere between three and twenty years. *Totem and Taboo* was written three years after *Leonardo* while *Civilization and Its Discontents* was written twenty years after. Meanwhile, the essay "Some Character Types Met with in Psycho-Analytic Work," which contains a section on "criminals from a sense of guilt" was written six years after *Leonardo*. In the case of the superego, the difference is thirteen years as *The Ego and the Id* was written in 1923. Of course, there are antecedents to both guilt and the superego which predate *Leonardo*, most notably, the Oedipus complex and the self-observing censor, which are both developed in *The Interpretation of Dreams* written in 1900, ten years before *Leonardo*.

6   Jacques Lacan, *The Seminar of Jacques Lacan, Book VII: The Ethics of Psychoanalysis, 1959–1960*, ed. Jacques-Alain Miller and trans. Dennis Porter (New York: Norton, 1992), 319.
7   Jacques Lacan, *The Seminar of Jacques Lacan, Book VI: Desire and Its Interpretation*, ed. Jacques-Alain Miller and trans. Bruce Fink (Cambridge: Polity, 2019), 476.
8   Jacques Lacan, *The Seminar of Jacques Lacan, Book XI: The Four Fundamental Concepts of Psychoanalysis*, ed. Jacques-Alain Miller and trans. Alan Sheridan (New York: Norton, 1981), 265.
9   For a comprehensive account of capitalism's consequences for the psyche, see Todd McGowan, *Capitalism and Desire: The Psychic Costs of Free Markets* (New York: Columbia University Press, 2016).
10 Lacan, *Ethics*, 219.
11 Lacan, *Ethics*, 319.
12 Lacan, *Ethics*, 321.
13 Lacan, *Ethics*, 193.
14 Lacan says of the pervert, especially the sadist, this: "It is very clear that, for him, the Other exists," Jacques Lacan, in *The Seminar of Jacques Lacan, Book X: Anxiety*, ed. Jacques-Alain Miller and trans. A.R. Price (Cambridge: Polity, 2014), 164. Stephanie Swales comments: "While the obsessive negates the Other in the effort to regain lost jouissance, the Other is necessary for the pervert," Stephanie Swales, in *Perversion: A Lacanian Psychoanalytic Approach to the Subject* (New York: Routledge, 2012), 88.
15 Jacques Lacan, *The Seminar of Jacques Lacan, Book XX: On Feminine Sexuality, the Limits of Love and Knowledge, 1972–1973 (Encore)*, ed. Jacques-Alain Miller and trans. Bruce Fink (New York: Norton, 1998), 3.
16 For an incisive critique of the American Dream see Mari Ruti, *Penis Envy and Other Bad Feelings: The Emotional Costs of Everyday Life* (New York: Columbia University Press, 2021).
17 Lacan, *Ethics*, 314.
18 Lacan, *Ethics*, 230.
19 Lacan, *Ethics*, 152.
20 Lacan, *Anxiety*, 180.

Part Two

1   Jacques Lacan, *The Seminar of Jacques Lacan, Book VII: The Ethics of Psychoanalysis, 1959–1960*, ed. Jacques-Alain Miller and trans. Dennis Porter (New York: Norton, 1992), 94.
2   Sigmund Freud, "On Narcissism: An Introduction," trans. C.M. Baines, in *The Standard Edition of the Complete Psychological Works of Sigmund Freud*, ed. James Strachey, vol. 14 (London: Hogarth, 1957), 88, 89.
3   Freud, "Narcissism," 88.

4 Lacan, *Ethics*, 94.
5 Lacan, *Ethics*, 112.

Chapter 5

1 Sigmund Freud, "Instincts and Their Vicissitudes," trans. C.M. Baines, in *The Standard Edition of the Complete Psychological Works of Sigmund Freud*, ed. James Strachey, vol. 14 (London: Hogarth, 1957), 122.
2 Sigmund Freud, "On Narcissism: An Introduction," trans. C.M. Baines, in *The Standard Edition of the Complete Psychological Works of Sigmund Freud*, ed. James Strachey, vol. 14 (London: Hogarth, 1957), 94.
3 For Freud, the abandonment of the world of objects is characteristic of the psychotic. The psychotic, he writes, "seems really to have withdrawn his libido from people and things in the external world, without replacing them by others in phantasy. When he *does* so replace them, the process seems to be a secondary one and to be part of an attempt at recovery, designed to lead the libido back to objects." Freud, "Narcissism," 74, original emphasis.
4 Sigmund Freud, "Two Encyclopedia Articles," trans. James Strachey, in *The Standard Edition of the Complete Psychological Works of Sigmund Freud*, ed. James Strachey, vol. 18 (London: Hogarth, 1955), 256, original emphasis.
5 Jacques Lacan, *The Seminar of Jacques Lacan, Book VII: The Ethics of Psychoanalysis, 1959–1960*, ed. Jacques-Alain Miller and trans. Dennis Porter (New York: Norton, 1992), 58.
6 Lacan, *Ethics*, 112.
7 Kenneth Reinhard, "Universalism and the Jewish Exception: Lacan, Badiou, Rosenzweig," *Umbr(a): A Journal of the Unconscious* 1, (2005): 44.
8 Sigmund Freud, *Three Essays on the Theory of Sexuality*, trans. James Strachey, in *The Standard Edition of the Complete Psychological Works of Sigmund Freud*, ed. James Strachey, vol. 7 (London: Hogarth, 1953), 149 n.
9 Sigmund Freud, *Project for a Scientific Psychology*, trans. James Strachey, in *The Standard Edition of the Complete Psychological Works of Sigmund Freud*, ed. James Strachey, vol. 1 (London: Hogarth, 1966), 331, original emphasis.
10 Steven Pinker, for example, claims, "The mind is what the brain does; specifically, the brain processes information, and thinking is a kind of computation." Steven Pinker, *How the Mind Works* (New York: Norton, 1997), 21. Curiously, Pinker situates his project as an overcoming of psychoanalysis: "*How the Mind Works* is my attempt to synthesize an emerging view of human nature that, I believe, is superseding psychoanalysis as the idea behind Psychological Human." Pinker, *How the Mind Works*, vii. I suppose the irony of overcoming psychoanalysis by killing Freud is lost on Pinker.

11   Freud, *Project*, 331, original emphasis. The word that Strachey translates here as "thing" is the ordinary German word *Ding*. Strachey is correct to translate *Ding* as *thing* with a lowercase "t" because in German all nouns are capitalized thus there is nothing in the German to warrant its transformation into a proper noun. As *Das Ding* gets taken up by Lacan, however, it becomes a proper noun. To my mind, this transformation of *Das Ding* into a proper noun feels licentious. It has the effect of turning what for Freud was an ordinary word into a piece of jargon. For this reason, when referring to *the thing*, I have chosen not to use capitals. At the same time, I will not "correct" the text when quoting Lacan, since for him it was a proper noun.
12   Freud, *Project*, 366.
13   Freud, *Project*, 383, original emphasis.
14   Lacan, *Ethics*, 52.
15   Benjamin writes of history: "As flowers turn toward the sun, what has been strives to turn—by dint of a secret heliotropism—toward that sun which is rising in the sky of history." Walter Benjamin, "On the Concept of History," trans. Harry Zohn, in *Walter Benjamin: Selected Writings, Volume 4: 1938–1940*, eds. Howard Eiland and Michael Jennings (Cambridge, MA: Belknap Press, 2006), 390.
16   Lacan, *Ethics*, 52, original emphasis.
17   Bruce Fink, *Against Understanding, Volume 2: Cases and Commentary in a Lacanian Key* (New York: Routledge, 2014), 218.
18   Sigmund Freud, "The Uncanny," trans. Alix Strachey, in *The Standard Edition of the Complete Psychological Works of Sigmund Freud*, ed. James Strachey, vol. 17 (London: Hogarth, 1955), 248 n., original emphasis.
19   Freud, "The Uncanny," 248 n.
20   Lacan, *Ethics*, 71.
21   Bruce Fink, *Fundamentals of Psychoanalytic Technique: A Lacanian Approach to Practitioners* (New York: Norton, 2007), 4.
22   Fink, *Fundamentals of Psychoanalytic Technique*, 4.
23   Fink, *Fundamentals of Psychoanalytic Technique*, 2.
24   Lacan, *Ethics*, 98.
25   Lacan, *Ethics*, 187.
26   Lacan, *Ethics*, 103, original emphasis.
27   Jacques Lacan, *The Seminar of Jacques Lacan, Book XX: On Feminine Sexuality, The Limits of Love and Knowledge, 1972–1973 (Encore)*, ed. Jacques-Alain Miller and trans. Bruce Fink (New York: Norton, 1998), 94.
28   Lacan, *Ethics*, 45.
29   Lacan, *Ethics*, 45.
30   Immanuel Kant, *Critique of Pure Reason*, trans. Paul Guyer and Allen W. Wood (Cambridge: Cambridge University Press, 1998), 185.
31   Lacan, *Ethics*, 63, original emphasis.
32   Lacan, *Ethics*, 114.
33   Lacan, *Ethics*, 114.

34 Lacan, *Ethics*, 229, original emphasis.
35 Lacan, *Ethics*, 119.
36 Lacan, *Ethics*, 119.
37 Lacan writes, "In this connection the human factor will not be denied otherwise than in the way that I defined the Thing just now, namely, that which in the real suffers from the signifier." Lacan, *Ethics*, 125.
38 Lacan, *Ethics*, 125.
39 Lacan, *Ethics*, 120.
40 Lacan, *Ethics*, 121.
41 Lacan, *Ethics*, 141.
42 Mari Ruti, *Distillations: Theory, Ethics, Affect* (New York: Bloomsbury Academic, 2018), 112.
43 Lacan, *Ethics*, 141.
44 For Plato's critique of art as imitation or *mimesis*, see Books III and X of Plato, *The Republic*, trans. Paul Shorey, in *The Collected Dialogues of Plato: Including the Letters*, eds. Edith Hamilton and Huntington Cairns (Princeton: Princeton University Press, 2009), 575–844.
45 Lacan, *Ethics*, 141.
46 Alenka Zupančič, *The Shortest Shadow: Nietzsche's Philosophy of the Two* (Cambridge, MA: MIT Press), 173, original emphasis.
47 Zupančič, *Shortest Shadow*, 136.
48 Jacques Lacan, *The Seminar of Jacques Lacan, Book VIII: Transference*, ed. Jacques-Alain Miller and trans. Bruce Fink (New York: Polity, 2015), 100.

Chapter 6

1 There is a happy ending to this story, as I didn't give into any of these urges.
2 Sigmund Freud, *Project for a Scientific Psychology*, trans. James Strachey, in *The Standard Edition of the Complete Psychological Works of Sigmund Freud*, ed. James Strachey, vol. 1 (London: Hogarth, 1966), 318, original emphasis.
3 Sigmund Freud, *Civilization and Its Discontents*, trans. Joan Riviere, in *The Standard Edition of the Complete Psychological Works of Sigmund Freud*, ed. James Strachey, vol. 21 (London: Hogarth, 1964), 67.
4 Jacques Lacan, *The Seminar of Jacques Lacan, Book VII: The Ethics of Psychoanalysis, 1959–1960*, ed. Jacques-Alain Miller and trans. Dennis Porter (New York: Norton, 1992), 41.
5 Jacques Lacan, *The Seminar of Jacques Lacan, Book X: Anxiety*, ed. Jacques-Alain Miller and trans. A.R. Price (Cambridge: Polity, 2014), 167.
6 Matthew 7:9–11.
7 Freud, *Project*, 318, original emphasis.
8 Sigmund Freud, *Three Essays on the Theory of Sexuality*, trans. James Strachey, in *The Standard Edition of the Complete Psychological Works of Sigmund Freud*, ed. James Strachey, vol. 7 (London: Hogarth, 1953), 136.

9   Freud, *Three Essays*, 148.
10 Freud, *Three Essays*, 148.
11 Freud, *Three Essays*, 148.
12 Freud, *Three Essays*, 148.
13 Freud, *Three Essays*, 149.
14 Lacan, *Anxiety*, 166.
15 Freud, *Three Essays*, 150.
16 Freud, *Three Essays*, 180.
17 Jacques Lacan, *The Seminar of Jacques Lacan, Book VIII: Transference*, ed. Jacques-Alain Miller and trans. Bruce Fink (Cambridge: Polity, 2015), 236, 237.
18 Elsewhere in *Three Essays*, Freud does indeed call so-called normative sexuality a problem in its own right: "Thus from the point of view of psycho-analysis the exclusive sexual interest felt by men for women is also a problem that needs elucidating and is not a self-evident fact based upon an attraction that is ultimately of a chemical nature." Freud, *Three Essays*, 146 n.
19 Sigmund Freud, "Instincts and Their Vicissitudes," trans. C.M. Baines, in *The Standard Edition of the Complete Psychological Works of Sigmund Freud*, ed. James Strachey, vol. 14 (London: Hogarth, 1957), 122.
20 Jacques Lacan, *The Seminar of Jacques Lacan, Book IV: The Object Relation*, ed. Jacques-Alain Miller and trans. A.R. Price (Cambridge: Polity, 2020), 29.
21 Lacan, *Ethics*, 58.
22 Freud, "Instincts and Their Vicissitudes," 123.
23 Freud, "Instincts and Their Vicissitudes," 122.
24 Freud, *Three Essays*, 149.
25 Freud, "Instincts and Their Vicissitudes," 122.
26 Sigmund Freud, "Analysis Terminable and Interminable," trans. Joan Riviere, in *The Standard Edition of the Complete Psychological Works of Sigmund Freud*, ed. James Strachey, vol. 23 (London: Hogarth, 1964), 252.
27 Mari Ruti, *A World of Fragile Things: Psychoanalysis and the Art of Living* (Albany, NY: SUNY Press), 143.
28 Lacan, *Ethics*, 52.
29 Ruti, *Fragile Things*, 147.

Chapter 7

1 Plato, *The Symposium*, trans. Michael Joyce, in *The Collected Dialogues of Plato: Including the Letters*, eds. Edith Hamilton and Huntington Cairns (Princeton: Princeton University Press, 2009), 542.
2 Plato, *Symposium*, 544.
3 Sigmund Freud, *Three Essays on the Theory of Sexuality*, trans. James Strachey, in *The Standard Edition of the Complete Psychological Works of Sigmund Freud*, ed. James Strachey, vol. 7 (London: Hogarth, 1953), 222.

4   Jacques Lacan, *The Seminar of Jacques Lacan, Book XI: The Four Fundamental Concepts of Psychoanalysis*, ed. Jacques-Alain Miller and trans. Alan Sheridan (New York: Norton, 1981), 167.
5   Freud, *Three Essays*, 222.
6   Sigmund Freud, *Civilization and Its Discontents*, trans. Joan Riviere, in *The Standard Edition of the Complete Psychological Works of Sigmund Freud*, ed. James Strachey, vol. 21 (London: Hogarth, 1964), 66.
7   Freud, *Civilization and Its Discontents*, 65.
8   Freud, *Civilization and Its Discontents*, 67.
9   Freud, *Civilization and Its Discontents*, 67.
10   Freud, *Civilization and Its Discontents*, 68.
11   Freud, *Civilization and Its Discontents*, 66.
12   Freud, *Civilization and Its Discontents*, 66-7.
13   Sigmund Freud, "Instincts and Their Vicissitudes," trans. C.M. Baines, in *The Standard Edition of the Complete Psychological Works of Sigmund Freud*, ed. James Strachey, vol. 14 (London: Hogarth, 1957), 136.
14   Sigmund Freud, "Negation," trans. Joan Riviere, in *The Standard Edition of the Complete Psychological Works of Sigmund Freud*, ed. James Strachey, vol. 19 (London: Hogarth, 1961), 237.
15   Freud, "Instincts and Their Vicissitudes," 136.
16   Jacques Lacan, *The Seminar of Jacques Lacan, Book VII: The Ethics of Psychoanalysis, 1959-1960*, ed. Jacques-Alain Miller and trans. Dennis Porter (New York: Norton, 1992), 52.
17   Lacan, *Ethics*, 118.
18   Alenka Zupančič, *The Shortest Shadow: Nietzsche's Philosophy of the Two* (Cambridge, MA: MIT Press), 136.
19   Lacan, *Ethics*, 118.
20   Molly Rothenberg points out that this retroactive dynamic of losing the object by finding it is already at work in Lacan's theory of the mirror stage. The child loses (the object of) mastery over its body only when it finds the "'orthopedic' form of its totality" in the mirror. Jacques Lacan, "The Mirror Stage as Formative of the *I* Function as Revealed in Psychoanalytic Experience," in *Écrits: The First Complete Edition in English*, trans. Bruce Fink (New York: Norton, 2006), 78. Personal communication.
21   "Steve Jobs: 'There's Sanity Returning,'" by Andy Reinhardt, *Business Week*, May 25, 1998. https://www.bloomberg.com/news/articles/1998-05-25/steve-jobs-theres-sanity-returning.
22   This is a paraphrase of the accusation that Leonardo "frittered away his time when he could have been industriously painting to order and becoming rich." Sigmund Freud, *Leonardo da Vinci and a Memory of His Childhood*, trans. Alan Tyson, in *The Standard Edition of the Complete Psychological Works of Sigmund Freud*, ed. James Strachey, vol. 11 (London: Hogarth, 1957), 65.
23   Freud, *Leonardo*, 70 n.
24   Lacan, *Ethics*, 114.

Chapter 8

1. Sigmund Freud, "On Narcissism: An Introduction," trans. C.M. Baines, in *The Standard Edition of the Complete Psychological Works of Sigmund Freud*, ed. James Strachey, vol. 14 (London: Hogarth, 1957), 87.
2. Freud, "Narcissism," 88.
3. Freud, "Narcissism," 74.
4. Freud, "Narcissism," 75.
5. Freud, "Narcissism," 87.
6. Freud, "Narcissism," 93.
7. Freud, "Narcissism," 76.
8. Sigmund Freud, *Three Essays on the Theory of Sexuality*, trans. James Strachey, in *The Standard Edition of the Complete Psychological Works of Sigmund Freud*, ed. James Strachey, vol. 7 (London: Hogarth, 1953), 222.
9. Freud, "Narcissism," 100.
10. Freud, *Three Essays*, 222.
11. Freud, "Narcissism," 101.
12. Freud, "Narcissism," 90–1.
13. Freud, "Narcissism," 89–90.
14. Lacan states, "You can, in fact, see it emerge in a narcissistic relation, an imaginary relation. At this level the object introduces itself only insofar as it is perpetually interchangeable with the love that the subject has for its own image." Jacques Lacan, *The Seminar of Jacques Lacan, Book VII: The Ethics of Psychoanalysis, 1959–1960*, ed. Jacques-Alain Miller and trans. Dennis Porter (New York: Norton, 1992), 98.
15. Freud, "Narcissism," 91.
16. Freud, "Narcissism," 94.
17. Freud, "Narcissism," 94.
18. Freud, "Narcissism," 88.
19. Freud, "Narcissism," 94.
20. Many believe that the friend is Lou Andreas-Salomé and the poet is Rainer Maria Rilke.
21. Sigmund Freud, "On Transience," trans. James Strachey, in *The Standard Edition of the Complete Psychological Works of Sigmund Freud*, ed. James Strachey, vol. 14 (London: Hogarth, 1957), 305.
22. Freud, "Transience," 306.
23. Freud, "Transience," 305.
24. Freud, "Transience," 309.
25. Secondary revision is the dream process that pulls all the disparate elements of a dream together into a coherent narrative. Freud writes, "[I]t fills up the gaps in the dream-structure with shreds and patches. As a result of its efforts, the dream loses its appearance of absurdity and disconnectedness and approximates to the model of an intelligible experience." Sigmund Freud, *The Interpretation of Dreams (Second Part)*, trans. James Strachey, in

The Standard Edition of the Complete Psychological Works of Sigmund Freud, ed. James Strachey, vol. 4 (London: Hogarth, 1953), 490.
26 Slavoj Žižek, *Sex and the Failed Absolute* (London: Bloomsbury, 2020), 187.
27 Freud, "Transience," 305.

Part Three

1 See Jean-Paul Sartre, *Search for a Method*, trans. Hazel E. Barnes (New York: Vintage, 1968).
2 What is translated as "group" is the German word *Masse*, which translates more literally as "mass." Strachey claims that he chose *group* for the sake of uniformity between Freud's account and the other accounts of mass psychology with which Freud interacts. However, it seems to me that this unnatural translation of Freud's *Masse* comes from the same motivation that led Strachey to translate *Trieb* as "instinct," namely, to give Freud's language a more scientific inflection, as the word *mass* in English gives off a very different connotation than *group*—something more akin to *mob*—which isn't present in German.
3 Sigmund Freud, *Group Psychology and the Analysis of the Ego*, trans. James Strachey, in *The Standard Edition of the Complete Psychological Works of Sigmund Freud*, ed. James Strachey, vol. 18 (London: Hogarth, 1955), 139, original emphasis.
4 Freud, *Group Psychology*, 139.

Chapter 9

1 Sigmund Freud, *Leonardo da Vinci and a Memory of His Childhood*, trans. Alan Tyson, in *The Standard Edition of the Complete Psychological Works of Sigmund Freud*, ed. James Strachey, vol. 11 (London: Hogarth, 1957), 122, 122–3.
2 Jacques Lacan, *The Seminar of Jacques Lacan, Book XI: The Four Fundamental Concepts of Psychoanalysis*, ed. Jacques-Alain Miller and trans. Alan Sheridan (New York: Norton, 1981), 38.
3 Lacan, *Four Fundamental Concepts*, 158.
4 Freud, *Leonardo*, 63.
5 Freud, *Leonardo*, 122.
6 Sigmund Freud, *Group Psychology and the Analysis of the Ego*, trans. James Strachey, in *The Standard Edition of the Complete Psychological Works of Sigmund Freud*, ed. James Strachey, vol. 18 (London: Hogarth, 1955).
7 Freud, *Group Psychology*, 105, 106.

8   Freud, *Group Psychology*, 106, original emphasis.
9   Sigmund Freud, *Civilization and Its Discontents*, trans. Joan Riviere, in *The Standard Edition of the Complete Psychological Works of Sigmund Freud*, ed. James Strachey, vol. 21 (London: Hogarth, 1964), 114.
10 Freud, *Group Psychology*, 101.
11 Freud, *Group Psychology*, 102.
12 Freud, *Group Psychology*, 98.
13 Sigmund Freud, "Mourning and Melancholia," trans. Joan Riviere, in *The Standard Edition of the Complete Psychological Works of Sigmund Freud*, ed. James Strachey, vol. 14 (London: Hogarth, 1957), 249. What Freud is calling a "special agency" will eventually become *the ego ideal* in *Group Psychology*.
14 Freud, *Group Psychology*, 108.
15 Freud, *Group Psychology*, 108.
16 Sigmund Freud, "On Narcissism: An Introduction," trans. C.M. Baines, in *The Standard Edition of the Complete Psychological Works of Sigmund Freud*, ed. James Strachey, vol. 14 (London: Hogarth, 1957), 94, original emphasis.
17 1 Corinthians 11:1.
18 Freud, *Group Psychology*, 116.
19 Freud, *Group Psychology*, 100.
20 Curiously, Freud overlooks this aspect of the unidentifiability of Jesus in the "Postscript" of *Group Psychology* when he claims that the Church differs from the army on this question of the identifiability of the leader: "Every Christian loves Christ as his ideal and feels himself united with all other Christians by the tie of identification. But the Church requires more of him. He has also to identify himself with Christ and love all other Christians as Christ loved them." Freud, *Group Psychology*, 134. There is, however, a case to be made for Freud's position, as Todd McGowan reminds me, in Christian theology, in Jesus, God reveals himself in human form—that is to say, in Jesus, God reveals himself to be lacking. And insofar as the Christian God is a lacking God, the Christian is able to fully identify with Christ. Of course, even in this view, structural inaccessibility still persists in the Church insofar as rank exists everywhere in the Church (with the rare exceptions, like, the Quakers): priests, bishops, pastors, deacons, elders, and the like. Each of these ranks, like the army officer's rank itself, mark that aspect with which the rank and file Christian cannot identify. Personal communication.
21 Personal communication.
22 On aphanisis, Lacan states, "If he is apprehended at his birth in the field of the Other, the characteristic of the subject of the unconscious is that of being, beneath the signifier that develops its networks, its chains and its history, at an indeterminate place." Lacan, *Four Fundamental Concepts*, 208.
23 Freud, *Group Psychology*, 110; Freud, "Narcissism," 100.
24 For example, in his likening of the group to hypnosis, Freud contends, "The replacement of the directly sexual impulsions by those that are inhibited in their aims promotes in both states a separation between the ego and the

ego ideal, a separation with which a beginning has already been made in the state of being in love." Freud, *Group Psychology*, 143. It seems to me that there is something directly satisfying in the group's investment in the leader—which, perhaps, is unlike hypnosis—that Freud overlooks.
25 Jacques Lacan, *The Seminar of Jacques Lacan, Book I: Freud's Papers on Technique, 1953–1954*, ed. Jacques-Alain Miller and trans. John Forrester (New York: Norton, 1988), 222.
26 The pervert, according to Lacan, makes of themselves "an idol offered to the desire of the other" and "offers himself loyally to the Other's jouissance." Lacan, *Freud's Papers on Technique*, 222 and Jacques Lacan, *The Seminar of Jacques Lacan, Book X: Anxiety*, ed. Jacques-Alain Miller and trans. A.R. Price (Cambridge: Polity, 2014), 49. Stephanie Swales adds, "the pervert places himself in the position of the object, and that this object is not the object-cause of the Other's desire, but the object-cause of the Other's jouissance." Stephanie Swales, *Perversion: A Lacanian Psychoanalytic Approach to the Subject* (New York: Routledge, 2012), 56.
27 Edmundson writes, "We fall in love not only with 'sexual objects' (as Freud charmingly calls them) but, individually and collectively, with power. Though badly in need of sane and measured authority"—what is "sane and measured authority"?—"we swoon before the authoritarian." Mark Edmundson, "Introduction," in *Beyond the Pleasure Principle and Other Writings* (London: Penguin, 2003), vii.
28 Joan Copjec, *Read My Desire: Lacan against the Historicists* (Cambridge, MA: MIT Press, 1995), 150. Copjec writes, "one elects a master who is demonstrably fallible—even, in some cases, incompetent. What may first appear to be a stumbling block turns out on closer inspection to be a solution: Americans love their masters not simply in spite of their frailties but because of them." *Read My Desire*, 149.

Chapter 10

1 Alain Badiou, *Lacan: Anti-Philosophy 3*, trans. Kenneth Reinhard and Susan Spitzer (New York: Columbia University Press, 2018), 127.
2 Badiou, *Lacan*, 127, 128.
3 Badiou, *Lacan*, 128.
4 Badiou, *Lacan*, 131.
5 Badiou, *Lacan*, 129.
6 Badiou, *Lacan*, 184, original emphasis.
7 Badiou, *Lacan*, 130. Bruce Fink, for example, says, "I'm very suspicious, myself, of taking concepts that were developed in the clinical setting for transformative psychotherapeutic work and trying to apply them everywhere else." Bruce Fink, *Against Understanding, Volume 1: Commentary and Critique in a Lacanian Key* (New York: Routledge, 2014), 217.

8 Sigmund Freud, *Group Psychology and the Analysis of the Ego*, trans. James Strachey, in *The Standard Edition of the Complete Psychological Works of Sigmund Freud*, ed. James Strachey, vol. 18 (London: Hogarth, 1955), 115.
9 Freud, *Group Psychology*, 139, original emphasis.
10 Freud, *Group Psychology*, 139.
11 Freud, *Group Psychology*, 115, 127.
12 Freud, *Group Psychology*, 103.
13 Freud, *Group Psychology*, 94.
14 Freud, *Group Psychology*, 97.
15 Freud, *Group Psychology*, 112–13.
16 Reiterating his claims from "Narcissism" that achieving an ideal produces satisfaction, Freud writes, "There is always a feeling of triumph when something in the ego coincides with the ego ideal." Freud, *Group Psychology*, 131. When the ego fully coincides with the ideal, this is mania: "On the basis of our analysis of the ego it cannot be doubted that in cases of mania the ego and the ego ideal have fused together, so that the person, in a mood of triumph and self-satisfaction, disturbed by no self-criticism, can enjoy the abolition of his inhibitions, his feelings of consideration for others, and his self-reproaches." Freud, *Group Psychology*, 132.
17 Is group psychology one of those extra-clinical applications that draw Fink's suspicions?
18 Sigmund Freud, "On the Universal Tendency to Debasement in the Sphere of Love," trans. Joan Riviere, in *The Standard Edition of the Complete Psychological Works of Sigmund Freud*, ed. James Strachey, vol. 11 (Hogarth: London, 1957), 179.
19 Freud, "Debasement," 183.
20 Freud, "Debasement," 185, 180.
21 Freud, "Debasement," 183.
22 Freud, "Debasement," 185.
23 One can imagine a feminine retort: no woman should be debased because there is no woman who cannot be debased.
24 Freud, "Debasement," 186.
25 Jacques Lacan, *The Seminar of Jacques Lacan, Book VIII: Transference*, ed. Jacques-Alain Miller and trans. Bruce Fink (Cambridge: Polity, 2015), 237.
26 Jacques Lacan, *The Seminar of Jacques Lacan, Book X: Anxiety*, ed. Jacques-Alain Miller and trans. A.R. Price (Cambridge: Polity, 2014), 168.
27 Lacan, *Anxiety*, 166–7.
28 That we ever felt ourselves to be whole is, for Lacan, a function of the imaginary: "the sight alone of the whole form of the human body gives the subject an imaginary mastery over his body." Jacques Lacan, *The Seminar of Jacques Lacan, Book I: Freud's Papers on Technique, 1953–1954*, ed. Jacques-Alain Miller and trans. John Forrester (New York: Norton, 1988), 79.
29 Lacan, *Anxiety*, 41, 101, original emphasis.

30 Sigmund Freud, "Fetishism," trans. Joan Riviere, in *The Standard Edition of the Complete Psychological Works of Sigmund Freud*, ed. James Strachey, vol. 21 (London: Hogarth, 1964), 154.
31 Octave Mannoni, "'I Know Well, but All the Same …'," in *Perversion and the Social Relation*, eds. Molly Anne Rothenberg, Dennis Foster, and Slavoj Žižek (Durham: Duke University Press, 2003), 70. Mannoni goes on: "Of course, the fetishist does not use a phrase of this sort to describe his perversion: *he knows well* that women do not have a phallus, yet he cannot add a 'but all the same,' since his 'but all the same' is his fetish." Mannoni, "'I Know Well'," 70, original emphasis.
32 Lacan, *Anxiety*, 174, original emphasis.
33 Saint Agatha's breasts were cut off as part of her torture.
34 Lacan, *Anxiety*, 163.
35 Lacan, *Anxiety*, 162.
36 Lacan, *Anxiety*, 166, 167, emphasis added.
37 Freud, "Debasement," 179.
38 Lacan, *Transference*, 52, 179.
39 Lacan, *Transference*, 34.

Chapter 11

1 See Sigmund Freud, *Totem and Taboo*, trans. James Strachey, in *The Standard Edition of the Complete Psychological Works of Sigmund Freud*, ed. James Strachey, vol. 13 (London: Hogarth, 1955), Chapter 4. Regarding the primal father, Joan Copjec helpfully explains this: "That he is unthinkable within this regime of brothers does not gainsay the fact that the *institution* of the regime is inexplicable without him. For if we did not posit his existence, we would be incapable, without resorting to psychologism, of explaining how the brothers came together in this fashion." Joan Copjec, *Read My Desire: Lacan against the Historicists* (Cambridge, MA: MIT Press, 1995), 12, original emphasis.
2 Sigmund Freud, *Group Psychology and the Analysis of the Ego*, trans. James Strachey, in *The Standard Edition of the Complete Psychological Works of Sigmund Freud*, ed. James Strachey, vol. 18 (London: Hogarth, 1955), 123.
3 Freud, *Group Psychology*, 124.
4 Freud, *Group Psychology*, 124.
5 Freud, *Group Psychology*, 121, 123–4.
6 Freud does indeed take up the question of murder in the "Postscript" to *Group Psychology*.
7 Jacques Lacan, *The Seminar of Jacques Lacan, Book X: Anxiety*, ed. Jacques-Alain Miller and trans. A.R. Price (Cambridge: Polity, 2014), 279.
8 Freud, *Group Psychology*, 125, 126.

9   Freud does consider the possibility of the hypnotist using "a bright object" or "a monotonous sound" in lieu of their mysterious power. But Freud quickly eschews the significance of this technique, saying it is "misleading and has given occasion to inadequate physiological theories." Freud, *Group Psychology*, 125.
10 Copjec, *Read My Desire*, 150.
11 Jacques Lacan, *The Seminar of Jacques Lacan, Book XI: The Four Fundamental Concepts of Psychoanalysis*, ed. Jacques-Alain Miller and trans. Alan Sheridan (New York: Norton, 1981), 270. Slavoj Žižek has used this principle in Lacan to critique antisemitism to great effect; he writes, "To 'identify with a symptom' means to recognize in the 'excesses', in the disruptions of the 'normal' way of things, the key offering us access to its true functioning." Slavoj Žižek, *The Sublime Object of Ideology* (New York: Verso, 1989), 128.
12 Lacan, *Anxiety*, 316.
13 Sigmund Freud, *Inhibitions, Symptoms and Anxiety*, trans. Alix Strachey, in *The Standard Edition of the Complete Psychological Works of Sigmund Freud*, ed. James Strachey, vol. 20 (London: Hogarth, 1959), 90.
14 Lacan, *Anxiety*, 317.
15 Sigmund Freud, "From the History of an Infantile Neurosis," trans. Alix Strachey and James Strachey, in *The Standard Edition of the Complete Psychological Works of Sigmund Freud*, ed. James Strachey, vol. 17 (London: Hogarth, 1955), 29.
16 Lacan, *Anxiety*, 312.
17 Lacan, *Anxiety*, 312.
18 Lacan, *Anxiety*, 313.
19 Lacan, *Anxiety*, 313, original emphasis.
20 Lacan, *Anxiety*, 313.
21 Lacan states, "In the main, it's not true that the child is weaned. He weans *himself*." Lacan, *Anxiety*, 327, original emphasis.
22 Lacan, *Anxiety*, 314.
23 Lacan, *Anxiety*, 312.
24 Lacan, *Anxiety*, 317.
25 Lacan, *Anxiety*, 316.
26 For example: "Children who are making use of the susceptibility to erotogenic stimulation of the anal zone betray themselves by *holding back* their stool till its accumulation brings about violent muscular contractions and, as it passes through the anus, is able to produce powerful stimulation of the mucous membrane." Sigmund Freud, *Three Essays on the Theory of Sexuality*, trans. James Strachey, in *The Standard Edition of the Complete Psychological Works of Sigmund Freud*, ed. James Strachey, vol. 7 (London: Hogarth, 1953), 186, emphasis added.
27 Lacan, *Anxiety*, 316.
28 Lacan, *Anxiety*, 313.
29 Lacan, *Anxiety*, 315.

30 Lacan, *Anxiety*, 337.
31 Lacan, *Anxiety*, 331.
32 Lacan claims that ignorance is one of the three "passions for being"—love and hate are the other two. Jacques Lacan, "The Direction of the Treatment and the Principles of Its Power," in *Écrits: The First Complete Edition in English*, trans. Bruce Fink (New York: Norton, 2006), 424.
33 Lacan, *Anxiety*, 317.
34 Alenka Zupančič, "Squirrels to the Nuts, or, How Many Does It Take to Not Give up on Your Desire?," in *Lubitsch Can't Wait: A Theoretical Examination*, eds. Ivan Novak, Jela Krečič, and Malden Dolar (Ljubljana: Slovenian Cinematheque, 2014), 179.
35 Lacan, *Four Fundamentals*, 276.

Chapter 12

1 Mari Ruti has persistently—and I believe, convincingly—critiqued the self-destructive, suicidal strain of Lacanian thought. See, for example, Mari Ruti, *The Ethics of Opting Out: Queer Theory's Defiant Subject* (New York: Columbia University Press, 2017).
2 The idea of the image can be found throughout Lacan's work. Here is one example: "What we have here is a first capture by the image in which the first moment of the dialectic of identifications is sketched out. It is linked to a gestalt phenomenon, the child's very early perception of the human form." Jacques Lacan, "Aggressiveness in Psychoanalysis," in *Écrits: The First Complete Edition in English*, trans. Bruce Fink (New York: Norton, 2006), 91.
3 Paul Eisenstein, *Traumatic Encounters: Holocaust Representation and the Hegelian Subject* (Albany: SUNY Press), 31.
4 Jacques Lacan, *The Seminar of Jacques Lacan, Book X: Anxiety*, ed. Jacques-Alain Miller and trans. A.R. Price (Cambridge: Polity, 2014), 320.
5 Lacan, *Anxiety*, 328.
6 Sigmund Freud, *Three Essays on the Theory of Sexuality*, trans. James Strachey, in *The Standard Edition of the Complete Psychological Works of Sigmund Freud*, ed. James Strachey, vol. 7 (London: Hogarth, 1953), 161.
7 Lacan states, "At this level, the subject already has to give what he is … as something irreducible with respect to what is imposed upon him as a symbolic imprint." Lacan, *Anxiety*, 328.
8 Lacan describes alienation in the following way: "The *vel* of alienation is defined by a choice whose properties depend on this, that there is, in the joining, one element that, whatever the choice operating may be, has as its consequence a *neither one, nor the other* …. If we choose being, the subject disappears, it eludes us, it falls into non-meaning. If we choose meaning, the meaning survives only deprived of that part of non-meaning that is, strictly speaking, that which constitutes in the realization of the subject,

the unconscious. In other words, it is of the nature of this meaning, as it emerges in the field of the Other, to be in a large part of its field, eclipsed by the disappearance of being, induced by the very function of the signifier." Jacques Lacan, *The Seminar of Jacques Lacan, Book XI: The Four Fundamental Concepts of Psychoanalysis*, ed. Jacques-Alain Miller and trans. Alan Sheridan (New York: Norton, 1981), 211, original emphasis.

9   Lacan, *Four Fundamental Concepts*, 257.
10 Lacan, *Anxiety*, 261.
11 Lacan, *Anxiety*, 322.
12 For Lacan, meaning emerges in the field of the Other. He states, "If we choose being, the subject disappears, it eludes us, it falls into non-meaning. If we choose meaning, the meaning survives only deprived of that part of non-meaning that is, strictly speaking, that which constitutes in the realization of the subject, the unconscious. In other words, it is of the nature of this meaning, as it emerges in the field of the Other, to be in a large part of its field, eclipsed by the disappearance of being, induced by the very function of the signifier." Lacan, *Four Fundamental Concepts*, 211.
13 Lacan writes, "The jubilant assumption of his specular image ... thus seems to me to manifest in an exemplary situation the symbolic matrix in which the *I* is precipitated." Jacques Lacan, "The Mirror Stage as Formative of the *I* Function as Revealed in Psychoanalytic Experience," in *Écrits: The First Complete Edition in English*, trans. Bruce Fink (New York: Norton, 2006), 76.
14 Lacan, *Four Fundamental Concepts*, 92.
15 Todd McGowan, *Universality and Identity Politics* (New York: Columbia University Press, 2020), 63–4.
16 McGowan, *Universality and Identity Politics*, 63.
17 McGowan, *Universality and Identity Politics*, 8.
18 Alenka Zupančič, "Squirrels to the Nuts, or, How Many Does It Take to Not Give up on Your Desire?," in *Lubitsch Can't Wait: A Theoretical Examination*, eds. Ivan Novak, Jela Krečič, and Malden Dolar (Ljubljana: Slovenian Cinematheque, 2014), 177.
19 Zupančič, "Squirrels to the Nuts," 178.
20 Zupančič, "Squirrels to the Nuts," 179.
21 Zupančič, "Squirrels to the Nuts," 179.
22 To be clear, Zupančič does recognize Belinski's objective status. She writes, "The chief male protagonist, Professor Adam Belinski, is a Czech refugee. This status of his is of crucial importance in the structure of the movie." Zupančič, "Squirrels to the Nuts," 174. Only she doesn't link Cluny's act to that status.
23 Zupančič, "Squirrels to the Nuts," 176.
24 McGowan, *Universality and Identity Politics*, 76.
25 McGowan, *Universality and Identity Politics*, 60.
26 McGowan, *Universality and Identity Politics*, 23.
27 McGowan, *Universality and Identity Politics*, 61.

28 McGowan, *Universality and Identity Politics*, 61–2.
29 McGowan writes this of life in the universal: "Opting for the universal forces us to confront how our identity is enmeshed in that of the other. Instead of securing identity, it uproots it. The universal allows us to exist in common by taking away the security that comes from living amid other identities." McGowan, *Universality and Identity Politics*, 87.
30 Lacan, *Anxiety*, 315.
31 Lacan, *Anxiety*, 317. McGowan avows something similar when he writes, "Universal solidarity doesn't leave anyone out because it takes those who don't belong as its starting point. Universal solidarity is solidarity with those who don't belong formed through the universality of nonbelonging." McGowan, *Universality and Identity Politics*, 68.

Conclusion

1 Sigmund Freud, *Three Essays on the Theory of Sexuality*, trans. James Strachey, in *The Standard Edition of the Complete Psychological Works of Sigmund Freud*, ed. James Strachey, vol. 7 (London: Hogarth, 1953), 168.
2 Sigmund Freud, *Beyond the Pleasure Principle*, trans. James Strachey, in *The Standard Edition of the Complete Psychological Works of Sigmund Freud*, ed. James Strachey, vol. 18 (London: Hogarth, 1955), 62.
3 Freud, *Beyond the Pleasure Principle*, 13.
4 Freud, *Beyond the Pleasure Principle*, 16, original emphasis.
5 Freud, *Beyond the Pleasure Principle*, 16.
6 Freud, *Beyond the Pleasure Principle*, 20.
7 Freud, *Beyond the Pleasure Principle*, 20–2.
8 Freud, *Beyond the Pleasure Principle*, 21.
9 Freud, *Beyond the Pleasure Principle*, 23.
10 Freud, *Beyond the Pleasure Principle*, 62.
11 Freud, *Beyond the Pleasure Principle*, 42.
12 Freud writes, "It was still an easy matter at that time for a living substance to die; the course of its life was probably only a brief one …. till decisive external influences altered in such a way as to oblige the still surviving substance to diverge ever more widely from its original course of life and to make ever more complicated détours before reaching its aim of death. These circuitous paths to death, faithfully kept to by the conservative instincts, would thus present us today with the picture of the phenomenon of life." Freud, *Beyond the Pleasure Principle*, 38–9, original emphasis.
13 Freud, *Beyond the Pleasure Principle*, 36, original emphasis.
14 Sigmund Freud, "The Economic Problem of Masochism," trans. Joan Riviere, in *The Standard Edition of the Complete Psychological Works of Sigmund Freud*, ed. James Strachey, vol. 19 (London: Hogarth, 1961), 159.
15 Freud, *Beyond the Pleasure Principle*, 8, original emphasis.

16 Freud, *Beyond the Pleasure Principle*, 63.
17 Freud, *Beyond the Pleasure Principle*, 63.
18 Freud, *Beyond the Pleasure Principle*, 29, 63.
19 Freud, *Beyond the Pleasure Principle*, 62.
20 Freud, *Beyond the Pleasure Principle*, 16, emphasis added.
21 Freud, *Beyond the Pleasure Principle*, 7.
22 Freud, *Beyond the Pleasure Principle*, 52–3.
23 Jacques Lacan, "Position of the Unconscious," in *Écrits: The First Complete Edition in English*, trans. Bruce Fink (New York: Norton, 2006), 719.
24 Freud, *Beyond the Pleasure Principle*, 48, original emphasis.
25 Sigmund Freud, *Leonardo da Vinci and a Memory of His Childhood*, trans. Alan Tyson, in *The Standard Edition of the Complete Psychological Works of Sigmund Freud*, ed. James Strachey, vol. 11 (London: Hogarth, 1957), 78.

Index

A
acute nostalgia, 97–100, 102–4, 105, 128
the aim, 7, 26, 53, 68, 90, 94
   death drive, 174, 177
   genius, 40, 67, 71, 179
   inhibited, 117–18, 135, 138, 146, 147
   the mind, 29
   nonsexual, 10, 35–7, 47
   sexual, 34–6, 42, 46
   sublimation, 10, 30, 37, 41, 47–8, 135
   thinking, 32
   uninhibited, 117, 139
alienation, 6, 161–2, 201 n. 8
American Dream, 61–2
Anna O., 119
anti-intellectual, 19, 32–3, 37, 39–40, 48–9
aphanisis, 128
Apostle Paul, 124
Aristophanes, 38, 98, 99, 100, 102, 104
the army, 125–6, 196 n. 20
Arrival (Villeneuve), 114–15

B
Badiou, Alain, 13, 133–5, 157, 169
bare death, 179
Bladerunner 2049 (Villeneuve), 141
the breast, 128
   debased object, 142–4
   ego, 100
   genius, 106
   lost object, 99, 101–3
   the object, 69, 88–9, 108, 109, 140–1
   yieldable object, 153–6
Breuer, Josef, 119

C
castration, 94, 155
Cézanne, Paul, 83–4
Christianity, 121
the church, 125, 126, 196 n. 20
Cluny Brown (Lubitsch), 160, 162, 166, 168
Coca-Cola, 98–9, 104
Coition of a Hemisected Man and Woman (da Vinci), 38–9, 105
cool indifference, 10, 14, 17–18, 20, 123
Copjec, Joan, 130, 149, 199 n. 1

D
da Vinci, Leonardo, 9
   abandonment of art, 11–14
   art, 21–3
   authority, 119–20
   genius, 9, 38, 65
   hypocrisy, 14, 17, 19
   intellectual work, 20, 21
   interest in science, 11–2
   love and hate, 14–15, 17
   research instinct, 38–9
   suspension of passion, 17–18, 19
death, 171, 175, 203 n. 12
   absolute expenditure, 174
   accumulation of stimulus, 179
   contradictory, 179, 180
   the death drive, 175–6
   dualism, 178
   return to quiescence, 173, 175
   source of life, 180
the death drive, 8, 50–1, 171, 173
   death, 179
   dualism, 175, 178
   internal to drive, 176, 178
   life, 179
   monism, 178

the pleasure principle, 174, 176–7
split, 177
the debased father, 150
debasement, 137, 139–40, 144
   disavowal, 142
   fantasy, 141, 143, 152
   the group, 148, 149, 150
   the logic of, 142, 143, 145
desire
   analyst's, 158
   capitalism, 58–9
   the cause of, 141–2
   conformity with, 63–4
   debasement, 138–40, 149
   deciduous object, 140
   drive, 56
   the ethics of, 154
   genius, 63, 123, 127
   giving ground on, 55–9, 128, 145, 165
   the good, 59, 62, 64
   guilt, 59–61
   to hold back, 155
   ignorance, 156–7
   the image, 161
   inhibition, 151–2, 168
   lack, 56
   leader, 149, 150
   learning, 4
   object, 87, 94, 104, 143–4
   object *a*, 149, 154
   ontological, 58
   original narcissism, 129
   the other, 60, 61–2, 119, 130, 145, 161
   pain, 60, 62, 64
   sign of renunciation, 56–7, 63
   sublimation, 33, 64, 144
   superego, 62
   to yield, 153
disavowal, 142
dissatisfaction, 7, 36, 47
   genius, 40
   satisfaction, 42–3
   sublimation, 6, 37, 41, 188

Double Indemnity (Wilder), 21
the drive, 4, 25, 27, 34, 51, 54, 68, 108, 144, 171
   brooding, 32
   death, 179
   the death drive, 174–7
   ethics, 63
   excessive, 5, 8, 99
   forepleasure, 45, 48, 49, 65
   genius, 7, 10, 33, 37, 40, 67
   the group, 135
   hunger, 90–1, 93
   instinct, 5–6
   lacking, 88, 91, 94–5, 97, 98, 103, 106, 109
   masochism, 42–3, 50
   mental stimulus, 27–9
   monism, 178
   nonsexual aim, 37
   renunciation, 55–7
   satisfaction, 37
   sexual aim, 35–6
   sublimation, 23, 33, 36, 41, 46–8, 102, 118

E
Edmundson, Mark, 130
the ego, 26, 102, 154
   genius, 123, 127
   the group, 124, 157, 169
   guilt, 54
   ideal, 128–9, 136
   identification, 120, 122, 125
   inhibition, 151
   misrecognition, 100–1, 109
   narcissism, 107–10, 112
   superego, 61
Eisenstein, Paul, 127, 159, 163
endpleasure, 44–7, 48
enjoyment (*see also* jouissance), 23, 43, 71, 74, 110, 113–14, 141
Ex Machina (Alex Garland), 71
excrement, 39, 159, 160, 163, 169

F
Fink, Bruce, 72, 73–4, 198 n. 17
The Flavor of Green Tea over Rice (Ozu), 145–6
forepleasure, 40, 43, 44–51, 64, 65, 102, 169
freedom, 53, 55, 163, 165
Freud, Sigmund, 4
   Aristophanes, 99–100
   classicism, 68
   dualism, 175–9
   group psychology, 137
   guilt, 55
   Lacan, 103
   Leonardo, 9–10, 16–17, 38–9, 119
   lost breast, 101–2
   mana, 149
   original narcissism, 128
   the pleasure principle, 27, 30, 50–1, 174
   the primal father, 150
   sexuality, 159
   sublimation, 33, 41, 67

G
Galton, Francis, 1–2, 3
genius
   acceptance of null, 95
   awareness of the lost object, 106
   beyond narcissism, 112
   cession of the image, 169
   changes the object, 78, 80
   contradiction, 49, 50, 86
   death drive, 179
   deemphasize of the object, 102
   desire, 64
   eugenics, 1
   failure, 9, 31, 180
   fidelity to inquiry, 22, 30, 37–8, 48
   forepleasure, 48, 64
   group psychology, 117
   guilt, 55
   infantile sexual researches, 39, 173
   innate, 1, 2, 9, 17
   as intervention, 158
   pain, 41, 49
   pleasure, 23, 40, 49
   pleasure principle, 27, 30, 48, 49
   as a problem, 49
   refusal of love and hate, 20, 30
   rejection of authority, 120, 123, 127, 130
   renunciation of satisfaction, 36–7, 40, 56
   the subject of, 51, 63, 158
   sublimation, 7, 33
   the thing, 71–2, 76
   transience, 114–16
   willpower, 18
Gladwell, Malcolm, 3–4
The Godfather (Coppola), 16
the good, 58–9, 59–64, 76, 130
The Grand Canyon, 112, 115–16
the group, 16, 117–18, 158
   the army, 135–6
   artificial, 118, 124, 136, 147, 149, 157
   the Church, 126
   Cluny Brown (Lubitsch), 164, 165, 167, 169
   debasement, 148
   disintegration, 127
   encountering the thing, 146
   the far right, 149
   genius, 127, 130–1, 148, 151
   grievance, 153
   idealization, 123–4
   identification, 120–1
   ignorance, 157
   illusion, 136
   image, 159
   inhibition, 137, 152, 157
   internal cruelty, 122
   the leader, 129, 150
   psychoanalysis, 133–5
   psychoanalytic, 169
   sublimated, 159, 160
guilt, 53, 57–8, 61
   genius, 64
   giving ground, 55–6, 59

renunciation, 54
sublimation, 63
superego, 62

H
hate, 16, 19, 26-7, 125
hedonist, 179-80
Hegel, Georg Wilhelm Friedrich, 4
Hereditary Genius, 1

I
the ideal, 17, 109, 138
  debasement, 143-4
  genius, 130, 146
  of immortality, 113-14, 115
  original narcissism, 111-2, 128-9, 136
idealization, 123-4, 147, 157
  compensation, 129-30, 150
  enucleation, 143
  genius, 127
  imaginary, 133, 135, 136
  species of identification, 124-6
identification, 120-2, 147, 164
  genius, 123, 127
  idealization, 123-6
  imaginary, 133, 135, 136
  internal cruelty, 122
ignorance, 15-16, 73
  genius, 169
  passion, 156-7, 159, 164
the image, 121-2, 133, 144, 159-60, 168
  cession, 169
  meaning, 160-1
  oblativity, 162
  remainder, 159-60, 163, 168, 169
  the thing, 163-4
infantile sexual researches, 31-3, 37, 39-40, 173
inhibition, 118, 135, 157, 159, 169
  debasement, 144
  desire, 152-3, 154
  intervention, 152, 155-6
  the object *a*, 151, 154

the primal horde, 147-8
restriction, 151
sublimation, 137
intellectual, 20, 21, 31-3, 37-8, 40, 173

J
Jobs, Steve, 104-5, 106
jouissance (*see also* enjoyment), 43, 61, 64, 80, 142

K
Kant, Immanuel, 2, 37, 77
Kierkegaard, Soren, 1, 20

L
Lacan, Jacques, 4, 7, 65-6, 80-1
  Cause freudienne, 133
  the death drive, 178
  Freud, 55, 57-8, 67, 88-9, 103
  the group, 169
  lack of politics, 134
  Mannerism, 93
  modernism, 68
lack, 56
  belonging, 168-9
  debasement, 142
  the drive, 93-4, 97
  ethics, 57, 63
  the good, 59, 62
  the object, 104-6, 143, 151
  ontology, 58, 60, 94, 99
the leader, 8, 16, 123-4, 136, 147
  buddy style, 126-7
  debasement, 149-51
  idealization, 125, 133, 169
  identification, 124-5
  Jesus Christ, 126
  original narcissism, 127, 129-30, 157
libido, 33, 35, 53, 66, 111, 177
  split, 108-9
life, 173, 178-80
love, 14-17, 26, 64, 98, 166-7
  identification, 123

infatuation, 111–2
Lacan, 145–6
leaders, 130, 150
narcissistic, 75–6, 107, 112
parental, 110
transience, 113, 115

M
Malabou, Catherine, 2
Mannoni, Octave, 142
masochism, 42–3, 45, 50
The Matrix (Wachowski and Wachowski), 59
McGowan, Todd, 163, 165–6, 167
Mona Lisa, 13, 182 n. 6

N
Nachträglichkeit, 103
narcissism (*see also* original narcissism), 75–6, 90, 107–9, 115
  active, 110–1
  the group, 136
  passive, 111–2
  the thing, 77
null, 78, 160, 163
  genius, 95
  the object, 80, 83, 105–6
  signifier, 158

O
the object (*see also* object *a*), 7, 26–7, 29, 67, 87–9, 97–8, 107–9, 163, 164
  art, 83–4
  debasement, 137–40, 141–2
  desire, 58–9, 60
  the drive, 47, 56, 63, 90–5
  the ego, 100–2, 122
  ethics, 63–4, 154
  genius, 65–6, 67, 71–2, 76–8, 80, 95, 105–6, 112, 115, 146
  the group, 124
  grouping, 140, 143–4, 153
  idealization, 123–4
  identification, 125
  loss, 104, 109–10
  love, 145
  macaroni, 83
  narcissism, 75–6, 90, 107, 109, 110–2
  original narcissism, 128, 131
  refinding, 98–9
  refound, 102–4
  the solution, 29, 33, 40
  sublimation, 37, 41, 46, 67–8, 82, 85
  the symbolic, 77, 81
  the thing, 68–71, 73, 76, 79–80, 81–2
  transience, 113–14
  the vase, 83
  yieldable, 155–7, 169
object *a*, 149–51, 156, 169
  yielding of, 153–4, 155, 156–8, 159
the object of desire, 139–40, 144
  debasement, 140–2, 145
  desire, 143–4
  object *a*, 149
the object of love, 138–40, 144–5, 149
  debasement, 140–2
  desire, 143–4
original narcissism, 65–6, 109, 116, 130, 150, 159
  ambiguity, 128
  active narcissism, 110
  compensation, 129
  genius, 127, 130–1, 146, 169
  the group, 153, 157
  passive narcissism, 111–2
  transience, 112, 114, 115
  yielding of, 154, 157
Outliers, 3

P
pain, 25, 28, 41, 44, 47, 56, 177
  desire, 60, 62, 64
  forepleasure, 45–6, 48–50, 51
  the mind, 30
  the pleasure principle, 39–40

qualitative, 42
signal, 26–7
sublimation, 31, 33
perverse dividend, 130, 136, 150–1, 152, 157
Phillips, Adam, 185 n. 31
Pinker, Steven, 189 n. 10
pleasure (*see also* endpleasure *and* forepleasure), 25, 41, 44, 51, 64, 90, 95, 99
  compulsive brooding, 32, 34
  the death drive, 171–3, 174, 176–7, 180
  enjoyment, 43
  genius, 23, 40
  intellectual, 29–30, 40
  masochism, 42
  preparatory acts, 43–4
  signal, 26–7
  sublimation, 31, 42, 46
the pleasure principle, 25, 39, 41, 51
  contradictory, 49–50
  the death drive, 171–2, 174, 176–7, 179–80
  endpleasure, 44, 45
  genius, 30, 40, 48
  love and hate, 26–7
  masochism, 42
  sublimation, 31, 37, 41
  as watchman, 50, 175
Prévert, Jacques, 79
The primal father, 147, 151
The primal horde, 147
psychoanalysis, 2, 6, 63
  Freud, 27, 137
  genius, 66
  the group, 117–18, 133–5, 157
  human beings, 25
  ontological insight, 88, 97
  original narcissism, 65

R
Raiders of the Lost Ark (Spielberg), 81
Rear Window (Hitchcock), 74–5

Reitler, Rudof, 38–9
Rothenberg, Molly, 193 n. 20
Ruti, Mari, 83–4, 95

S
Saint Agatha of Catania (de Zubaran), 92, 143–4, 149, 150
The Shawshank Redemption (Darabont), 98
the signifier, 60, 77, 81, 128, 146
  Cluny Brown, 164, 169
  dignified, 105
  fabricated, 82–3, 158
  missing, 76, 78, 80, 105
  the object, 67, 81
  promoted, 84–6, 158
  the thing, 82
  transience, 116
the solution, 151
  art, 21
  genius, 33, 37–8, 48, 55, 102
  infantile sexual researches, 31
  the object, 29–30, 32, 40
subjective cession, 160
  the act, 154, 155, 159, 164
  ethics, 64, 154
  the object *a*, 153–4, 155
sublimation, 4, 5–6, 10, 31, 32–3, 65, 120, 179
  aim of dissatisfaction, 36–7, 41–2
  aim without an object, 37, 102
  change of object, 66, 67, 79
  contradiction, 30–1
  creation, 81
  debasement, 144–5
  forepleasure, 40, 43, 46–7, 51
  genius, 7, 37
  the group, 118, 131, 135–6
  love, 64
  masochism, 42
  pleasure, 23
  renunciation, 53, 55, 56, 63–4
  standard interpretation, 33–5
  the thing, 68, 78, 80–1, 82, 85

the superego, 55
   American Dream, 62
   belief in the other, 62
   difference between Freud and
      Lacan, 57–8, 63
   internalized aggression, 54
   renunciation of satisfaction, 56–7
The Symposium, 38, 98

T
the thing, 80, 163, 164
   antagonistic, 72
   ethics, 68, 71, 85
   genius, 71–2, 76, 80
   muting, 73–4, 76, 82, 145
   negativity, 77–8, 81
   radical difference, 71, 73
   representing, 81–2, 83, 84
   revelation of, 79
   unassimilable, 69
   useless, 80, 105
transience, 112–14, 115–16, 130
Trump, Donald, 127, 129–30

U
the universal, 31, 48, 167, 168

V
Vasari, Giorgio, 11
Vertigo (Hitchcock), 92–3, 138–40

Z
Žižek, Slavoj, 7, 114–15, 200 n. 11
Zupančič, Alenka, 84, 103, 158,
   164–5, 202 n. 22
de Zurbarán, Francisco, 92, 143–4, 149

Volumes in the Series:

Mourning Freud
by Madelon Sprengnether
Does the Internet Have an Unconscious?: Slavoj Žižek and Digital Culture
by Clint Burnham
In the Event of Laughter: Psychoanalysis, Literature and Comedy
by Alfie Bown
On Dangerous Ground: Freud's Visual Cultures of the Unconscious
by Diane O'Donoghue
For Want of Ambiguity: Order and Chaos in Art, Psychoanalysis, and Neuroscience
by Ludovica Lumer and Lois Oppenheim
Life Itself Is an Art: The Life and Work of Erich Fromm
by Rainer Funk
Born After: Reckoning with the German Past
by Angelika Bammer
Critical Theory between Klein and Lacan: A Dialogue
by Amy Allen and Mari Ruti
Transferences: The Aesthetics and Poetics of the Therapeutic Relationship
by Maren Scheurer
At the Risk of Thinking: An Intellectual Biography of Julia Kristeva
by Alice Jardine, edited by Mari Ruti
The Writing Cure
by Emma Lieber
The Analyst's Desire: The Ethical Foundation of Clinical Practice
by Mitchell Wilson
Our Two-Track Minds: Rehabilitating Freud on Culture
by Robert A. Paul
Norman N. Holland: The Dean of American Psychoanalytic Literary Critics
by Jeffrey Berman
Psychological Roots of the Climate Crisis: Neoliberal Exceptionalism and the Culture of Uncare
by Sally Weintrobe

Circumcision on the Couch: The Cultural, Psychological and Gendered Dimensions of the World's Oldest Surgery
by Jordan Osserman
The Racist Fantasy: Unconscious Roots of Hatred
by Todd McGowan
Antisemitism and Racism: Ethical Challenges for Psychoanalysis
by Stephen Frosh
The Ethics of Immediacy: Dangerous Experience in Freud, Woolf, and Merleau-Ponty
by Jeffrey McCurry
Analyzed by Lacan: A Personal Account
by Betty Milan
Visual Culture in Freud's Vienna
by Mary Bergstein
Genius After Psychoanalysis
by K. Daniel Cho